The Other Enlightenment

OFF THE FENCE: MORALITY, POLITICS, AND SOCIETY

The series is published in partnership with the Centre for Applied Philosophy, Politics & Ethics (CAPPE), University of Brighton.

Series Editors:

Bob Brecher, professor of moral philosophy, University of Brighton

Robin Dunford, senior lecturer in globalisation and war, University of Brighton

Michael Neu, senior lecturer in philosophy, politics and ethics, University of Brighton

Off the Fence presents short, sharply argued texts in applied moral and political philosophy, with an interdisciplinary focus. The series constitutes a source of arguments on the substantive problems that applied philosophers are concerned with: contemporary real-world issues relating to violence, human nature, justice, equality and democracy, self and society. The series demonstrates applied philosophy to be at once rigorous, relevant, and accessible—philosophy-in-use.

The Right of Necessity: Moral Cosmopolitanism and Global Poverty, by Alejandra Mancilla
Complicity: Criticism between Collaboration and Commitment, by Thomas Docherty
The State and the Self: Identity and Identities, by Maren Behrensen
Just Liberal Violence: Sweatshops, Torture, War, by Michael Neu
The Troubles with Democracy, by Jeff Noonan
Against Borders: Why the World Needs Free Movement of People, by Alex Sager
Digital Working Lives: Worker Autonomy and the Gig Economy, by Tim Christiaens
The Other Enlightenment: Self-Estrangement, Race, and Gender, by Matthew Sharpe

The Other Enlightenment

Self-Estrangement, Race, and Gender

Matthew Sharpe

ROWMAN & LITTLEFIELD
Lanham • Boulder • New York • London

Published by Rowman & Littlefield
An imprint of The Rowman & Littlefield Publishing Group, Inc.
4501 Forbes Boulevard, Suite 200, Lanham, Maryland 20706
www.rowman.com

86-90 Paul Street, London EC2A 4NE, United Kingdom

Copyright © 2023 by The Rowman & Littlefield Publishing Group, Inc.

All rights reserved. No part of this book may be reproduced in any form or by any electronic or mechanical means, including information storage and retrieval systems, without written permission from the publisher, except by a reviewer who may quote passages in a review.

British Library Cataloguing in Publication Information Available

Library of Congress Cataloging-in-Publication Data

Names: Sharpe, Matthew, 1975- author.
Title: The other Enlightenment : self-estrangement, race, and gender / Matthew Sharpe.
Description: Lanham : Rowman & Littlefield, 2023. | Series: Off the fence : morality, politics and society | Includes bibliographical references and index.
Identifiers: LCCN 2022041069 (print) | LCCN 2022041070 (ebook) | ISBN 9781538160213 (cloth) | ISBN 9781538160237 (paperback) | ISBN 9781538160220 (epub)
Subjects: LCSH: Enlightenment—Europe. | Other (Philosophy)—History—18th century. | Self-perception—History—18th century. | Sex—Philosophy—History—18th century. | Race relations—Philosophy—History—18th century.
Classification: LCC B802 .S465 2023 (print) | LCC B802 (ebook) | DDC 190.9/033—dc23/eng/20221024
LC record available at https://lccn.loc.gov/2022041069
LC ebook record available at https://lccn.loc.gov/2022041070

∞™ The paper used in this publication meets the minimum requirements of American National Standard for Information Sciences—Permanence of Paper for Printed Library Materials, ANSI/NISO Z39.48-1992.

Dedication
For my wife, in gratitude
"It is better to will the good than to know . . . "
—Petrarch

Contents

Preface: Argument ... ix

Introduction: The Enlightenment Beleaguered ... 1

Chapter 1: Locke, Bayle, Critique, and Toleration ... 21

Chapter 2: Paris–Persia: Othering (and Sexing) the Enlightenment ... 43

Chapter 3: Voltaire's Smiling Philosophy ... 63

Chapter 4: Eyesight from the Blind: Diderot, Saunderson, and Humans Born Blind ... 87

Chapter 5: Enlightenment, Race, Slavery, and Anti-Colonialism ... 109

Chapter 6: The Enlightenment, Sexuality, and Gender ... 135

Conclusion: What Was the Enlightenment? ... 157

Bibliography ... 165

Index ... 177

About the Author ... 181

Preface
Argument

This book can be presented as taking its orientation from two comments. The first, ironically, given how he is often understood, is from Michel Foucault in his work *The Birth of the Clinic*, when he observed that: "the two great mythical experiences on which the philosophy of the eighteenth century wished to found its beginning: the foreign spectator in an unknown country and the man-born-blind restored to the light."[1] The second, scarcely less ironic, comes from the anti-enlightenment historian Hippolyte Taine's *Origins of Contemporary France*, who remarks with bitterness, but (as we will argue) telling accuracy:

> Montesquieu looks at France through the eyes of a Persian, and Voltaire, on his return from England, describes the English, an unknown species. Confronting dogma and the prevailing system of worship, accounts are given, either with open or with disguised irony, of the various Christian sects, the Anglicans, the Quakers, the Presbyterians, the Socinians, those of ancient or of remote people, the Greeks, Romans, Egyptians, Muslims, and Guebers, of the worshippers of Brahma, of the Chinese and of pure idolaters.[2]

Lest readers be in any confusion, I want to start by stating the contentions of *The Other Enlightenment* in axiomatic fashion. The book you are about to read argues that:

- The central critical and philosophical exercise or practice of key thinkers of the French enlightenment was "self-estranging" or "self-othering", which was carried out in a variety of literary, poetic, dramatic, satirical, and philosophical mediums.
- This philosophical practice has different modalities:

- exploring the intellectual, cultural, moral, aesthetic, or political practices of other cultures, and presenting these to members of our in-group;
- imagining how "we" and our customs appear through the eyes of an Other; whether Persians visiting Paris (Montesquieu), Quakers, American Indians, Brahmins, or Chinese sages (Voltaire), the blind, dreaming, or Tahitians (Diderot);
- presenting the (for us) evident flaws and problems facing other individuals or groups (for example, religious intolerance) in such a way as *it is clear that we share these others' faults*.
- These modalities have critical functions, central to answering the question "What is enlightenment?" when it comes to the great, widely neglected French *philosophes* of the eighteenth century, being:
  - above all, to challenge our epistemic egoism, the deeply set individual and corporate tendencies we face, anatomized in Western thought by Francis Bacon, John Locke, and Pierre Bayle, to "relate everything to ourselves", understanding and potentially judging everything new and different against our own taken-for-granted norms and assumptions;
  - to realize that there are other ways of thinking, being, living, and acting than our own recent or present ways, and that therefore these ("our") ways are not inevitable, unquestionably best, and unchangeable;
  - to realize that our own ways of thinking, being, living, and acting will appear different and strange to others, who will be able to readily identify what in our practices are contingent, unnecessary, or even irrational, by comparison with their norms;
  - to recognize that where we might be inclined initially to see the other as only exotic or "inferior", they have virtues and capabilities which may in different ways be "superior" to our own, and from which we could learn;
  - to recognize our own faults, wrongs, and limitations, by seeing the faults, problems, and limitations facing others, *and recognizing ourselves in them*;
  - to as such open up the possibility of an expanded, cross-cultural, or cosmopolitan dialogue between different individuals and groups, predicated on a sense of curiosity, openness, and humility, rather than egoism, arrogance, and fear.
- That the preconditions for the development and literary-philosophical staging of enlightenment self-estrangement lie in the limited skepticism characterizing Francis Bacon's identification of the "idols of the mind", John Locke's explorations of the limits of human understanding, and the sources of ignorance and error, and the historically informed philosophical criticism of Pierre Bayle.

- That in a complex historical process which remains to be fully studied, since 1960 these critical dimensions of the enlightenment have been widely misrepresented, and the classic enlightenment texts neglected, by what is broadly called "postmodernism", "post-structuralism", or "French theory", whose advocates actually celebrate some practices of self-othering, and its ethics, but present this as "anti-enlightenment".
- That the enlightenment practice of self-othering critique, opening onto what Genevieve Lloyd calls "a cosmopolitan ideal nourished by what can be seen as an expansive form of skepticism", represents a cultural legacy which is increasingly needed, as virulently anti-liberal political movements on the Far Right increasingly menace the Capitols of pluralistic forms of polity looking back to enlightenment ideals.

NOTES

1. Michael Foucault, *The Birth of the Clinic*, trans. M. Sheridan Smith (London: Tavistock, 1973), 64–65.
2. Hippolyte A. Taine, *The Origins of Contemporary France, Volume 1, The Ancient Regime*, trans. John Durand (Project Gutenberg, 2008 [1880]), chapt. 3, sec. 4, https://www.gutenberg.org/files/2577/2577-h/2577-h.htm.

Introduction
The Enlightenment Beleaguered

"How many postmodernists does it take to change a lightbulb?"
"None; the enlightenment is dead."

—Joke, proverbial

INSIDE THE POST-TRUTH CAVE

The year 2016, the time of Brexit and the first ascent of Donald Trump, was also the year in which the term "post-truth" became a buzzword. Like all such half-popular, half-profound terms, "post-truth" is ambivalent. For some, it meant a culture in which political decisions were based on emotions, not facts or science. For others, it was a period in which politicians no longer needed to even *care* if what they were claiming was true. In another view, "post-truth" is what follows from a culture in which increasing numbers of citizens get their news selected by algorithms on social media platforms. These feed them what they "like", not what may be true, or even attempting to be so. For yet others, "post-truth" announced the final breakdown of public trust in experts, when it came to everything from climate change to the sanctity of democratic elections. For all comers, what "post-truth" amounted to was a climate in which "everyone was entitled to their own opinion". But no one could persuade others from different "filter bubbles" by appeals to reason or evidence that their opinions were any better or worse.[1]

Of course, it was possible to doubt the "post-" idea in all of this, the latest in a generation or so of such "afters". Politicians have never been on easy terms with independent inquiry and telling nothing but the truth. They have always known the power of rhetoric to move people's emotions, especially in crowds. Different twentieth-century regimes were no strangers to the cynical deployment of propaganda to create mass false consciousness and manufacture consent. People in general have never relished hearing contrary opinions to their own. We prefer information which confirms our own and our tribes' biases. So, human beings have arguably been "post-truth" on several of these models from soon after we sprang up in the Garden or were evicted from it. In 1749, the year when Denis Diderot was jailed for his "Letter on the Blind" (chapter 4), to take one example, rumours were swirling around Paris that Louis XV was abducting small children to bathe in their blood for the betterment of his health.[2] This is two hundred and seventy years ago. But it is hardly a million miles away from core delusions in today's "QAnon", a post-truth phenomenon if ever there was one.

Then again, the post-truth condition sounded a lot like what had been called "postmodernism" or "post-structuralism", for those of us who went through higher education in the later 1980s or 1990s. Both of these terms, too, are ambivalent. Many of the thinkers—like Gilles Deleuze, Jean Baudrillard, Jacques Derrida, or Michel Foucault, to whose work they were applied—never used them. Nevertheless, the terms can serve as shorthand for a constellation of opinions which developed in the transatlantic (and Australasian) reception of these thinkers' work in the bridgehead disciplines of literary and cultural studies, before percolating more widely into philosophy and other social sciences.[3]

In this doxastic constellation, there is no rational, mind-, or "discourse"-independent truth out there, waiting to be discovered by inquirers with sufficient courage, insight, impartiality, tenacity, or method. There are only perspectives or standpoints on the world held by different individuals, types, or groups. And these perspectives are more or less incommensurable. They can be studied, reconstructed, and juxtaposed. But none is truer to an "objective world" than the others. Each is instead the expression of a particular individual's, group's, or culture's way of seeing things; and on some accounts, their ways of being, living, and evaluating their experiences.

Attempts by any individual or group to lay claim to a culture-transcending "Truth", by appeals to forms of impartial knowledge, reasoning, experimental verification, or objectivity, are ("in truth"?) power plays: the expressions of a will to power, unconscious drives, and/or a fearful closure to Otherness. Such truth-claims cannot be defended by appeal to any perspective-independent standards. The highest value, on the predominant Left-liberal versions of the postmodernist perspective, is hence a generous openness to difference, which carries forwards older Leftist concerns for history's excluded, forgotten, and exploited. So, we should accept that difference goes all the way down and give up on all nostalgia for ancient values like "truth", "objectivity", or "the good", understanding their deep implications in historical violences.

Nevertheless, an old paradox faces the progressive postmodernist perspective, which also attends other forms of liberal toleration. Should we be open to others who express their difference by, precisely, posing essentialist claims to the truth of their views, or, worse, the right to impose them on others? Should we tolerate the intolerant other? More than this, if we accept that the world just is an irreducibly pluralistic cacophony of different post-truth standpoints, isn't it a rational move at this point for members of different groups to consciously embrace an unashamedly groundless decisionism: "Here we stand, and no matter how others think or feel, we can assert our rights as we see fit, and with as much right as they".

The paradox has deep political consequences. For such decisionism is exactly the form of steely-jawed self-assertion in a normative void which thinkers of the Far Right advocate. Benito Mussolini famously pronounced fascism a species of relativism; the philosopher Martin Heidegger's famous rectorship speech announcing his allegiance to Nazism did so on the basis of a notion of *völkisch* "self-assertion" by the German people against the decadent liberal-modern world.[4] If no principles can decide between perspectives, this is to say, are things not left to adjudication on "the field of Mars"?—that is, the contest of competing forms of particularistic self-assertion, backed by any means of persuasion each "we" can muster, including even violence, for those enraged enough?

To be sure, the liberal postmodernist will charge against the Right relativist that the latter's position is closed to difference and other perspectives. Their relativism was never meant to open the door to forms of exclusionary hatred. The "best" perspective is one that tolerates or even celebrates all others'.[5] But the Rightist can reply that their intolerance, prejudice, and particularistic self-assertion just is *their* unique way of expressing their difference, and as such, the highest right. At this point, the postmodernist liberal cannot in principle oppose the others' bellicose form of difference without skirting hypocrisy. We know that mediatic culture warriors delight in highlighting this, calling down "intolerance" on "political correctness", "wokeness", "SJWs", etc. Postmodern relativism, propounded out of a desire to empower the excluded, is hence rebounding in post-truth upon its generous proponents. We can only assert our decision in favour of inclusion on a normatively level playing field with others who mimetically announce their avowedly "identitarian" credentials, but as a means to limit and eventually overthrow liberal toleration.[6]

Is there no middle, or *other*, ground then open to us in the period of culture wars? Or are we forever to be torn between the identitarian New Right which, cynically aping ideas and phrases from the New Left, asserts national, ethnic, or racial differences as the primary data of history; and a broadly postmodernist New Leftism, which asserts that, within pluralistic nations, cultural, gender, racial, and sexual difference are the primary data? Is the "culture war" between these positions, characterised by increasing incivility on both sides, and increasingly openly insurrectionary actions from the Right, the inevitable reality of a post-truth situation from which there can be no civil exit?

The argument of this book is that such excluded third positions (plural) do exist. But they must be recovered and argued for against advocates of more established positions. We start with the observation that one thing uniting the two sides in today's culture wars is a shared hostility to "the enlightenment". For the illiberal Right, the enlightenment is denounced, accurately, as the period in which religious toleration, freedom of conscience, the philosophical commitment to the equality of human beings, and the liberal rule of law first emerged in the West, informing the American and French revolutions, and paving the way for more recent struggles for social justice.[7] For these figures, the enlightenment and its champions are the beginning of the multicultural "nihilism" which weakens "Western identity", and levels out natural hierarchical differences or "rank orderings" between the sexes as well as races.

For the postmodernist Left, by contrast, the enlightenment is charged with remaining insufficiently open to religious, ethnic, and cultural differences. Its proponents, to a man—although tellingly, it is Immanuel Kant or the nineteenth-century thinker W. G. F. Hegel, not Montesquieu, Voltaire, Condillac, d'Holbach, or Diderot who are often presented as exemplary[8]— are charged with propounding forms of universalism whose hidden end was always to illicitly impose a particular gendered, racial standpoint on all others. In such a purview, the enlightenment and its champions represent the intellectual highpoint of white privilege, and the universalist ideologies underlying the worst crimes of racism, chattel slavery, and colonialism.

As Dennis Rasmussen has done the most to document, the alleged sins of the enlightenment, for its manifold critics in the postmodern period, are legion.[9] For some, "it" (for it was one thing) enshrined a naïvely over-optimistic understanding of human nature and unsustainable, Eurocentric metanarrative(s) of history as uniformly progressive. The enlightenment outlook was characterised by an overconfidence in reason's powers and compass (if not a secularized, heretical "faith", for some theological critics). This caused its advocates to produce far-ranging rationalist systems, blind to the relativity of truth-claims and the plurality of incommensurable perspectives and language-games (Nietzsche, Lyotard), the oppressive potentials of the instrumental, objectifying powers of reason (Adorno and Horkheimer, Heidegger), and the insidious relationship between knowledge and power (the Frankfurt School, Foucault, the *nouveaux philosophes*).[10] The enlightenment's faith in universal truth- and value-claims led to a focus on disembedded individuals and their rights rather than communal ties and duties, for communitarian critics. It downplayed the feminine, the sensual, the embodied, and the singular, as well as the ludic and the literary, in the rush to claim a scientific universal rationality. It led moderns to be closed or hostile to individuals and groups, including women, different or other to white bourgeois males, for many feminist and post-colonialist theorists.[11] All the while, the enlightenment's hostility to revelation robbed modern human beings of existential orientation, abandoning them to a godless, soulless, materialism, according to the *lumières'* oldest, their theological critics.[12]

Each of these criticisms is important. Especially those challenging the basic normative credentials of the enlightenment seem to this author to be devastating, *if they were demonstrably accurate*. Nevertheless, the argument of this book is that these criticisms cannot be upheld, if we return to the key French enlightenment *philosophes*, led by the works of the great trio of Montesquieu, Voltaire, and Denis Diderot. One striking feature of many debates surrounding "the enlightenment" and "the enlightenment project" or "enlightenment rationality" today, however, is how just *how little* these three giants of the period are considered. Victor Hugo claimed that the eighteenth century itself could be adequately named "the age of Voltaire". Voltaire was known in his own lifetime as the "patriarch" of the enlightenment, and the first generations of the anti-modernist Right in the nineteenth century knew the *philosophes* as their principal foes. Yet today, when the same enlightenment is subjected to the withering criticisms we just inventoried, the works of the patriarch, as well as Montesquieu and Diderot (the other contender for *most* significant *philosophe*), are left widely unconsulted and uncited.

This is not to deny that important critical literatures on these figures, and this extraordinary period of European and French intellectual history, continue to be produced within the academy in French studies, literary studies, history, and history of ideas disciplines.[13] But a second striking feature of the contemporary debates on "the enlightenment" is how little its different, radical critics who hail from other disciplines actually consult enlightenment scholars' works; and, on the other hand (it has to be said), how little eighteenth-century scholars seem to pay attention to, and protest against, the often deeply inaccurate representations of the figures and ideas they work upon hailing from their colleagues in other locales in the humanities.[14]

In one way, this book began with two experiences too long ago for the author to comfortably confess. The first has a very specific setting in the author's memory. As a sixteen- or seventeen-year-old, having secured a copy of Voltaire's *Candide* in pursuit of the fond aim to "read all the classics", I devoured a slim little Dover Thrift translation of Voltaire's tale in one sitting. I remember laughing so hard I almost wept, while at the same time marvelling at the lightness of touch, and understated *compassion*, with which Voltaire's little *conte* could detail the most horrific litany of natural catastrophes and human infamies with the restrained innocence of a children's fairy tale. I did not at that time know much of Leibniz, Pope, or Rationalist philosophy. But Christianity had been part of our school education, and Voltaire seemed to me to have produced a definitive *reductio ad absurdum* of the human tendency to claim that we know or are able explain a good deal more than we actually can.

The second experience dates from several years later, attending a university class in literary studies on modernism. The lecturers and tutors were strongly encouraging us to read (and where possible, cite) figures whom I had previously been unaware of in my undergraduate studies in history and philosophy: *à la mode* French thinkers like Jacques Derrida, Michel Foucault, or Roland Barthes. Anyway, "the enlightenment" was being presented in those classes in ways that I remember having extraordinary difficulties squaring with my earlier encounter with the author of *Candide*, whose *Philosophical Dictionary* I had in the meantime also relished. *The excessive rationalism, Eurocentrism, humourlessness, and utopianism which my teachers were attributing to "the enlightenment" all seemed to me to be exactly Voltaire's targets in* Candide *and* The Philosophical Dictionary. Clearly, something was amiss. Needless to say, as an introverted undergrad student, I said nothing. The discordance sat with me for well over a decade, before I returned to reading the original eighteenth-century originals, having completed my PhD and several studies on more recent thinkers and ideas.

Looking back, I can see that in these two experiences, I had spanned the continuing divide that still characterises academic literature on the enlightenment today. On one hand, there are specialised studies attentive to the texts, history, and context of the *lumières'* writings, in which all of the extraordinary art, culture, history, philosophy, satire, criticism, and passion for ethical and social reform which drives their work remains visible. On the other hand, there are the *lumières'* own presently estranged, more politically engaged successors in other disciplines. These carry forward the enlighteners' aim to respond to and better the social conditions of the excluded. But they have ceased reading the eighteenth-century texts, accepting cyclopean—which is to say, one-eyed or half-blind—accounts of their own intellectual antecedents.

The first aim of this book, in what the author takes to be an enlightenment spirit, is to try to span this divide. The enlightenment and its ways of thinking, writing, and acting are too important, and too continually significant in shaping who "we" are in the liberal-democratic West, both strengths and weaknesses, to be left to scholarly specialists. This is a fate Voltaire and Diderot would have found especially grating, given their own aims as *philosophes*, to spread the light of learning to wider public audiences. At the same time, if academic and public debates on class, race, gender, and sexuality are to break out of the culture wars between New Left and New Right forms of identitarian particularisms; and if we are to rediscover new modes of pluralism and civility which can halt what some are calling the present period's "fascist drift", this book proposes that public debates need a more nuanced and more accurate understanding of the key thinkers and ideas of the enlightenment.

THE ENLIGHTENMENT AGAINST SYSTEMS AND THE FIGURE OF THE *PHILOSOPHE*

An introduction is not the place to present all of the premises of a book. An author also wants readers to read on! Nevertheless, several things need to be addressed, so readers new to enlightenment literature and *philosophie* can have a better working understanding of what it meant for Montesquieu, Voltaire, and Diderot to identify themselves, and be identified, as *philosophes*.

Firstly, it has to be said straightaway that the idea of the enlightenment *philosophes* as system-building rationalists is misguided, in several basic ways.[15] Anyone who has tried to locate Voltaire's or Diderot's "system" in their *oeuvres* will be able to report their frustrations. Continental thinkers who celebrate Friedrich Nietzsche's hostility to system-building should know that, in this way at least, he was walking a path trodden by the *philosophes* whose "free thinking" he otherwise mostly reviled.[16] As we will see in chapters 3 and 4 in particular, the predominant attitude of the *philosophes* towards rationalist system-building philosophy like that undertaken in the seventeenth century by René Descartes and Baruch Spinoza is captured in the entry "System" in the *Encyclopedia*. Diderot writes:

> Now, such systems, far from dispelling the chaos of metaphysics, are only fit to dazzle the imagination by their bold consequences, to seduce the mind by the false lights of evidence, to nourish obstinacy in believing the most monstrous errors, to eternalize disputes as well as the bitterness and the anger with which they are maintained . . . There are systems that deserve the praise people give them, and even some works that compel our admiration, they resemble those palaces in which taste, comfort, splendour, and magnificence compete to produce an artistic masterpiece, but their foundations are so weak that they appear supported only by a magic spell.[17]

The neo-Kantian Ernst Cassirer is hence closer to the literature, and the kinds of thinking and expression which characterised the French enlightenment, when he writes:

> The eighteenth century takes reason in a different and more modest sense [than the seventeenth-century Rationalists]. It is no longer the sum total of "innate ideas" given prior to all experience, which reveal the absolute essence of things. Reason is now looked upon . . . as . . . the original intellectual force which guides

the discovery and presupposition of truth . . . a kind of energy, a force which is fully comprehensible only in its agency and effects.[18]

Decisive here, as will be revealed in chapters 1 through 3, is in fact the thought of the British seventeenth-century experimental or empirical philosophers, in the lineage of Francis Bacon and John Locke: the former of whom Diderot and other *lumières* revered, and the latter of whom Voltaire thought the wisest metaphysician, precisely because of his refusal to base his reasoning on assumptions and axioms which could not be certified by repeatable experiences and observations. For these thinkers, the human mind is so limited and "uneven" that one must work to derive adequate inductive principles from experience.[19] In doing so, we need to first of all be awake to the ways in which our intelligences are finite and prey to a variety of egoistic passions and predilections which push us to more readily accept what we *wish*, rather than what verifiable evidences suggest to be so.[20]

The *philosophes* in the French enlightenment came to take on a different identity, either to that which was recognised in the rationalists of the previous century, or to what we recognise in academia today. As Stephane van Damme has considered, the term *philosophie* itself was changing its sense during this period in France. In the universities, philosophy remained integrated within the Arts Faculties. So, including in the *Encyclopédie*, it kept its old Aristotelian sense, as being the organizational knowledge of knowledges, seeking after the first principles of all sciences.[21] But precisely *none* of the key *philosophes* involved in the French enlightenment, led by Montesquieu, Voltaire, and Diderot, were university scholars. Many, following Montesquieu, Voltaire, and Diderot, blended more traditional philosophical theorizing with literary productions of the kind which will be central to this book. By the middle of the eighteenth century, Daniel Brewer observes, the meaning of the term *philosophe* in France had begun to morph away from a professor in the Arts Faculty to a distinct cultural type: "He is a man who rejects nothing, who constrains himself in relation to nothing, and who leads the life of a *philosophe*."[22] As such, these *philosophes* were of increasing interest to agents of the Church and Throne, as a source of social disruption and "bad morals".

There is undoubtedly a carryover from the ancient Greek and Roman, pre-Christian sense of philosophy as a way of life at work in these thinkers' conception of the *philosophe*.[23] We can see this, for instance, in Voltaire's entry for "philosopher" in his *Philosophical Dictionary*, which opens by declaring that philosophers set out models of virtuous living,[24] and the *Encyclopedia*'s own famous "philosopher" entry by Du Marsais, which presents the *philosophe* as an amiable amalgam of Stoic, Epicurean, and Ciceronian traits.[25] This philosopher "wants to enjoy like a wise housekeeper the goods that nature offers him" and "to find pleasure with others", rather than withdraw into solitary contemplation. Indeed, "civil society" is as a "deity" for him, which he reveres, and to which he aspires to contribute. "To write is to act", for Voltaire and the *philosophes*: not simply to interpret the world, but to *intervene* in it, to use a French expression.

With that said, as Catherine Wilson has well examined, the enlightenment *philosophes* were far more directly interested in understanding the social preconditions and manifestations of humans' propensities to folly, error, ignorance, and prejudice than the ancients they admired had been. Alongside the passions and forms of individual folly and suffering addressed by the Hellenistic and Roman philosophers, "the targets of the philosophes included colonialism, luxury, austerity, hypocrisy, antifeminism (but also some forms of feminism), monarchy, aristocracy, clergy, religion, physicians, and the arts and letters".[26]

Finally, it is in light of these subjects and concerns that we need to understand the most striking difference between the work of the enlightenment philosophers and other, better-known understandings of this vocation today. This is the farrago of literary forms in which Montesquieu, Voltaire, and Diderot communicated, in order to convey and advertise their ideas: letters, fictions, satires, dramas, tragedies, epics, poems, dictionary and encyclopedia entries . . . The moniker "the age of reason" which has so often been pinned to the enlightenment is hence potentially very misleading. For a start, it was only specific kinds of "reason" which the enlighteners were interested in defending, in contrast to the highly deductive, specialised forms of reasoning taught in the Arts Faculties. These new forms of seeking knowledge were both shaped by, and continued in dialogue with, the "natural philosophy" that had revolutionised European understandings of nature since 1600. The point here is that the enlightenment philosophers were interested in speaking to, and contributing to enlightening, a growing reading public outside of the universities, convents, and monasteries: men and women from the growing French middle classes, as well as thoughtful aristocrats. For they understood that it would be such men and women who could be the vanguard of social change in the causes they cared about: religious toleration (chapter 3), the development of new forms of experimental inquiry and the spread of the new philosophies (chapter 4), and then, increasingly, the abolition of slavery (chapter 5), the re-founding of political authority on the consent of the governed, and the liberation of women from continuing disadvantage, and of Europeans from extant marriage customs (chapter 6).

The leading enlightenment *philosophes*, including the three thinkers we'll focus on here, understood that *many more people are engaged by characterisations, drama, tragedy, and comedy*—the stock in trade of narrative arts—*than by technical argumentation*. The literature of the *philosophes* is hence, exactly, often *literature*, or even what the French call *belles lettres*.[27] The idea that the great French enlighteners were stony-faced utopian social engineers, closed to everything elusive and playful, is frankly bizarre, when what the period produced is a literature which has been described as "of such delicate wit as no other literature has ever matched."[28]

THE ENLIGHTENMENT(S) AS FERMENT, NOT "PROJECT"

Finally in this introduction, we need to make what in technical terms is called a "meta" comment, on the very idea of the enlightenment. The use of the definite article ("the") suggests a single movement or phenomenon, *an* "enlightenment" which unfolded in a fairly discrete period of time. Everyone in this period and movement, "the enlightenment", are presented by this moniker as if they were thinking the same things or developing the same ideas. At some point, maybe around 1721 (with the appearance of our first text, *Persian Letters*), this period of intellectual and wider history began.

At a later point, perhaps with the death of Diderot in 1784, or perhaps with the French Revolution itself (1789), it ended. People then were no longer "in" the enlightenment, as they had not previously been "in" it before 1721. Having all thought "enlightenment" things, or perhaps, in Alasdair MacIntyre's influential term, shared in a singular "enlightenment project", everyone now pulled up stumps on that project.[29] They began doing other things—perhaps "romantic" things, to use a similar historicising category. We saw the kind of overgeneralisations at work here, in fact, with Cassirer's "eighteenth century" above. It is as if in 1700 or 1701, a memo went around European intellectual circles that systematising rationalism was "in the past", and experimental, fallible, self-limiting modes of reasoning were the next thing.

Of course, history doesn't work like this. Neither does intellectual history. Declaring "for" or "against" a singular enlightenment is hence a fallacy (*dicta simpliciter* is the old word for it). It is like declaring "for" or "against" "the Greeks", when there are after all some notable differences between Achilles and Socrates, Alcibiades and Aristides the Just, Athens and Sparta. The work of Jonathan Israel in the last decades has the great merit of alerting people to the idea that there were *at least two* enlightenments, a moderate and a radical.[30] It is also important to remark that there were different national enlightenments, operating in relative autonomy (as well as dialogue) with each other, in addition to the French enlightenment, the Scottish, the American, and the later German enlightenments.[31]

Our position here is different (and we will state our criticisms of Israel's particular claims in the course of the text [4.1, 5.2, 5.4]). Rather than a "project", which implies an extraordinary degree of direct coordination which the record doesn't bear out, *the enlightenment was a period of extraordinary intellectual ferment*: of questions, as much as new answers, and of debates, rather than the hardening of an unlikely single orthodoxy. It originated in what chapters 1 and 2 identify as four sources of the "decentering" of European self-consciousness, in the early modern period: the Renaissance, the Protestant Reformation, what we now call "the scientific revolution[s]" after Copernicus, Kepler, and Galileo, and the discovery of the "new" worlds in South, meso-, and North America, as well as in the Far East.[32] Each of these developments had called into question the sufficiency of the Christian worldview, which had been accepted by most of Europe, and undergirded its modes of socio-political organization, for over a millennium. In the ensuing intellectual uncertainty, the enlightenment saw ongoing debates between philosophers, naturalists, and men (and women) of letters on the roles in shaping human experience played by climate, luxury, education, geography, religion, population, free trade, law, and manners.[33] As the author has put it elsewhere:

> The "little flock" of the *lumières* disagreed between themselves, and oscillated within themselves, on the educability of the masses, the bases and the limits of knowledge, the nature and social role of religions, deism or atheism, whether knowledge or civilisation aids or hinders people's pursuits of happiness, the roles and relations of the arts, sciences and philosophy, the nature and meaning (or senselessness) of history, free will or determinism, the nature and limits of government, the comparative merits of the ancients and the moderns, and the ([revealed,] natural, affective, conventional or rational) bases of morality.[34]

This is not to deny that a degree of unity emerged from these impassioned debates on many, especially ethical questions: notably, the primary value of toleration, the unsustainability of basing morality on biblical religion, the unjustifiability of colonial exploitation and the slave trade, the need for educational reform, and the equal intellectual and aretaic (that is, virtue-achieving) capacities of women. But it is to underline that looking for a single set of "enlightenment ideas" that one could lay out as in a list is a mistaken endeavour. The later Michel Foucault was discerning when he stressed that "enlightenment" is hence best thought of as a process, way or ways of thinking, rather than any achieved outcome[s][35]—outcomes which the enlighteners' embrace of critical, cumulative, and collective inquiry led them to hope (and expect) would in many cases be soon improved upon. This way of thinking, it seems to me, was well described by Immanuel Kant in his *Critique of Judgment*, when he named three requirements of "common human understanding":

> They are these: (1) to think for oneself; (2) to think from the standpoint of everyone else; (3) always to think consistently. The first is the maxim of unprejudiced thought, the second that of enlarged thought, the third that of consistent thought. The first is the maxim of a never-passive reason. To be given to such passivity, consequently to heteronomy of reason, is called prejudice . . . As to the second maxim belonging to our habits of thought, . . . : [it can be fulfilled] if [a person] detaches himself from the subjective personal conditions of his judgement, which cramp the minds of so many others, and reflects upon his own judgement from a universal standpoint (which he can only determine by shifting his ground to the standpoint of others). The third maxim—that, namely, of consistent thought—is the hardest of attainment, and is only attainable by the union of both the former, and after constant attention to them has made one at home in their observance.[36]

In reading Montesquieu, Voltaire, and Diderot over the last decade, this passage from the third *Critique* has often sprung to the author's mind. It is above all Kant's second maxim on "thinking from the standpoint of others", with the "enlarged thought" that it would make possible, that this book argues was at the heart of the works of Montesquieu, Voltaire, and Diderot. Indeed, we will show how central it is to their philosophical fictions, and to their philosophies more widely. This kind of enlarged thought ought still to be taught and celebrated as amongst the highest virtues for the citizens of any pluralistic societies, just as its opposite, closed-minded and sectarian self-assertion, should be recognised and opposed as the crucible of intolerance, illiberalism, and cruelty, not some higher "strength" or authenticity.

CHAPTER SYNOPSIS

Chapter 1 presents an account of the historical and intellectual preconditions of the French enlightenment texts which we are going to examine in chapters 2 through 6. The Italian and Northern renaissances, the breakdown of religious consensus with the Reformation, the increasing independence being declared by the new "natural philosophy" from clerical and theological control, and the resulting change in Europeans' understanding of the natural world, engendered the pervasive cultural uncertainty that created the ferment which became the French enlightenment. The thought of Francis Bacon and John Locke were especially significant. They suggested new ways of doing philosophy, beginning in an awareness of the "idols of the human mind", the sense-based limits of human understanding, our innate propensities to go down well-trodden erroneous paths, and the need to base philosophical inquiries on forms of controlled, collective experimentalism. The chapter closes by looking at Pierre Bayle's extraordinary *Various Thoughts on the Occasion of a Comet*. We argue that this text was significant for bringing together the kind of skeptical, self-limiting inquiry valorized by Bacon and Locke, with a call for the kinds of religious toleration which the *Encyclopedists* and other *philosophes* would advocate for in France after 1720.

Chapter 2 introduces the fourth source of decentering European self-consciousness which precipitated the debates and concerns of the French enlighteners: the wealth of travel writing flooding back into Europe from mercenaries, missionaries, and adventurers in the sixteenth and seventeenth centuries. We turn in this light to Montesquieu's marvelous *Persian Letters*. Montesquieu herein sets up what we argue is the template for enlightenment "enlarging" of thought. He uses the conceit of two Islamic Persians visiting Christian Paris, and corresponding with people back home, to show how what "we" Europeans take to be inevitable, rational, and unchangeable appears to others in very different lights. He also uses implicit criticisms of Persian institutions and mores as a displaced "other scene" in which to criticize European intolerance, absolute monarchy, and, above all, treatment of women.

Chapter 3 is on Voltaire, the enlightenment's "patriarch", and its most famous and widely read advocate for toleration. We first examine how Voltaire's *Letters on the English* walks in the trail carved out by *Persian Letters*, using a conversation with a Quaker to unsettle Catholic assumptions of moral and religious superiority, and his encounter with Bacon's, Locke's, and Newton's thought to contest regnant French Cartesian philosophical thinking. Next, we look at the wonderful philosophical tale, *Micromégas*, another enlightenment travel tale in which our little planet's visitation by Voltaire's lovable 24,000-foot-tall giant from the planet Sirius is used to stage a self-estranging view down on human beings' fondness for war, and our tendency to take ourselves as cosmically central—a supposition which the astronomical (and microscopic) discoveries of the previous centuries had shown to be a proud, but all-too-small-minded illusion. *Candide* follows, Voltaire's definitive satirical attack on Rationalist theodicy, and the idea that we could know "all is well" (*tout est bien*), when the world is riddled with avoidable ignorance, injustices, and suffering. We close by examining Voltaire's biblical criticism and anti-clerical writings, especially in the post-1762 *écrasez l'infâme* period of his extraordinary public activism in favor of religious toleration. Again and again, we will see the force of Voltaire's later description of himself as a Socratic, "ignorant philosopher", whose skepticism in metaphysics was undergirded by a "primacy of practical reason" elevating moral reciprocity as the basis for toleration and social reform.

Chapter 4 examines Denis Diderot's 1749 "Letter on the Blind, for the Use of Those Who See", which we argue is yet another artful enlightenment travelogue: this one, from the land of the blind. We "sighted" folk assume we must be simply superior to the blind. Diderot delights in showing how much we can learn from the blind, and the ways in which their forms of experience and knowing are superior to the sighted. This includes, infamously, their putative ability to "see" by firsthand experience the ways that the seemingly ordered world of nature, which even Voltaire admired as the basis for his belief in a rational Deistic God, includes many exceptions, monsters, and transitional forms, like the blind themselves. Any form of thinking which does not proceed from a post-Lockean examination of how our experience shapes our knowledge-claims is truly "blind", Diderot's "Letter" suggests. On the other hand, enlightenment—the awakening of people from the blindness of faith and unexamined tradition—must proceed "like a blind-folded man" in unsteady, frequently checked steps towards a truer understanding of the world.

After the first four chapters examine key enlightenment texts, excavating the practices of self-othering at their heart from behind layers of misunderstanding, like the sea-God Glaucus, the final two chapters turn to the subjects of colonialism, racism, and slavery (chapter 5), and sexuality and gender (chapter 6), each so controversial today. These chapters aim to show that critical generalizations about "the enlightenment" as a period wholly characterised by racial and sexual prejudices do not stand up to the experience of reading the primary enlightenment texts, notably in their impassioned advocacy for the abolition of African slavery. We examine in these chapters two more extraordinary, widely forgotten classics of the enlightenment: the Abbé Raynal's *History of the Two Indies*, in whose later editions Diderot played no small part, and Diderot's own *Supplement to Bougainville's Voyage*.

These chapters also mark out the end of a trajectory, from imaginary to real, as it were. Chapter 6 centrally looks at Olympe de Gouges and Mary Wollstonecraft, in whose thought and advocacy feminism emerges, transforming the imaginative self-othering staged in Montesquieu, Voltaire, Diderot, and other *philosophes* into the direct voicing by the Other of women's equal dignity, capacity, and claims to vindication.

AUDIENCE, ARRANGEMENT, AND STYLE

This book is written for academics and non-academics. It reconstructs texts from the past which aimed to transform the world, in ways and on issues which are still divisive (and decisive) for many societies today: its opening and close therefore return from the past to present debates and prospects.[37]

I've aimed to employ a style which is precise but clear, unclouded by technical language. Where information which I anticipate will be new to non-specialist readers is introduced, it is exactly "introduced". Wherever possible, I've chosen the simpler rather than the more technical word. Likewise, I've tried (not always with success) to use shorter sentences, rather than longer, more convoluted academic constructions.[38] Interested specialists will find in the footnotes the details of the historical, critical, and philosophical sources on which the analyses draw. I accordingly anticipate the odd reader who will be unhappy on either side of the specialist–non-specialist divide, and can only extend due apologies.

Likewise, you don't write a book like this without anticipating heated criticisms from commentators on either side of the culture wars. I have aimed to belong to no culture-war country, as Pierre Bayle would direct. But I make no attempt to conceal my concerns about the forms of anti-enlightenment despotism (too softly labelled "populism") that are rising globally, including in the heartlands of the enlightenment and its transatlantic satellites. Diderot, as so often, said it well:

> He that could force us to good, could also force us to evil. The first despot, fair, firm, and enlightened, is a scourge; a second, a bully, fair, firm, and enlightened, is a greater scourge; a third that looks like the first two, by forgetting the rights of the people, consummates their slavery.[39]

Gratitude for reading the draft in its entirety to Tim Neal and Dr. Benjamin Waters; for reading particular chapters, to Dr. Maria Rae, Matthew Anderson, Matthew King, and the different participants in the academia session on the draft introduction in June 2021. Above all, the author wishes to express his gratitude to his 2019 Honors class at Deakin University, wherein many of these ideas, as well as many others, were explored with honesty, openness, and enthusiasm. These are good work memories.

NOTES

1. On post-truth, see James Ball, *Post-Truth: How Bullshit Conquered the World* (London: Biteback Publishing, 2018); and Quassim Cassam, *Vices of the Mind: From the Intellectual to the Political* (Oxford, UK: Oxford University Press, 2019).

2. Anthony S. Curran, *Diderot and the Art of Thinking Freely* (New York: Other Press, 2019), 84.

3. On the transatlantic reception of "French theory", see Robert Holub, *Crossing Borders: Reception Theory, Poststructuralism, Deconstruction* (Madison: University of Wisconsin Press, 1992). For accounts of the original thinkers, see Gary Gutting, *Thinking the Impossible: French Philosophy since the 1960s* (Oxford, UK: Oxford

University Press, 2013; David West, *Continental Philosophy: An Introduction* (London: Wiley-Blackwell, 2010). For important criticisms, see Jurgen Habermas, *Philosophical Discourse of Modernity*, trans. Frederick G. Lawrence (Cambridge: Massachusetts Institute of Technology Press, 1987); Manfred Frank, *What Is Neostructuralism?*, trans. Sabine Wilke and Richard Gray (Minneapolis: University of Minnesota Press, 1989); and Terry Eagleton, *The Illusions of Postmodernism* (Cambridge, UK: Blackwell Publishers, 1996).

4. "Everything I have said and done in these last years is relativism by intuition. If relativism signifies contempt for fixed categories and those who claim to be the bearers of objective immortal truth . . . then there is nothing more relativistic than Fascist attitudes and activity. . . . From the fact that all ideologies are of equal value, that all ideologies are mere fictions, the modern relativist infers that everybody has the right to create for himself his own ideology and to attempt to enforce it with all the energy of which he is capable", Mussolini wrote in *The Turning*. See Franz Neumann, *Behemoth: The Theory and Practice of National Socialism, 1933–1944* (Chicago: Ivan R. Dee, 2009), 462–63; Roger Kimball, "Introduction: The Dictatorship of Relativism", *The New Criterion*. On Heidegger's rectorship speech, see Matthew Sharpe, "Rhetorical Action in the *Rektoratsrede*: Calling Heidegger's *Gefolgschaft*", *Philosophy & Rhetoric* 51, no. 2 (2018): 176–201; on Heidegger's Nazism, see Emmanuel Faye, *Martin Heidegger: The Introduction of Nazism into Philosophy*, trans. Michael B. Smith (New Haven and London: Yale University Press, 2009); for statements concerning the "ontological" basis of the Nazi state in the unitary, "decisional" "self-assertion" of a Volk, see Martin Heidegger, *On Hegel's Philosophy of Right*, trans. Andrew J. Mitchell (London: Bloomsbury, 2014): 152, 158, 177, 183, 185. On this text, see Matthew Sharpe, "The State as the Being of the Volk: State, Führer and the Political in Heidegger's Seminars during the Kairos", in Thanos Zartaloudis, ed., *Law and Philosophical Theory: Critical Intersections* (London: Rowman & Littlefield, 2018), 199–217.

5. See, e.g., Alexis Papazoglou, "The Post-Truth Era of Trump Is Just What Nietzsche Predicted", *The Conversation*, December 14, 2016, which runs this line concerning the German thinker of the Second Reich.

6. See Leo Strauss, "Preface", in *Spinoza's Critique of Religion* (Chicago: University of Chicago Press, 1965), 6–7. This is to identify a precondition, at the ideological level, of how liberalism can devolve into fascism, or indeed to some other non-liberal state. The idea that it is a sufficient explanation, as if ideas determined all things, is another story.

7. See Ronald Beiner, *Nietzsche, Heidegger, and the Far Right* (Philadelphia: University of Pennsylvania Press, 2018); also for an impassioned defense of the enlightenment against these critiques, Jonathan Israel, *A Revolution of the Mind: Radical Enlightenment and the Intellectual Origins of Modern Democracy* (Princeton, NJ, and Oxford: Princeton University Press, 2010), vii–ix.

8. See, for example, Gayatri Spivak, *Critique of Postcolonial Reason: Towards a History of the Vanishing Present* (Cambridge, MA: Harvard University Press, 1999); Dipesh Chakrabarty, *Provincialising Europe: Postcolonial Thought and Historical Difference* (Princeton, NJ: Princeton University Press, 2007; Amy Allen, *The End of*

Progress: Decolonising the Normative Foundations of Critical Theory (New York: Columbia University Press, 2017).

9. See Dennis Rasmussen, *The Pragmatic Enlightenment: Recovering the Liberalism of Hume, Smith, Montesquieu, and Voltaire* (Cambridge, UK: Cambridge University Press, 2013) and "Contemporary Political Theory as an Anti-Enlightenment Project", in *Rethinking the Enlightenment: Between History, Philosophy, and Politics*, ed. Geoff Boucher and Henry Martyn Lloyd (Lanham, MD: Lexington Books, 2018), 39–59.

10. See note 3 above; also Thomas McCarthy, "The Critique of Impure Reason: Foucault and the Frankfurt School", *Political Theory* 18, no. 3 (1990): 437–69.

11. Compare Daniel Gordon, "On the Supposed Obsolescence of the French Enlightenment", in Daniel Gordon, ed., *Postmodernism and the Enlightenment* (London: Routledge, 2001), esp. 211–12.

12. See, for example, Charles Taylor, *A Secular Age* (Cambridge, MA: Harvard University Press, 2018); John Milbank, *Theology and Social Theory* (London: Wiley-Blackwell, 1990); Christopher Brittain, "Washing His Hands of the Enlightenment: A Critique of John Milbank", *Theology and the Crisis of Engagement Essays on the Relationship of Theology and the Social Sciences,* ed. Jeff Nowers, Nestor Medina (Eugene, OR: Pickwick Publications, Wipf and Stock, 2014), 58–76.

13. This literature is huge and will be a constant interlocutor in these notes. See for an opening: Daniel Brewer, *The Enlightenment Past: Reconstructing Eighteenth-Century French Thought* (Cambridge, UK: Cambridge University Press, 2008); Anthony Pagden, *The Enlightenment and Why It Still Matters* (Oxford, UK: Oxford University Press, 2013), 1–18; James Schmidt, ed., *What Is Enlightenment? Eighteenth-Century Answers and Twentieth-Century Questions* (Berkeley: University of California Press, 1996); Tzvetan Todorov, *In Defence of the Enlightenment*, trans. Gila Walker (London: Atlantic Books, 2010); Will and Ariel Durant, *The Story of Civilization, Vol. IX, The Age of Voltaire* (New York: Simon & Schuster, 1965); Ira Wade, *The Structure and Form of the French Enlightenment, Volume 1: Esprit Philosophique* (Princeton, NJ: Princeton University Press, 1977a); *The Structure and Form of the French Enlightenment, Volume 2. Esprit Revolutionnaire* (Princeton, NJ: Princeton University Press, 1977b); Vincenzo Ferrone, *The Enlightenment: History of an Idea*, trans. Elisabetta Tarantino (Princeton, NJ: Princeton University Press, 2015); Genevieve Lloyd, *Enlightenment Shadows* (Oxford: Oxford University Press, 2013); Peter Gay, *The Enlightenment: An Interpretation, Volume I: The Rise of Modern Paganism* (New York: W. W. Norton & Co., 1995a); *The Enlightenment: An Interpretation, Volume II: The Science of Freedom* (New York: W. W. Norton & Co., 1995b); Dan Edelstein, *The Enlightenment: A Genealogy* (Chicago: University of Chicago Press, 2010); Gertrude Himmelfarb, *The Roads to Modernity. The British, French and American Enlightenments* (London: Vintage, 2008); Jonathan Israel, *Enlightenment Contested: Philosophy, Modernity, and the Emancipation of Man, 1670–1752* (Oxford: Oxford University Press, 2006); *Radical Enlightenment: Philosophy and the Making of Modernity, 1650–1750* (Oxford: Oxford University Press, 2001); *Democratic Enlightenment: Philosophy, Revolution and Human Rights, 1750–1790* (Oxford: Oxford University Press, 2013).

14. See Henry Martyn Lloyd, "Introduction", in Lloyd and Boucher, *Rethinking the Enlightenment*.

15. See on this also Matthew Sharpe and Michael Ure, *Philosophy as a Way of Life: History, Dimensions, Directions* (London: Bloomsbury, 2021), 205–12.

16. Nietzsche's "free spirits" are not "free thinkers", since they call Judaeochristian morals, based in the morality of the "Jewish prophets," into question, whereas Voltaire et al. want to secularize them, and do not go far enough. Such morality indeed limits the kinds of actions the free thinkers would support. See Friedrich Nietzsche, "Free Spirits", Part 2, *Beyond Good and Evil*, trans. R. J. Hollingdale (London: Penguin, 2003); Domenico Losurdo, *Friedrich Nietzsche: Aristocratic Rebel* (Leiden: Brill, 2020), esp. 456–59, 703–09.

17. Denis Diderot, "System", in Stephen J. Gendzier trans., *The Encyclopedia of Diderot and d'Alembert Collaborative Translation Project* (Ann Arbor: Michigan Publishing, University of Michigan Library), online at http://hdl.handle.net/2027/spo.did2222.0001.321. See Élodie Cassin, "Esprit systématique et esprit de système", *Labyrinthe* 34, no. 1 (2010), at http://labyrinthe.revues.org/4051; and see Denis Diderot, "Philosophy", in *The Encyclopedia of Diderot and d'Alembert Collaborative Translation Project*, trans. Julia Wallhager (Ann Arbor: Michigan Publishing, University of Michigan Library, 2015), last accessed 28 April 2021, <http://hdl.handle.net/2027/spo.did2222.0003.145>: esp. the following: "The obsession with system does no less harm to the progress of truth. By obsession with system, I do not mean the approach that connects various truths to each other so to form proofs which is nothing else but the true philosophical mind—rather I mean to designate the one that makes plans and forms systems of the universe to which it then wants to adjust phenomena by will or force. . . . It is certain that nothing is more praiseworthy than the practice adopted by the Academy of Sciences, to see, to observe, to set down in its registers observations and experiences, and to leave the desire to make a complete system for posterity when there is enough material for this; but this time is still far away, if indeed it will ever come. What thus makes the obsession with system so opposed to the progress of truth is that it is no longer possible to correct those who have imagined a system that has some appearance of verisimilitude. They preserve and very tightly hold on to everything that can serve in any way to confirm it; and, on the other hand, they do not take into consideration almost any of the objections that are opposed to it, or rather, they rid themselves of them by some frivolous distinction. They draw inner satisfaction from the sight of their work and the esteem that they hope to receive from it; they do not concentrate on anything except the image of truth that emerges from their opinions. They fixate on this image but never pay any sustained attention to the other side of their feelings, the one that would reveal its falseness to them. Add the prejudices and the passions to this . . . ," etc.

18. Ernst Cassirer, *The Philosophy of the Enlightenment* (Boston, MA: Beacon Press, 1955), 13.

19. For the mind as "uneven mirror", see Francis Bacon, *Novum Organum*, in *The Works of Francis Bacon . . . : Translations of the Philosophical Works, Vol. VIII*, ed. James Spedding et al. (New York: Hurd and Houghton, 1869), book II, 41.

20. On Bacon, Locke, and surrounding Royal Society thinkers, see Sorana Corneanu, *Regimens of the Mind* (Chicago: University of Chicago Press, 2011).
21. Stéphane van Damme, "The Philosophe/Philosopher", in Daniel Brewer, ed., *The Cambridge Companion to the French Enlightenment* (Cambridge, UK: Cambridge University Press, 2014), 153–66.
22. Daniel Brewer, cited in van Damme, "The Philosophe/Philosopher", 55.
23. See especially Pierre Hadot, *Philosophy as a Way of Life*, trans. M. Chase (London: Wiley-Blackwell, 1995).
24. Voltaire, "Philosopher", in *Philosophical Dictionary*, trans. Thomas Besterman (London: Penguin, 2004), 334.
25. Voltaire, "Philosopher"; cf. César Chesneau Du Marsais, "Philosopher", in Dena Goodman trans., *The Encyclopedia of Diderot and d'Alembert Collaborative Translation Project* (Ann Arbor: Michigan Publishing, University of Michigan Library), online at http://hdl.handle.net/2027/spo.did2222.0000.001; Sharpe and Ure, *Philosophy as a Way of Life*, 213–14.
26. Catherine Wilson, "The Enlightenment Philosopher as Social Critic", *Intellectual History Review* 18, no. 3 (2008): 416.
27. See notably Roger Pearson, *The Fables of Reason: A Study of Voltaire's "Contes Philosophiques"* (Oxford, UK: Oxford University Press, 1993).
28. Durant and Durant, *Age of Voltaire*, 497–98.
29. See for criticism of this MacIntyrean coinage, which has become currency of the realm, Robert Wolker, "Projecting the Enlightenment," in *After MacIntyre: Critical Perspectives on the Work of Alasdair MacIntyre*, ed. John Horton and Susan Mendus (Notre Dame, IN: University of Notre Dame Press, 1994).
30. Jonathan Israel, *A Revolution of the Mind: Radical Enlightenment and the Intellectual Origins of Modern Democracy* (Princeton, NJ: Princeton University Press, 2010), vii–ix; *Enlightenment Contested*; *Radical Enlightenment*.
31. For a recent summary of the debates on multiple enlightenments, see Ritchie Robertson, *The Enlightenment: The Pursuit of Happiness, 1680–1790* (New York: HarperCollins, 2021), 37–41. See, for example, Gertrude Himmelfarb, *The Roads to Modernity: The British, French and American Enlightenments* (London: Vintage, 2008). Himmelfarb contrasts the Scottish and French enlightenments, assigning many of the attributes which this book locates in Voltaire, Montesquieu, and Diderot to the Scots, but not (excepting Montesquieu, and we believe contestably) in the *philosophes*.
32. I am here indebted to Ira Wade, *Intellectual Origins of the French Enlightenment* (Princeton, NJ: Princeton University Press, 1971).
33. See esp. Henri Vyverberg, *Human Nature, Cultural Diversity, and the French Enlightenment* (Oxford, UK: Oxford University Press, 1989).
34. See Matthew Sharpe, "From Amy Allen to Abbé Raynal: Critical Theory, the Enlightenment and Colonialism", *Critical Horizons* 20, no. 2 (2019): 178–99.
35. Michel Foucault, "What Is Enlightenment?", trans. Catherine Porter, in *Ethics: Subjectivity and Truth, Vol. 1 of The Essential Works of Foucault, 1954–1984*, ed. Paul Rabinow (New York: New Press, 1997).

36. Immanuel Kant, *Critique of Judgment* (translated with introduction and notes by J. H. Bernard (2nd ed., revised) (London: Macmillan, 1914), §40, "Taste as a kind of *sensus communis*".

37. Cf. for comparison, Rumy Hasan, *Modern Europe and the Enlightenment* (Sussex, UK: Sussex University Press, 2021).

38. Non-specialists may find especially the chapter on Diderot demanding, on the *philosophe*'s wonderfully rich "Letter on the Blind". Evidently, I have done my best here to try to throw light on some of the many layers. Interested readers are directed towards Katherine Tunstall, *Blindness and Enlightenment: An Essay: With a New Translation of Diderot's "Letter on the Blind" and La Mothe Le Vayer's "Of a Man Born Blind"* (London: Continuum, 2011).

39. Diderot, *Essai sur les règnes de Claude et de Néron et sur la vie et les écrits de Sénèque pour servir d'introduction à la lecture de ce philosophe* (Paris: L'Imprimerie de J. J. Smith et al., 1792 [orig. 1782]), 424.

Chapter 1

Locke, Bayle, Critique, and Toleration

SOCIETY, RELIGION, AND THE NEW KNOWLEDGES: THE THREEFOLD DECENTERING OF EARLY MODERN EUROPE

We live in a period in which the enlightenment has received a very hostile critical press, looking back from the later twentieth century. It will therefore be helpful to start here by looking *forwards* at our subject, beginning by recovering an understanding of the historical context of the writings of Montesquieu, Voltaire, Diderot, and the other *lumières*.

Around 1720, when the first of our texts, *Persian Letters*, was conceived, European nations were led almost exclusively by absolute monarchs. The exception was the Netherlands, which had been a republic since 1581 (with the Union of Utrecht).[1] The Low Countries also represented a haven of toleration, which played host to the exiled René Descartes and Pierre Bayle, and seeded what Margaret C. Jacob was the first to call "the radical enlightenment".[2] Britain, soon to become a socio-political ideal for Montesquieu and Voltaire, had experienced the "glorious" peaceful revolution of 1689, becoming a constitutional monarchy, with some protection of civil liberties, but a very limited franchise.[3]

Elementary education was universally offered only in Württemberg, the Dutch republic, and the Duchy of Weimar, and had recently been achieved in Scotland (1696) and France (1698). In Britain, there were church-based charity schools for lower-class boys and girls (for reading, writing, sewing, knitting, spinning, and religion). In France, every town had an elementary school with a teacher chosen by local Catholic bishops or curates. Secondary schools were run there by the Jesuits, whilst nunneries provided secondary education for girls. In Britain, public schools were for upper-class Anglican boys exclusively. Otherwise, education was delivered by private tutors to the privileged.[4] In France, women could receive anything like an advanced education only in nunneries (see ch. 6).[5] Except (again) in the Dutch republic, universities were in decline. It is a striking fact that *none of the great philosophers or scientists of the later seventeenth century were university men*. Oxford and Cambridge were denounced by everyone from Francis Bacon to Edward Gibbon, and Adam Smith as decrepit and hostile to the new learnings.

Turning from the palaces of learning to the privies, even bathrooms were a privilege of the few. Cities had rudimentary sewers. In England in the eighteenth century, 59 percent of children died before the age of five, 64 percent before reaching the age of ten (especially of the whooping cough). Abandonment of infants was piously scorned and widely practiced. Between 1771 and 1779, 32,000 infants were admitted to the Paris Foundling Hospital, around 80 percent of whom perished. Venereal disease was widespread, as was prostitution in the capitals. Voltaire would estimate in his lifetime about a 20 percent mortality rate in France through smallpox, and an average longevity of twenty-seven years. Scything across the century of the enlightenment, there would be epidemics in France (1719), Sweden (1749), Vienna (1763, 1767), Tuscany (1764), and London (1766, 1770). The plague had visited London (1665), Vienna (1679), Prague (1681), and Prussia (1709) within living memory. Scarlet fever, malaria, dysentery, pneumonia, diphtheria, and yellow fever from the Americas were all common, a situation dramatized vividly for us in Voltaire's *Candide* (3.4).[6]

Brutal physical punishment for criminal offenders, administered publicly, was the norm.[7] This was still the age of honorific duels, sometimes fatal, in England and France. England had achieved *habeus corpus* and trial by jury. But there were gallows in every district of London. Most crimes in England attracted the capital sentence, and in the period of the enlightenment the number of capital crimes would grow from 50 in 1689 to 160 by 1820, including for such offences as forgery, theft of over forty shillings, shoplifting above 5 shillings, setting fire to a cornfield, and of course homosexuality (as in France and elsewhere). Prisons everywhere were hotbeds of disease: 75 percent of British prisoners died of typhus, Dr Johnson estimated. In France, the Crown had the capacity through *lettres de cachet* (secret letters) to imprison anyone *without public trial*—a fate which would soon befall Voltaire—as well as to make What Laws His Majesty Wished. French judges were able to use torture to elicit confessions, and call down hanging and drawing and quartering upon convicted offenders.

Everywhere in Europe, including in France, publications were officially censored. Even in the republican Netherlands, the radical philosopher Spinoza could only publish one book in his own lifetime, the *Tractatus*

Theologico-Politicus (1670), which still occasioned a scandal. Protestant countries and Britain were somewhat more lenient than the Catholic kingdoms. The very multitude of German principalities was a bonus for authors, who could readily "go next door" to publish sensitive items. In France, all the books of the age of enlightenment would have to receive (or not) the "Great Seal" of the monarch or regent.[8] After 1757, and the regicide attempt against Louis XV by Robert-François Damiens (known to recent readers from the colourful opening to Foucault's *Discipline and Punish*), censorship was tightened.[9] Reprobates could be flogged and receive nine years in galleys for buying or selling Voltaire, or other censored authors.

Nevertheless, the cultural world of this almost-unrecognizable, pre-enlightenment Europe had been changing over the previous three hundred years. The fourteenth and fifteenth centuries had seen the recovery of many of the long-lost or hidden texts of pagan antiquity: works of poetry, history, and philosophy which had animated the Italian, then wider European "Renaissance", and exercised a first decentering of medieval Catholicism.[10] The sixteenth century had then seen the Protestant Reformation emerge in the German states, led by Martin Luther, then spread to Calvinist Geneva, and much of Northern Europe: a second, religious decentering of the old *ordo*. The arrival of a competitor form of Christianity to the One and Universal Catholic Church had not occasioned civil peace. In 1524–1525, the German peasants' war (following widespread revolt, acerbically denounced by Luther himself) saw the death of at least 100,000 peasants. Following the establishment of Protestant "Huguenots" in France, the French religious (and dynastic) wars would span four decades (1562–1598), taking an estimated two to four million lives, including the infamous Saint Bartholomew's Day massacres of Huguenots in Paris in 1572. The years between 1568 and 1648 saw continued warring in the Low Countries (Netherlands) between Spanish Catholics and Dutch, mainly Calvinist republicans (led by elected *staedholders*). Between 1618 and 1648, finally, long-brewing religious and political disagreements within Bohemia in the Holy Roman Empire led to another bloody thirty years' war (killing between 25 percent and 40 percent of the population in some provinces).

The 1648 Treaty of Westphalia ended the ten decades of strife within the Holy Roman Empire, granting monarchs the right to determine the religion of their own kingdoms. In 1689, following the Glorious Revolution, the British Act of Toleration was extended to non-Anglican Protestants, although not Catholics. In France, however, after 1650, the Sun King Louis XIV came under increasing Catholic pressure to revoke the tolerant Edict of Nantes, brokered by Henri IV, who would soon become an icon of the enlightenment, and the subject of one of Voltaire's epics. Following 1660, over 500

Protestant churches were again torn down. Huguenots were prevented from advancing within guilds (1664) or establishing new colleges (1666). In 1685, the revocation of the Edict of Nantes unleashed what Jules Michelet called the "holy terror". Some 400,000 Huguenots, including the philosopher Pierre Bayle, fled France to the Low Countries and elsewhere amidst torture, forced confessions, the closure of Huguenot businesses, and expropriation of their lands.[11] In 1721, when we take up our scene with *Persian Letters* in chapter 2, you could not openly worship as a Protestant in some French provinces. In a way which is vital to understanding the fierce anti-clericalism of the French enlightenment, that is to say:

> [w]hereas in Switzerland, Germany, Holland, and England reformation had served to express rebellion against the church, no such vehicle of resentment remained in France: the reaction against Romanism found it safer to be utterly sceptical than openly Protestant. The French Renaissance, unimpeded by Protestantism, passed directly into the Enlightenment after the death of [Louis XIV].[12]

Meanwhile, European culture and learning had been undergoing a third radical set of changes, with the advent of new forms of understanding the natural world, beginning with Copernicus's *De revolutionibus orbium coelestium* of 1543 and progressively upsetting the foundational premises of both the biblical, and Ptolemaic-Aristotelian, conceptions of nature. The educated European of 1600, excepting a small minority of Copernicans, understood the cosmos to be finite, spherical, and geocentric.[13] The heavenly bodies were held to be perfect, moving in perfect spheres in a "fifth element", aether, wholly different from anything we experienced "here below". Comets were seen as divine signs (see ch. 1), the Earth as being around six thousand years old (following the Bible), and mathematics was considered applicable only to heavenly bodies. As for nature on Earth, including the animal kingdom, it, as it were, had no history. All species had been created by God in the beginning, as described in the book of Genesis.

By 1700, incredibly, nearly all of these consensus beliefs had been challenged or overthrown. The physical universe was now understood to be very large, if not infinite (per Giordano Bruno, who burned for his ideas). Our solar system was conceived as heliocentric; the moon and other heavenly bodies had been seen through telescopes to be imperfect; and moons had been seen orbiting around Jupiter. The very planets were proven to move in ellipses, not circles; and comets in mathematisable parabolas. The same physical laws, led by the gravity mathematised by Isaac Newton in his *Principia Mathematica* (1687), were seen as applying both above and below. Terrestrial motion and acceleration were known to be likewise reducible to mathematical laws, following the work of Galileo, Hooke, Boyle, Huygens, and Newton. Only the biblical account of the age of the Earth, and the divine creation of all species "in the beginning" survived the "century of genius", although these suppositions too would be called into doubt by the end of the eighteenth century.

In mathematics, the seventeenth century had seen the development of differential calculus (Newton and Leibniz, simultaneously), and the beginning of statistics (with Graunt and Perry). In optics, diffraction had been grasped, the microscope and telescope produced, and Hooke and Huygens had developed the wave theory of light. The new science of meteorology had taken form, and geology's first researches on fossils had begun to suggest the deep, pre-Adamic antiquity of the globe. In geography, monographs had charted the new worlds of Canada, Mexico, Brazil, Tibet, Mongolia, and China; Cassini's world map had charted precise latitudes and longitudes.

In physics, Huygens's pendulum clocks had mastered keeping time and measuring longitude at sea; atmospheric pressure had been discovered (by Pascal and Torricelli); the nature of electricity had attracted study (by Gilbert, Kircher, and others); and above all, Newton's basic laws of physics (gravity, the conservation of energy, the law of equal and opposite reaction) had reshaped the understanding of the solar system. In chemistry, fire's need for oxygen ("a little vital quintessence" [Boyle]) was now understood. In biology, microscopic cells had been discovered by Hooke, the cataloguing of over 18,000 plant species had been undertaken by Ray (1670), the sexuality of plants had been grasped, and protozoa, spermatozoa, and the anatomy of insects studied.

Similar leaps had occurred in anatomy and physiology, and medicine had progressed from "physic" and "laying on of hands" to Athanasius Kircher's discovery of the microscopic organisms at work in diseases, the beginning of drug treatments, Thomas Sydenham's cataloguing of diseases, even the first intravenous injections and blood transfusions.[14]

These extraordinary developments in Europeans' understandings of the natural world posed profound dilemmas. They opened up both new possibilities and new sources of anxiety. Could the new knowledges be reconciled with the old faiths? Did the advent of the new knowledges instead speak to the need to develop new, more rational forms of religion, based not upon the Bible and putative revelations to exceptional prophets, but upon God's gift of reason to all human beings? Might morality stand independently of, and even criticise, the claims of ancient religious traditions like Christianity? And could the new methods of the sciences, so successful in charting the stars and revealing nature's minute workings, be applied to human morality and politics?

The highly volatile intellectual ferment which came to be called "the enlightenment" arose out of the felt need of a growing number of European intellectuals to address the many questions arising out of these scientific developments which had so profoundly decentred the European biblical sense of human cosmic centrality, against the background of the simultaneous breakdown of universal religious consensus in early modern Europe occasioned by the Reformation:

> Doubtless men would continue to form or favour conceptions of the world that would give hope and consolation, meaning and dignity, to harassed, fleeting lives; but how could the Christian *epos* of creation, original sin, and divine redemption stand up in a perspective that reduced the earth to a speck among a million stars? What was man that the God of such a universe should be mindful of him? How could the poetry of Genesis survive the explorations of geology? ... How could the miracles of Christ, not to mention those widely ascribed to the saints and Satan, be reconciled with the apparent reign of universal law? How could the soul or mind of man be immortal when it seemed so dependent on the nerves and other tissues visibly doomed to decay? What must happen when the religion is so challenged by a science daily growing in scope, achievements, and prestige? And what must happen to a civilization based upon a moral code based upon that religion?[15]

To pose such questions, whilst no longer accepting uncritical appeal to traditions: this description gives us a first approximation of what the French enlighteners would attempt.

BACON AND LOCKE ON THE CONDUCT AND LIMITS OF THE HUMAN UNDERSTANDING

This rush of natural philosophical discoveries was not the result of an unmotivated change in worldview, visited upon Europe by an inscrutable providence or "Being". The cumulative scale of the challenge they posed to established culture reflects how they emerged from new conceptions, methods, and cultures of collective inquiry that developed following 1600 in Europe and the British Isles in relative independence from theological supervision and sponsorship. Today, we call such conceptions of inquiry "scientific". But this word usage was only stabilised later. We are also wont to call them simply "rational". Yet this is also imprecise. For the Aristotelianism and scholasticism of the medieval and early modern universities were nothing if not highly "rational". It was these conceptions of inquiry that Galileo, Bacon, Descartes, Gassendi, and other early moderns all opposed.

What was more specifically *new* in the new forms of natural philosophy of the seventeenth and eighteenth centuries were ways of *discovering* truths about the natural world.[16] The new sciences responded in new ways to the vital question of where and how we get our premises (or "middle terms") for understanding the natural and social worlds. Aristotelian, Stoic, and scholastic logics were only too adept at ordering and reordering them. The British philosopher and statesman, Francis Bacon—whom Diderot and d'Alembert would laud in the *Encyclopédie* in 1751 as "the most universal and eloquent of philosophers"—was a decisive figure here (ch. 4).[17] Bacon's wide-ranging work both inspired scholars with the hope that a "new advancement of learning" could be possible, as well as, improbably, already sketching out a "new organon" (or method) by which such advancement could be effected.[18] Bacon strongly challenged the forms of Aristotelian philosophy taught in the universities of his time. This pedagogical program, he claimed, placed too great an emphasis on the rules for deducing and demonstrating conclusions from accepted ideas, without adequately explaining how we can generate true observations and inductions concerning natural phenomena in the first place.[19]

For Bacon, human beings face what later philosophers call an underdetermination of our competing theories by the data. People have accordingly been only too capable of producing any number of internally coherent but mutually inconsistent understandings of the world: think of Christianity, Islam, Judaism, Aristotelianism, Platonism, Stoicism, Epicureanism, and so forth.[20] In a characteristic metaphor, Bacon depicts the existing, incommensurable but internally coherent intellectual systems as so many stage settings ("idols of the theatre") in which different theoretical stories are played out. All of them are plausible enough to attract followers, and many are as exciting as stage dramas. But it is impossible to decide which of their stories is truest to the shared world of natural kinds or "forms" actually out there: what Bacon calls the "book of God's works".[21]

Bacon argues powerfully that the human mind is, as it were, "preprogramed" to form erroneous, partial, and flattering opinions about the world. Principally at issue here is what he famously calls the "idols of the [human] tribe (*tribus*)". For Bacon, if we are to avoid intellectual errors, we need to become aware of how:

- human beings are wont to overgeneralise on the basis of too few cases, especially if some of the cases in question are striking and memorable;
- once they form opinions, people tend to only seek out confirmations of what they already believe to be right or true ("confirmation bias"); hence,
  - we prefer to ignore and explain away contradictory evidences ("negative instances") to our beliefs;

- or else we "injuriously" turn upon (by attacking or "de-platforming") those who disagree with us, shooting the messengers;
- above all, our understanding is not a "dry light", unsaturated by individual and shared interests, passions, and prejudices, which push us to hold for true what we would *like* to be so, rather than patiently assessing all of the evidence and hearing all relevant testimony.[22]

As different individuals, Bacon additionally notes, we also each bring our own specific "idols of the cave" to our inquiries. These are predispositions to forming and favouring particular kinds of beliefs, shaped by our specific abilities and backgrounds. Some of us are more analytic, others more "sublime", and prone to seek out big pictures. Some favour everything old; others are only engaged by what is new. Each of us has to fight the tendency to falsely suppose that, since we may be gifted in some particular pursuits (say, analytic or continental philosophy, mathematics, or economics), that these are the truest or best approaches to all problems.[23] We all use natural languages, finally, exchanging words like shared coins. But these words were not coined to reflect more exacting understandings of the natures and causes of things than are required in peoples' everyday experiences. Due to our very words, these "idols of the marketplace", we thus find ourselves limited in the ways we see things in the world.[24]

On the basis of his extraordinary diagnosis of these four "idols of the mind" (of tribe, cave, marketplace, and theatre), Bacon proposed nothing short of a new logic for discovering things about the natural world in book II of his *Novum Organum*. This logic included detailed prescriptions for the practice of collective modes of "data collection", tabulation, and reportage, as well as what we now know as controlled experimentation to isolate the active and invariant causes of naturally occurring phenomena.[25] The new Baconian method is famously presented in the "Preface" to the *Novum Organum* as almost "mechanical" in its operations. But it participates in what Sorana Corneanu has described as a wider early modern tradition of writings interested in the cultivation of the mind.[26] This tradition, as Corneanu charts it, looked back to Marcus Tullius Cicero and other ancient philosophers who conceived philosophy itself as a means to transform, and better, the character of inquirers: a *cultura* or *medicina animi* (culture or medicine of the mind).[27] On the other hand, it embraced forms of Augustinian, Christian thought which stressed that the effect of the biblical fall on the human mind had been to limit and "tincture" its epistemic capacities.[28] This fall made the human mind, left to its own devices, like an "uneven mirror", rather than one which truly frames and reflects God's light.[29] Only by becoming aware of our characteristic propensities to form false judgements, in order to actively combat them as individuals and within new cultures of shared, critical inquiry, could we hope to advance our knowledge.[30]

The significance in pre-shaping the enlightenment of this idea of pursuing new knowledges, both through and as a means to cultivate new kinds of inquirers, is enormous. In academic philosophy, we tend to consider ethics (the theory of good character and right action) and epistemology (the theory of knowledge) as wholly separate things. At the same time, like everyone else, academics describe opinions as "just" or "unjust" and call ethical attitudes "warranted" or "unwarranted". For Bacon, and also for a second philosopher decisive in pre-shaping the French enlightenment, John Locke, the attempt to discover true knowledge of the world just *was* also an ethical task.[31] It was also one which inescapably implicates wider socio-political considerations.

Locke's *Essay on Human Understanding* remains a classic of modern epistemology. It is widely taught today, at least in extracts. Emphasis is placed on Locke's famous claims that the mind, until it experiences external things through the senses, is like a *tabula rasa* or clean slate (albeit a "slate" which is imbued with in-born capacities which may be developed).[32] The ideas we form about the world are hence based upon our experiences.[33] Locke's understanding of the origin of our ideas underlies the later label we use for his thought, saying that he was an "empiricist", from the Greek *empeiria*.[34] Yet, by emphasising just these aspects of Locke's position, we abstract Locke's text from its *cultura animi* lineage, as well as its historical context. And we largely don't teach those aspects of *The Essay on Human Understanding* which made it so vital for Voltaire, Diderot, and other French enlighteners, and which explain why they saw Locke's *Essay* as less an exercise in cold epistemology than as philosophical dynamite with which to shake the foundations of many established norms and beliefs.

In truth, Locke makes the ethical intentionality of his epistemological inquiry clear from the very opening of the *Essay*. His aim, he tells us, is to inquire into the "nature of the understanding", so that:

> by this enquiry ..., I can discover the powers thereof; how far they reach; to what things they are in any degree proportionate; and where they fail us: [for] I suppose it may be of use to prevail with the busy mind of man, to be more cautious in meddling with things exceeding its comprehension; to stop when it is at the utmost extent of its tether; and to sit down in a quiet ignorance of those things, which, upon examination, are found to be beyond the reach of our capacities.[35]

What should strike us about this passage is firstly the way that Locke's concerns with the human understanding are proposed with a view to proposing certain *virtues*. There is "caution" about what we claim to be true, lucidity about our own limits, a "learned ignorance" about what we can and do not know, and the patient ability (as he continues) "to content ourselves with what is attainable by us": a kind of epistemic moderation.[36] In his unpublished text, *On the Conduct of the Understanding*, planned as a fifth part to the *Essay*, Locke undertakes his own, post-Baconian diagnosis of the characteristic bad "habits" or "miscarriages" of the understanding which underlie the typical errors people make when they seek knowledge, and which we should set out to identify and overcome.[37] We claim to know more, and more certainly, than evidence warrants. Some of us get stuck in pedantic minutiae, whilst others sweep to overgeneralisations. Some people closed-mindedly overspecialise, while others range too widely. We mistake coincidences for causes, and are too readily seduced by sophisms, our own passions, and fine language. All the while, we too often read only in order to sample and "show off", rather than to comprehend and expand our outlooks.[38] For Locke, self-consciously echoing Bacon's diagnosis of the mind's idols in the *Novum Organum*, these errors reflect:

- the human tendency to over-rely upon existing epistemic, political, and religious authorities, as well as the prejudices that we imbibe as children from our parents and wider cultures;
- the influence of our wishes and fears on what we take to be plausible and true;
- the "haste" or "precipitancy" of leaping to conclusions given only inadequate, partial evidences;
- our egoistic inability to see our own faults, whilst being astutely aware of others', and;
- as in Bacon, a kind of inveterate human "laziness" or "sloth", so that once we accept an idea, we too readily identify with it as "ours", and as such something to be "defended" in argument, rather than improved upon in dialogue.[39]

Secondly, there is Locke's concern to establish *the limits* of human knowledge and capacity, central to books III and IV of the *Essay*. Any Lockean *paideia* (philosophical education) will primarily be a training in epistemic modesty. "I think that it is suitable to the modesty of philosophy not to pronounce dogmatically on topics where we lack the evidentness that could produce knowledge"[40], Locke makes clear—stealing a march by some years on Kant's critical philosophy, and its "transcendental dialectic". As Locke writes:

'Tis of great use to the Sailor to know the length of his Line, though he cannot with it fathom all the depths of the Ocean. 'Tis well he knows, that it is long enough to reach the bottom, at such Places, as are necessary to direct his

Voyage, and caution him against upon Shoales, that may ruin him. Our business is . . . not to know all things, but those which concern our Conduct.[41]

We are worlds away from utopian declarations on behalf of the all-conquering human mind like those often spliced out of Descartes or Bacon as speaking to the incorrigible *hybris* of "the enlightenment". Locke maintains that knowledge is the perception of the agreement between ideas, and he distinguishes three degrees of such agreement: intuitive knowledge, of the immediate connections between ideas; sensible knowledge, of objects immediately perceptible to our senses; and demonstrative knowledge, based on the deductive connections between ideas whose immediate connection is not evident.[42] *In all three degrees*, as Voltaire would soon stress (ch. 3, Locke goes to his own lengths to show *the limits* of our cognitive abilities. There are only a small number of connections between things which any human mind, however powerful, can intuitively grasp. Sensible knowledge, likewise, is as limited as our senses, so that when we so much as move our heads from left to right, what we see and thus immediately "know" changes. By the same token, our demonstrative knowledge of reality is limited to the extent that "we can't always find intermediaries" which connect distant ideas.[43] And in any case, as Bacon stressed, demonstrative truth-claims about the external world will be only as truthful as their first premises about things, drawn either from our limited sensible experience or our even more limited intuitions.

As far as Locke is concerned, the causes of human error and ignorance are legion. There is the narrow circle of what our senses can perceive, against the "whole vast extent of what there is",[44] a thought which will become the basis of Locke's scepticism about humans' capacities to establish truths in metaphysics. Some things are too remote in space or time to be experienced, like many secrets of astronomy; and the sheer scale of astronomical phenomena should serve to dwarf human pride, a thought we'll see Voltaire soon making great play with (ch. 3).[45] Other natural things, as microscopy had made clear, are so minuscule as to mostly escape our reckonings.[46] There is then the "lack of connection" between many of our ideas, even ideas as basic as those of mind and body, the principles of whose interactions remain a "hard problem" to this day. Again, we must admit ignorance of the essential realities of many of the ideas we conjure with, as, for example, that of "soul", or even of "matter", and one might soon enough add, "God".[47]

In this founding text of the enlightenment, therefore, Locke upholds the sobering thought that the extent of human ignorance is "infinitely larger" than the extent of what we do, or may ever, know:

> I don't think it is an insult to human excellence to be sure, as I am, that our knowledge would never reach to all we might want to know concerning the

ideas that we have, or to be able to surmount all of the difficulties and answer all of the questions that might arise concerning any of them.[48]

We see that any Lockean enlightenment this side of complete scepticism would have to begin with an acknowledgement of the limitations of our understanding, and integrate measures to combat the human predilections to error. We would also need to acknowledge the comic hybris at play in our propensity to shape our understandings of what *is* around our wishes and passions concerning what *ought to be*; and desist from proclaiming with unwarranted certainty on matters beyond the scope of what experience can certify. "These few narrow inlets" of the senses, and our resulting ideas, "are so disproportionate to the whole vast extent of what there is, as you will easily be brought to agree, unless you are so foolish as to think that your span—what you can experience and understand—is the measure of things".[49] For Locke, contra Protagoras, human edicts and wishes are not the measure of all things. The attempt to position them so is the pith of *un*enlightenment.[50]

Locke's philosophy has two further extraordinary implications which pave the road towards the French enlighteners, each of them pointing in noticeably socio-political directions. If knowledge is based on sense experience, firstly, there is no reason to suppose that the ideas of our particular tribe or religion are intrinsically superior to those of other cultures'. Others' ideas can instead be expected to differ vastly from ours, as much as do their experiences of climate, diet, culture, and geography (ch. 5). In his famous refutation of the idea of universal innate ideas in book I of the *Essay*, Locke hence pays great attention to the experiences and ideas of other cultures, as they had been reported from the new worlds (see ch. 2). In short, John Locke is what the postmodernist age celebrated as a "thinker of difference". There are cultures of the past, like Sparta and Rome, which thought about children so differently from us that they practiced "exposure" of weak infants (leaving them to die), which we find unconscionable. The Spanish poet-chronicler Garcilaso de la Vega reports even stranger customs amongst the people of Peru, which likewise challenge just how natural, inevitable, or uniquely God-given Europeans' mores might be.[51] "Had you or I been born in the bay of Soldana", Locke reflects—and readers should note the tension between Locke's continuing assumption of European superiority here[52], and the way that his empiricism renders this a contingent, not essential matter:

> possibly our thoughts and notions had not exceeded the brutish ones of the Hottentots that reside there, *and had the Virginia King Apochancana been educated in England*, he had been perhaps as knowing a divine, and as good a mathematician, as any in it, the difference between him and a more improved

Englishman lying barely in this, that the exercise of his faculties was bounded within the ways, modes, and notions of his own country.[53]

Secondly, Locke's position leads him to propose that the differences in perceived intelligence between different human beings, and potentially entire peoples, mustn't be based on unchangeable historical, traditional, or genetic inheritances. Decisive instead will be different individuals' access to different forms of experience and education. So it is that in his sections of the *Essay* on the causes of human errors[54], Locke laments that the majority of human beings have been so occupied by labour and necessity that they have had no *chance* to learn any higher studies. God has given everyone the capacity to know, he opines, but "the empire of custom" prevents most from developing this capacity. Nevertheless—and here's the rub—the empire of custom, unlike that of Nature or God, might in principle be reformed, since it is a human thing.

This progressive political implication is glimpsed by Locke himself, although it will only be developed by subsequent thinkers. Entire peoples are "hemmed in" by their laws and authorities, Locke observes.[55] The latter prevent them from accessing anything but the most basic education, instead "forcing them to swallow down" beliefs like medicine, "without knowing what they are made of or how they work, and having to settle that they will effect the cure".[56] Given how limited our individual knowledge is, Locke is unsurprised that most people so readily rely on hearsay, established traditions, and their own personal predilections: "This tenet has the support of revered antiquity, it comes to me with the passport of former ages, so I can safely accept it. Other men have been and are of the same opinion, so it is reasonable for me to embrace it too".[57] He is also aware of the political pressures that incentivize such conformity, "in this way winning the approval of those who can give him credit, promotion, or protection".[58] Nevertheless, the seed of enlightenment socio-cultural critique, spanning epistemology into political concerns, is unmistakably present in *The Essay on Human Understanding*. "If we could see the secret motives that influence the men of reputation and learning in the world, and the leaders of parties," Locke dryly states, "we wouldn't always find that they were to lead to their favored doctrines by embracing truth for its own sake".[59]

BAYLE, THE CRITIQUE OF SUPERSTITION, AND THE BIRTH OF TOLERATION

The final precursor to the French enlighteners, too often forgotten today, is John Locke's near-contemporary: the encyclopedic sceptic and first modern

Western defender of complete religious toleration, Pierre Bayle. Bayle's 1682 *Various Thoughts on the Occasion of a Comet* itself became the occasion for a scandal. Bayle's book patiently dismantles claims that comets could be signs from God presaging or precipitating disasters, in order to call Christians to repentance.[60] Like Bacon and Locke before him, Bayle laments the extent to which such beliefs are based upon inadequate, highly selective samplings and interpretations of the evidence. Specifically, he notes:

- the mechanism for comets exerting such divine influence on terrestrial affairs is opaque (§§11–14);
- many comets don't precede disasters, which nevertheless occur without these signs (§74);
- there are many more comets than there are such disasters (§43);
- comets are seen by non-Christians, and they were taken by pre-Christian pagans as missives from *their* false deities, hence encouraging further idolatry, not conversion to the True Faith (§§60, 62, 67, 70);
- moreover, the sources who report these signs, mainly poets and historians, are often unreliable, having a tendency to exaggerate the striking, unusual, exceptional, wonderful, or fearful to move copy (§§4–5).

Bayle agrees with Locke that most people believe superstitious things based on nothing more than hearsay and beliefs imbibed in childhood. It follows that:

[w]e would reduce the vote of an infinite number of people to the authority of two or three persons who, having pronounced a doctrine one supposed they had thoroughly examined, persuaded a number of others of it through the prejudice in favor of their worth, and . . . [a] natural laziness [which] found its account in believing in one fell swoop what they were told, rather than examining it carefully. (§7)

Any beliefs about mind-independent reality do not become probable or true based solely on grounds of the numbers of people who believe them, "except insofar as it has appeared true to several persons independently of every predisposition and solely by means of the force of judicious examination accompanied by exactitude and a great understanding of things" (§47).[61] We should hope that truths about the natural world become widely believed. But popular belief is not a sure mark of truth, as Christians can concur, since:

otherwise it would be necessary to say that the superstitions of the Romans had learned from the Tuscans in the matter of omens and prodigies and all the impertinences of the pagans concerning divination were so many incontestable truths, since everyone was as predisposed in favor of them as of the presages of comets. (§45)

For Bayle as for Bacon and Locke, any judicious inquiry into what is true or likely has to take into account confirmation bias, shaped by peoples' individual passions, as well as their group interests and ties. As we know in the age of QAnon, there is a real tendency people experience to favour any belief, however otherwise improbable, which "arouses and flatters the passions and ... agitates men through the various interests that attach them to society", including fear, anger, suspicion, and hatred (§22). People are especially wont to be carried away by fascination with anything exceptional or fearful: earthquakes, floods, storms, pandemics, the spectre of hidden cabals ... :

> And because minds seized by the fright of subjects that merit it are easily shaken by others that do not merit it as much, it seems to me also that men, having once been seized by fear of these great spectacles, could have subsequently been astonished over lesser things and passed insensibly to a general fear of everything uncommon, not knowing, for want of being good philosophers, that extraordinary effects, like the production of monsters, are as much pure effects of nature as those produced daily. (§65)[62]

It is very easy to see in Bayle's critique of the then-popular superstitions concerning comets as omens the germs of a far wider critique of the epistemic bases of revealed religions—a critique which he carries out in many entries, and extended footnotes, of his *Historical and Critical Dictionary* (see ch. 3).[63] Nevertheless, the scandal occasioned by *Various Thoughts on the Occasion of a Comet* originates elsewhere. For, in the context of rebutting the seemingly pious claim that God sends comets to warn people against lapsing into atheism, Bayle's book has the temerity to assert the unthinkable: that *a society of virtuous atheists* is in principle possible (§§144–161). Up until that time, it was universally maintained in Christian Europe that revealed religion was a necessary check on human egoism, passion, and folly, without which no crime would be impermissible, and no outrage remain unventured. Bayle counters, however, that allowing non-belief in some sanctioning God would only amount to licensing immorality only if we could be sure:

a) that people's moral conduct was actually shaped by their professed theological beliefs;
b) that belief in such a God was necessary for moral behaviour.

But Bayle is sceptical as to (a): "When one compares the morals of a man who has a religion with the general idea one has of the morals of this man, one is surprised to find no conformity between these two things," he asserts.[64] Today, we can, for instance, wonder how some Christians have come to embrace an openly adulterous, and clearly Godless, president in the United States. Bayle is trenchantly clear: "Let man be as reasonable [a] creature as you like; it is no less true that he almost never acts in accordance with his principles" (§136).

For (b), Bayle's urbane scepticism about the human propensity to what the Greeks called *akrasia* (lack of self-control) prompts him to venture a wholly naturalistic explanation of the wellsprings of human motivation and morality. It is not people's pious professions of faith in any Cause, secular or religious, which shape their moral choices: these "almost always accommodate [themselves] to the dominant passion of the heart or to the inclination of the temperament, to the force of adopted habits, and to the taste for or sensitivity to certain objects" (§135). There are crimes of lust, passion, and envy in all societies, independent of creed (§136). When we look at Christian history with non-partisan eyes, Bayle risks commenting, we see that even "those who believe in a paradise and a hell are capable of committing every sort of crime" (§138; §§138–140).

To those who declaim that the fear of God is necessary to correct human iniquity, Bayle echoes Bacon and Locke. "I will always call upon experience" to decide such matters, not appeal to any preestablished credo (§145). The true bases of morality, it seems to Bayle, lie in "the inclination to pity, to sobriety, to good-natured conduct", whose bases are not divine (§145). They hail "from a certain disposition of the temperament, fortified by education, by personal interest, by the desire to be praised, by the instinct of reason, or by similar motives that are met in an atheist as well as in other men" (§145). For this reason, a society of atheists would need laws, police, and a bailiff; but no more (or less) so than the good societies of Christendom.

We see, therefore, why, in his remarkable book on the history and concept of tolerance, *Toleration in Conflict*, critical theorist Rainer Forst assigns to Pierre Bayle a place of honour.[65] Above all in Bayle's 1685 *Philosophical Commentary on the Words of the Gospel: Compel Them to Come In*, Forst notes that Bayle produces a series of arguments in favour of tolerating religious dissent which at once complement his defenses of the possibility of virtuous atheists, and pave the way for Voltaire, Diderot, and others.[66] As Locke had done, Bayle firstly appeals to Protestant arguments about the freedom of the "erring conscience" (of someone who honestly believes in false deities) as something God has given individuals their own, inalienable responsibility for.[67] It is wrong, and ultimately useless, to force others to "come into" one's particular denomination, since they must freely choose their faith or their perdition. Moreover, advancing upon ideas present in *Various Thoughts*, Bayle asserts the natural sources of even "mistaken" religious professions: they lie not in sin, but in human conventions, as well as childhood and educational experiences. Anyone who grows up in an Islamic nation cannot be blamed for not arriving at adulthood a convinced Christian.[68] In a Cartesian fashion, Bayle also appeals to a "natural light" of reason which must be invoked to interpret scripture, and should prevent reading the Bible as recommending unnatural or immoral actions, even towards heretics or heathens.[69]

However, these arguments for toleration are not the most telling that he bequeaths to Montesquieu, Voltaire, Diderot, and his other *philosophe*-admirers. For Bayle is aware that those who persecute others are also following their erring consciences. They profess the same unshakable certainty as we do in our faith, about the God-given sanctity of their persecutory actions. Bayle's *Philosophical Commentary* also hence produces a further, epistemic argument to rule out the "conscientious persecutor", and which targets fanatics' claim to exclusive knowledge of the Truth.[70] To persecute others, Bayle argues, we must be certain that we and we alone are in possession of the absolute exonerating Truth. Yet, here joining Locke (and before him Montaigne[71]), Bayle argues that human understanding is so limited as to prevent any sectarian declaring rightfully that they possess such a Truth:

> Now it is impossible in our present state to know certainly that the Truth which appears to us such (I speak here of the Truths of Religion in particular . . .) is absolutely and really the Truth . . . for on the contrary, all the world agree, that the Truths God has reveal'd to us in his Word are deep and unsearchable Mysterys, which require the captivating our Understandings to the Obedience of Faith.[72]

The certainty we profess, in our postcode, nation, religion, ethnicity, or sect, is not a certitude of anything outside our own subjective conviction. It is an "equivocal mark of truth".[73] To see this, we need again only consider those *Others* we disagree with. For the same certitude "be found in the very Pagans, and the most abandon'd hereticks".[74] In Bayle as in Locke, therefore, the acceptance of the limits of the human understanding is tied to what postmodernism calls a thought of difference. Far from being reviled by the closed-minded enlighteners, this thought becomes foundational to their central ethico-political cause:

> I shan't, I say, make any Advantage of this Example to shew, that all that odd Variety of Worship is not unbecoming to the Grandeur of a Being infinitely perfect, who has left such a vast Diversity in Nature as an Image of his Character of Infinite . . . But as [Unity and Agreement among Men] is a thing more to be wish'd than hop'd for; as difference of Opinions seems to be Man's inseparable felicity, as long as his Understanding is so limited, and his Heart so inordinate; we should endeavor to reduce this Evil within to the narrowest limits: and

certainly the way to do this is by mutually tolerating each other, either in the same Communion, if the Nature of the Differences will permit, or at least in the same City.[75]

THE ENLIGHTENMENT TEMPLATE: SELF-CRITICISM, SELF-OTHERING, AND TOLERATION

With Pierre Bayle's radical defence of religious pluralism and toleration, we arrive in the anteroom of the eighteenth-century French enlightenment. To stress:

- If theological critics of the enlightenment were to be uncritically believed, we ought to have explored in this chapter a burgeoning, radical atheism, primed to burst with Voltaire and others into materialistic, God-denying flames. *We have approached instead only Bayle's principled defence of the legitimacy of religious dissent and agnosticism, and with these, the first gestures towards a wholly secular, naturalistic account of the bases of morality and legality.*
- If postmodern critics of the enlightenment were to be uncritically assented to, we should have found in Bacon, Locke, and Bayle the most strident assertions of human capacity, announcing the hybristic Promethean project of mastering all nature. *We have read instead their echoing calls to epistemic self-assessment and a heightened awareness of both the limits of human understanding and the inveterate sources of human partiality, bias, folly, and error.*
- If postcolonial critics of the enlightenment were to be uncritically accepted, finally, we should have found in the enlighteners' seventeenth-century heroes triumphant assertions of European superiority and inevitability, licensing colonial imperialisms (ch. 5). *Instead, we have seen increasing appeals to the divergence of human experience, rooted in the experimental empiricism sanctioned by Bacon, Locke, and the emerging natural sciences,* adduced less to enthrone European certainties than to call the same self-certainties into question.

It is this last critical thought, and the critical practice of self-othering it points towards, which we will see principally developed by Montesquieu in *Persian Letters*.

NOTES

1. Wade, *Esprit Philosophique*, 315–16.
2. Margaret C. Jacob, *The Radical Enlightenment: Pantheists, Freemasons and Republicans* (London: George Allen and Unwin, 1981).
3. Wade, *Esprit Philosophique*, 120–74a.
4. Durant and Durant, *Age of Voltaire*, 62–63.
5. Durant and Durant, *Age of Voltaire*, 186–87.
6. Durant and Durant, *Age of Voltaire*, 589–92.
7. See for the following paragraph Gay, *Science of Freedom*, 424–47.
8. Jacob, *Radical Enlightenment*; Israel, *Enlightenment Contested*, 97–118; 2013, 292–93, 427–33.
9. Durant and Durant, *Age of Voltaire*, 496–98. See Michel Foucault, *Discipline and Punish*, trans. Alan Sheridan (New York: Vintage, 1979), 3–6; also Curran, *Diderot and the Art of Thinking Freely*, 145–51.
10. Wade, *Intellectual Origins*, 61–130; 146–52.
11. Nannerl O. Keohane, *Philosophy and the State in France: The Renaissance to the Enlightenment* (Princeton, NJ: Princeton UP, 1980), 312–18.
12. Durant, *Age of Louis XIV*, 75.
13. The following paragraphs draw on the magisterial works of H. Floris Cohen, *How Modern Science Came Into the World: Four Civilizations, One 17th-Century Breakthrough* (Amsterdam: Amsterdam University Press, 2012); with Will and Ariel Durant, *The Story of Civilization, Volume VIII: The Age of Louis XIV* (New York: Simon & Schuster, 1963), 493–530 and Will and Ariel Durant, *The Story of Civilization, Volume IX: The Age of Voltaire* (New York: Simon & Schuster, 1965), 507–85; and Henry Smith Williams, *History of Science, Volumes II–IV* (New York, London: Harper & Brothers, 1904).
14. The advances had been made possible, and animated by, new "places of learning" (Bacon, *Advancement of Learning* (London: J. M. Dent & Sons, 1973), II, Proem, 3), as well as instruments for learning. In Britain, the "invisible college" of the 1640s, then the Royal Society (1661), were both based on models set out by Francis Bacon in *The Advancement of Learning* and his visionary utopia, *The New Atlantis*. In France, the *Académie des Sciences* was given a Royal Charter in 1666; with further academies established at Schweinfurt (1652), Altdorf (1672), Uppsala (1710), and St. Petersburg (1714), and astronomical observatories at Paris (1667–1672) and the British National Observatory (1675). European scientists now commanded the air pump, microscope, telescope, barometer, wind gauges, barometers, thermometers, wheel barometers, and weather clocks (the last five, all discovered by Hooke).
15. Durant and Durant, *Age of Voltaire*, 95.
16. This, as against well-developed methods for ordering, presenting, disputing, and justifying what was already known from authoritative biblical and ancient sources.
17. Jean-Baptiste le Rond d'Alembert and Denis Diderot, "Preliminary Discourse", *The Encyclopedia of Diderot and d'Alembert Collaborative Translation Project*, trans. Richard N. Schwab and Walter E. Rex (Ann Arbor: Michigan Publishing,

University of Michigan Library, 2009), online at http://hdl.handle.net/2027/spo.did2222.0001.083.

18. Francis Bacon, *Advancement of Learning*; *Novum Organum*, in *The Works of Francis Bacon: Translations of the Philosophical Works, Volume VIII*, ed. James Spedding et al. (New York: Hurd and Houghton, 1869). References to these texts will be by book and aphorism or section number, in the former case using the section numerals introduced by W. A. Wright in 1869 for *Advancement*.

19. See Bacon, *Advancement* II, xiii, 3; cf. Proemium II, 12; *Novum Organum* I, 18–37, 62–63.

20. See Bacon, *Advancement*, II, viii, 5.

21. Bacon, *Novum Organum*, I, 44, 61–62.

22. Bacon, *Novum Organum*, I, 41, 45–58.

23. Bacon, *Novum Organum*, 62–68.

24. Bacon, *Novum Organum*, 59–60.

25. Matthew Sharpe, "The Topics Transformed: Reframing the Baconian Prerogative Instances", *Journal of the History of Philosophy* 56, no. 3 (2018): 429–454. It was the unchecked sway of these idols in shaping previous philosophies and intellectual culture, Bacon diagnoses, that has prevented European inquiries into nature from systematically advancing in the millennium since later antiquity. See Bacon, NO I 38–91 for the signs and causes of this stagnation in full.

26. Bacon, *Novum Organum*, Preface (p. 62); Corneanu, *Regimens of the Mind*, 14–45.

27. Marcus Tullius Cicero, *Tusculan Disputations*, Prefaces to book III; cf. Sharpe and Ure, *Philosophy as a Way of Life*, 110–11.

28. NO I 59; see Peter Harrison, *The Fall of Man and the Foundation of Modern Science* (Oxford, UK: Oxford University Press, 2009).

29. Bacon, NO I 41; *Advancement*, II, xiv, 9.

30. Bacon NO I, 108, 113–14.

31. For Locke's debts to Bacon, see Peter R. Anstey, "Locke, Bacon and Natural History", *Early Science and Medicine* 7, no. 1 (2002): 65–92.

32. John Locke, *Essay on the Human Understanding*, with an introduction by Mark G. Spencer (London: Wordsworth Classics of World Literature, 2014). References will be to book, chapter, section numbers.

33. A person born blind, whose eyes were restored to sight, could therefore be predicted to have no, or next to no, ideas about how things he has previously experienced with other senses would look—an "experiment" which became the centre of enlightenment debates, due to Locke's influence (chapter 4).

34. Locke, *Essay*, I 2–3. Students will also perhaps be taught Locke's key distinction between the primary and secondary qualities of things, as well as his claims concerning the nature of "the self", as based wholly on an individual's capacity to form a continuous set of memories. See *Essay*, I 4, 5; II 27.

35. Locke, *Essay*, I 1, 4.

36. Locke, *Essay*, I 1, 4: "We should not then perhaps be so forward, out of an affectation of an universal knowledge, to raise questions, and perplex ourselves and others with disputes about things, to which our understandings are not suited; and of

which we cannot frame in our minds any clear or distinct perceptions, or whereof (as it has perhaps too often happened) we have not any notions at all".

37. Locke, *On the Conduct of the Human Understanding*, at Conduct of Understanding (earlymoderntexts.com), §§4–5.

38. Respectively, Locke, *Conduct*, §§10–18, 21–22, 25–31, 38–39.

39. Locke, *Conduct*, §§10–18, 21–22, 25–31, 38–39.

40. Locke, *Essay*, I 1, 6.

41. Locke, *Essay*, I 1, 6.

42. Locke, *Essay*, IV 2, 1–7.

43. Locke, *Essay*, IV 2, 1; IV 3, 28.

44. Locke, *Essay*, IV 3, 23

45. Locke, *Essay*, IV 3, 24; IV 6, 12; cf. 3.2 below.

46. Locke, *Essay*, IV 32, 5.

47. Locke, *Essay*, IV 3, 6.

48. Locke, *Essay*, IV 3, 6.

49. Locke, Essay, IV 3, 23.

50. For all we know, he writes, matter may be able to think, and angelic beings with intelligences vastly greater than our own exist in the infinities of space.

51. Locke, *Essay*, I, 3, 9. See A. Talbot, "The Influence of Travel Literature on the Work of John Locke", in *The Great Ocean of Knowledge* (Leiden: Brill, 2010), 143–59.

52. We will return to Locke's support for slavery in the colonies in chapter 5. The point here is that his empiricism pushes against essentializing accounts of cultural differences as having biological bases, as against bases in the different experiences and histories of peoples.

53. Locke, *Essay*, I 3, 8 (emphasis added).

54. Locke, *Essay*, IV 12, 11–12.

55. Locke, *Essay*, IV 20, 4; IV 1, 11, where the absence of iron is held by Locke to explain the technological differences of American Indians to Europeans.

56. Locke, *Essay*, IV 12, 20

57. Locke, *Essay*, IV 20, 17.

58. Locke, *Essay*, IV 8, 20.

59. Locke, *Essay*, IV 20, 18.

60. Pierre Bayle, *Various Thoughts on the Occasion of a Comet* (Albany: State University of New York Press, 2000). In this section, section and page numbers in the text will be to this text and edition.

61. See Locke, *Essay*, IV 15, 5.

62. On the naturalness of "monsters", see chapter 4.2–4.5 below.

63. Pierre Bayle, *The Historical and Critical Dictionary. Selections*, trans. with an introduction and notes by Richard H. Popkin (Indianapolis/Cambridge: Hackett Publishing Co., 1965).

64. Bayle, *Various Thoughts*, §135.

65. Rainer Forst, *Toleration in Conflict: Past and Present* (Cambridge, UK: Cambridge University Press, 2013), 240.

66. Forst, *Toleration*, 239–41.

67. Pierre Bayle, *Philosophical Commentary on the Words of the Gospel*, ed. with an introduction by John Kilcullen and Chandran Kukathas (Indianapolis, IN: Liberty Fund, 2005), I, 3.

68. Bayle, *Philosophical Commentary* II, 10, 6; Bayle, *Supplement to the Philosophical Commentary on These Words of Jesus Christ, Compel 'Em to Come In*, in *Philosophical Commentary*, IV, 471.

69. Bayle, *Philosophical Commentary*, I, 2.

70. See Rainer Forst, "Pierre Bayle's Reflexive Theory of Toleration", *Nomos* 48 (2008): 97 ff..

71. See Michel de Montaigne, "The Apology of Raymond Sebond", in *The Complete Essays of Michel de Montaigne*, trans. Donald R. Frame (Stanford: Stanford University Press, 1965).

72. Bayle, *Philosophical Commentary* II, 10.

73. Bayle, *Philosophical Commentary* II, 10.

74. Bayle, *Philosophical Commentary* II, 10.

75. Bayle, *Philosophical Commentary* II, 6.

Chapter 2

Paris–Persia
Othering (and Sexing) the Enlightenment

PERSIAN LETTERS: A TRAVEL TALE IN REVERSE

Charles-Louis de Secondat, Baron de La Brède et de Montesquieu, is thankfully better known to posterity simply as Montesquieu. When his *Persian Letters* (*Lettres persanes*) first appeared in 1721, creating a sensation, Montesquieu judiciously concealed his own identity.[1] *Persian Letters* is a very strange candidate for a book which heralded an "age of reason" often criticised for being closed to the literary, the ludic, the sensual, the feminine, and the Other. The text consists of 161 letters written either by, or to, two Persian, Islamic men, Rica and Usbek, who have come to Christian Paris in 1711, or by people in their close networks. There are also letters from several of Usbek's wives and their keepers, back in Ispahan in Persia (see ch. 2). The "Preface" to *Persian Letters* uses a ruse which would often be staged throughout the enlightenment in order to dupe the censors. It underscores that the letters included in the little volume are but translations of the correspondence of others, not expressions of the author's own views. The two main characters, certainly, soon present themselves as each *sui generis*, and a study in contrasts. Rica, the younger man, is a far lighter spirit than his travelling companion. As he warms to his new surrounds, Rica's letters buzz with witty observations we'll return to (he eventually opts to stay in France). Usbek, by contrast, is introduced to us piously offering prayers at the tomb of the Virgin, Fatima, who gave birth to twelve prophets (L1, 4). From very soon afterwards, he is expressing gloomy misgivings about his travels amongst the heathens and longing to return home to his twelve wives, if only to watch over them in his seraglio (2.4).

Little apparent order, beyond the letters' chronology, at first meets the eye of the reader of *Persian Letters*. The epistles span a full gamut of philosophical, cultural, historical, and moral subjects. They range from gossip and social observation, through weighty political genuflections, into fables and fantasy. Rica, Usbek, and their Persian interlocutors undertake reflections and digressions on everything from the family, marriage, suicide, technology, the new philosophies, different punishments and their aims, the best form of government and its aims, to justice, tolerance, the right of subjects to rebel, sexual difference, the Papacy, European absolutism, monasticism, depopulation, human vanity, and the Divine Nature. To the extent that anything like a linear narrative does unfold in *Persian Letters*, it unfolds, as it were, "offstage". The letters Usbek receives from his increasingly disgruntled concubine-wives back home in Persia, and from their fraught eunuch keepers, describe a situation which by the end devolves into open revolt, as we'll see.[2]

Montesquieu would later insist that *Persian Letters* is bound together by a "secret and, in some respects, unknown chain" which underlies the apparent disorder, and which it behooves us as readers to seek out.[3] Usbek's first letter describes the two major characters as the first Persians who had come to the "heathen" West for the sake of an education; a definitively pre-enlightenment vocation which Usbek predicts would meet with ambivalence back home (L1, 4–5). As Montesquieu puts it, the two Persians "find themselves suddenly transported into Europe, that is, to another universe".[4] Part of the charm of the story comes from their culture shock, and the naïve (for us) wonder which Paris provokes in the visitors. "You must not expect from me an exhaustive account of the manners and customs of the Europeans", Rica thus writes in Letter 24 to his friend Ibben at Smyrna:

I have myself but a faint notion of them yet and have hardly had time to recover from my astonishment . . . we tread indeed the same earth; but it seems incredible, remembering in the presence of the men of this country those of the country in which you are (L24, 31, 32).

One link binding the epistolary sequence into a single chain is hence surely the "genesis and progress" of Rica's and Usbek's understandings of this (for them) "new world".[5] This is thus a tale not of two cities; it is a confrontation of two cultures, and of the ways in which this confrontation affects two men of quite different dispositions: the affable and open, curious Rica (2.3), and the more troubled Usbek (see below). Montesquieu's *Persian Letters* is *a kind of travel story, except in reverse*. It stages not European protagonists coming to grips with a non-Western culture and its (for them) "barbaric" practices, but non-Europeans visiting Paris, and sharing with each other and with *us* their astonishment at *our* strange customs.

To better understand what Montesquieu was up to in *Persian Letters*, we need accordingly now to undertake a brief digression of our own. We must situate this little masterpiece in the wake of the enormous flood of travel literature that circulated around Europe following 1492, from the (for us) "new worlds" the explorers had discovered, and to which imperialists had laid competing claims. For it is against this background—a fourth cause of the decentering of European Christendom (see chapter 1)—that *Persian Letters* was conceived and read, and needs again to be read today.

TRAVEL TALES AS ENGINE FOR ESTRANGING THE FAMILIAR (THE FOURTH DECENTERING OF EARLY MODERN EUROPEAN CULTURE)

If the great enlightenment scholar Ira Wade is correct, there were over 550 travel books printed in early modern Europe between 1480 and 1610 alone. (Locke's library, for one, was full of them [see ch. 1]).[6] Memoirs of soldiers, merchants, and missionaries in the New World, but also more philosophical treatments of non-European cultures, even the affairs of fictional interstellar travellers: all were eagerly sought out and consumed by a growing reading public. In the seventeenth century, a recognized class of professional travel writers emerged, relating information concerning the peoples, climates, and customs of Madagascar, the Near East, Africa, Turkey, China ("the Orient"), and the Americas. Colonialism had unleashed the worst in Europeans (see ch.5) and had long been visiting catastrophes on non-Europeans. However, many of the travel writers, like Louis-Armand de Lom d'Arce—Baron de Lahontan, and author of several hugely popular works documenting his time living amongst the American Indians—presented these Others in very different lights. Far from denouncing indigenous peoples' primitive savagery, these authors praised their health, vigour, and simple lives, their personal freedom, sexual mores, courage, moderation, and honesty, as well as the absence of courts, police, taxes, slaves, beggars, absolute rulers, and divisive revealed religions in their societies (see chapter 5).

On one hand, the European exposure to these different cultures and ways of life became the source of endless curiosity: "the slightest fact became a source of amazement: the climate, the longevity among the savages, the health of the natives, the fertility of the land, the riches of the country, the skill and industry of the inhabitants".[7] What Marc Lescarbot called the "marvelous difference in manners and fashions of life" also opened up a kind of exotic "other scene" before Europeans' imaginations, in which they could play out their own wishes, desires, and, of course, their *fears*.[8] Soon enough, bellicose ideological denigrations of the "heathens" and "barbarians" were competing with glowing Epicurean depictions of the inhabitants of the Americas, as well as the Pacific islanders, as "noble savages" (see chapter 6), enjoying the ways of life hitherto only dreamt of by Europeans in poetic and religious myths of a prelapsarian Golden Age.[9]

On the other hand, this confrontation with Others' cultural worlds added a further decentering dynamic to the religious and scientific decenterings of European Christendom's self-certainty that we examined in chapter 1, above. To encounter new worlds, as we glimpsed in our account of Locke (chapter 1), was also to be made to see that our way of experiencing things, and organizing social life, was not the inevitable way. The richly varied observations of other cultures which the seventeenth-century travel writers were able to assemble instead often left a definite impression (as, for instance, in Montaigne) of the relativity of morals. Our way was not the only way—*not by a long shot*. So, who could say any longer that it was simply the best?

Soon enough, some travel writers began to use their experiences of non-European cultures to hold up a comparative, critical mirror to contemporary European societies. In this cross-cultural mirror, all of the customs which egoism, habitude, ignorance, and pride had allowed Christians to think of as being indubitable showed up as much more contestable. Early modern travel writings thereby played a key role in enabling Europeans to *Other themselves*, and to see themselves through the eyes of Others. Many of these texts, Wade writes, hence proffered "not only [a] condemnation of contemporary life but propaganda for changing things; each work . . . potentially an attack and a blueprint for reform".[10]

The very existence of entire societies on other continents, unheard of in either the Bible or the classical pagans' writings, posed especially hard questions for Christian orthodoxies:

- Why had the universal Creator-God, a God of Love, not revealed His Truth to entire, unbaptized peoples for thousands of years, instead abandoning them to perdition?
- Could the sole election of the Jews by the Creator God any longer be seriously believed, or His sending His One Son to a particular continent amongst others, given the global spread of different, apparently wholly unconnected civilizations?
- Could humanity really have sprung from one, Edenic stock, given its dispersal over continents divided by great oceans?
- If not all humans (seemingly) underwent the Fall, what remains of the doctrine of the Atonement (or indeed, of the Incarnation and Passion)?

- Was there any need of a revealed religion to teach morality and cultivate virtue, since these Others were so clearly virtuous in many ways, with no prior knowledge of Moses or Christ?
- Could the chronology of the Old Testament any longer be believed, when the records, myths, and legends of other cultures suggested that the world and human civilization were perhaps far older?

Philosophically, other equally testing questions were posed by these travel writings. How could scholars understand both the clear divergences between the appearances, customs, and mores of different peoples, as well as their equally evident common features? At issue here is what Wade terms the "unifying" and "diversifying principles" key to enlightenment debates, which Henry Vyverberg has devoted an extended study to examining: "the diversifying principle proved the relativity of morality, while the unifying principle proved its basic oneness".[11] It was by facing such questions, prompted by Europeans' increased exposure to other cultures in the early modern period, that the first impulses were formed towards the development in the eighteenth century of modes of inquiry which clearly anticipate later modern disciplines such as sociology, ethnography, and anthropology.

Finally, there was one other feature of these travellers' tales which made them especially significant. This was simply *their popular appeal*. The broad circulation of these texts, as well as the fascinating allure of their contents for sedentary Europeans, meant that these kinds of theological, political, and philosophical questions became more and more widely asked and discussed than ever before. Looking back to chapter 1, we can say that this rush of travel writing represented a *fourth* decisive source of cultural decentering presaging the enlightenment's ferment, alongside those of the Renaissance, the Reformation, and the advent of the new knowledges of nature. Once more, to use Ira Wade's words in *The Intellectual Origins of the French Enlightenment*, it "prepared for the reform of man [sic] through knowledge of man in a medium where free-thinking is more understandable than systematic philosophy and where the audience is the largest possible for that moment".[12]
We are now set to return to Montesquieu and *Persian Letters*.

WE ARE (IN) THE OTHER: *PERSIAN LETTERS'* TWO-WAY MIRRORING

The brilliance and daring of Montesquieu's principal conceit in *Persian Letters* (hereafter in this chapter, *PL*), of a travel writing *in reverse*, can now be appreciated. For Europeans, the wonder of travellers' tales from other cultures lay in their accounts of exotic ways and customs, inviting readers to compare these to their own. The Others became so many mirrors to hold up to European societies, which enabled people to consider what might be done differently, or better. But Montesquieu positions his Persians, Rica and Usbek, as coming to Paris and experiencing *the same dumbstruck wonder at us which his contemporaries experienced in reading Jesuits' accounts of China, or the Baron de Lahontan's accounts of the American Indians*. *PL*'s readers were thereby invited to look at many of their own taken-for-granted customs, perhaps for the first times, through the eyes of Others. And how differently they were made to appear!

It is primarily in Rica's correspondence, urbane and ironic, that Montesquieu carries out this literary conceit. In Rica's epistles, we tour a Paris which harbours dervishes, an infatuated alchemist, women who pretend to be the same age as their daughters, a parade of old soldiers living in the past, idle and pompous judges, smart-alecky young fops planning ambitious social campaigns, fatuous, vain, and pedantic academics, uppity *nouveaux riches* obsessed with genealogical charts—even a puzzling, possibly allegorical tale about a blind man who can somehow play cards and who shows Rica some of the remotest corners of the city (L31, 41–42; see chapter 4). Rica finds especially curious the ways that educated French clerics debate ideas. They "enjoy supporting extraordinary opinions and reducing everything to a paradox" (L36, 49). Accordingly, their debates soon become needlessly warlike: "I can consequently assure you that no kingdom has existed with as many civil wars as the kingdom of Christ" (L27, 39). *Plus ça change* . . . ?

It is above all in Letter 22 where Rica gives the fullest expression of his wonder at the (for him) patent *irrationality* of French financial, political, and theological arrangements:

> Then again, the king is a great magician, for his dominion extends to the minds of his subjects; he makes them think what he wishes. If he has only a million crowns in his exchequer, and has need of two millions, he has only to persuade them that one crown is worth two, and they believe it. If he has a costly war on hand, and is short of money, he simply suggests to his subjects that a piece of paper is coin of the realm, and they are straightway convinced of it . . . What I have told you of this prince need not astonish you: there is another magician more powerful still, who is master of the king's mind, as absolutely as the king is master of the minds of his subjects. This magician is called the Pope. Sometimes he makes the king believe that three are no more than one [i.e., the Trinity]; that the bread which he eats is not bread [i.e., the host]; the wine which he drinks not wine [i.e., communion wine]; and a thousand things of a like nature (L22, 31).

When we read passages like this, we understand why *Persian Letters* was soon subject to censorship, and condemned for being too critical towards Throne and Altar. We can almost hear Karl Marx's pen scribbling the chapters of *Capital* on "commodity fetishism" as we read Rica's bewildered assessments of the kinds of financial goings-on that led to the crash of 1720, the year before *Persian Letters* was published. Meanwhile, the hallowed distance between Christian mysteries and the kinds of magic and superstition Christianity presented itself as overcoming are collapsed in the mouth of our Persian informant. Quietly underscoring the commonalities between Christianity and Islam, Rica and Usbek will elsewhere comically describe the Pope as a great "Mufti", and priests, Jesuits, and monks as "dervishes" (L23, 32; L27, 39; L47, 63–64; L54, 74–76; L119, 161, etc.).

Part of what is transpiring here is a felicitous by-product of censorship. Montesquieu is practicing the kinds of "art of writing" which Leo Strauss last century identified as characterizing authors facing persecution for the open expression of their ideas.[13] As a Catholic French subject, Montesquieu could not in his own name attack the Church or Louis XIV without courting trouble with the authorities. He couldn't mock the Pope, doubt transubstantiation, or poke fun at the vanities of clergymen, theologians, and scholars, without angling for the Bastille. But he could stage a Persian traveller decrying the irrationalities of Christian beliefs and practices, the absolute power of the monarch, and academics behaving badly. And he could also, to introduce now a second key mirroring device in *PL*, directly stage the venalities, ills, and injustices of Islamic institutions, in ways which nevertheless invited his readers to see that the same criticisms could be applied back home.

Take Letter 83. Usbek is purporting to reflect to his friend Mirza in Smyrna on the condemnable persecutory ravages of Shah Soliman. He writes as follows:

> You know, Mirza, that some ministers of Shah Soliman formed the design of obliging all the Armenians of Persia to quit the kingdom or become Mohammedans, in the belief that our empire will continue polluted, as long as it retains within its bosom these infidels ... The persecution of the Guebres by our zealous Mohammedans, has obliged them to fly in crowds into the Indies, and has deprived Persia of that nation, which labored so heartily, that it alone, by its toil, was in a fair way to overcome the sterility of our land ... Only one thing remained for bigotry to do, and that was, to destroy industry; with the result that the empire fell of itself, carrying along with it as a necessary consequence, that very religion which they wished to advance. If unbiased discussion were possible, I am not sure, Mirza, that it would not be a good thing for a state to have several religions (L83, 115–116).

To the reader of Montesquieu's day, these actions by the Shah could hardly fail to evoke the actions of Louis XIV, and the Revocation of the Edict of Nantes in 1685 (chapter 1). One need only replace "Huguenots" for the Armenians or Guebers, "Jesuits" for ministers, "King" for Shah,

"Catholics" for Mohammedans, and "France" for "Persia", to see what Montesquieu was up to. Like the proverbial "dream within the dream" which Freud's *Interpretation of Dreams* tells us often reveals the displaced truth, Montesquieu wants to issue a call to his contemporaries for "unbiased discussion" as to whether Louis XIV's expelling the industrious Huguenots was not a great national disaster. He wants to spark debate as to whether it might not be better for France to once more tolerate "several religions". So here, the effect of mirroring which we saw in Rica's ironic criticisms of Parisians' follies and foibles is effectively redoubled, or inverted. Instead of criticism *by* the Other of "our" irrationalities, we have the same irrationalities being critically decried *in* the "Other scene" of the Persia of Shah Soliman, since they cannot be directly challenged. (Freud later called this mechanism "displacement".)

Beyond duping the royal and churchly censors, why might Montesquieu have felt such ruses to be valuable in *Persian Letters*? There is, I believe, a philosophical as well as political reason. "It seems to me, Usbek", Rica remarks sagely in a key letter, Letter 58, "that our opinions are always influenced by a secret application to ourselves" (L58, 78). It is just as if he had read Bacon, Locke, or Bayle (chapter 1). "If triangles were to invent Gods", Rica continues, "they would give them three sides". We've seen this principle of epistemic egoism comically operative in Rica's description of the Pope as a Mufti, for example. But in Rica's defence, if a European went to his homeland in *PL*, Montesquieu would have her describing the Muftis as "bishops" or "priests". By contrast, confronting the Other, and glimpsing how they see us, promises the possibility that we not remain triangles, and can entertain the possibility that our Gods could have one, two, or many sides—and maybe no sides at all. It allows us to shake the individual and corporate egoism that sees us usually referring everything to ourselves, by reframing everything for an Other whose perspective we are learning to appreciate.

What is at stake in *Persian Letters*' mirror plays, in Genevieve Lloyd's words, is the opening up of "a cosmopolitan ideal nourished by what can be seen as an expansive form of skepticism".[14] When we can see how our practices and follies mirror those of Others, and when we can understand how our follies must look to them, we become more cautious about judging Others' ways so quickly as either wholly foreign, or wholly inferior, to our own. A new epistemic and ethical humility beckons, exactly of the kind we have seen Bacon, Locke, and Bayle propounding (chapter 1). Echoing themes from ancient Greek philosophical thought, like the Stoicism dear to Montesquieu (L13–14), Rica's Letter 58 hence concludes by assuming a view as if from above, looking down on humanity as if he were an interstellar traveller from another planet (chapter 3):

My dear Usbek, when I behold men, mere crawlers on this atom, the earth, which is but a point in the universe, proposing themselves as exact models for Providence, I know not how to harmonize such extravagance with such littleness (L58, 78).[15]

USBEK'S TRAVAILS, OR THE CHALLENGES OF ENLIGHTENMENT

Usbek, as we suggested earlier, is a deeply conflicted character. He has travelled out of a genuine desire to learn. Yet he soon confides he was also more or less forced into the venture to flee rivals in the royal court (L9, 11–12). He is deeply pious, yet we soon see him questioning the rationality of Islamic dietic proscriptions, on more seemingly Stoic grounds (L17, 28). Like Rica, but with more depth, he discerns very clearly the many problems facing eighteenth-century French society. It is his letters that give us the most extended philosophical reflections on forms of government, the virtue of republics (L11–14), the ills of despotism, the irrationalities of revealed religion (L17–18), the vagaries of power, and the relations between different systems of law, as well as scathing criticisms of the barbarities performed by the Spanish in the colonies, whom he charges with "having thought only of discovering to mankind the most extreme degree of cruelty possible" (L118, 164).

Yet, as we learn very quickly, Usbek is himself no stranger to the theologically sanctioned despotism which he despises in Europeans, and whose baleful effects in depopulating Persia he decries (L79, 111; L99, 136–37). As soon as the second Letter, we learn that Usbek is the absolute master of a seraglio of women in Ispahan, who are deprived of even the most basic liberties, effectively imprisoned in order to serve his every wish, even in his long absence. From early on, we also see how seriously he takes this position, and how jealously he guards his despotic prerogatives. Usbek repeatedly urges the castrated vizirs who rule over the seraglio in his name to ever-harsher restrictions and exactions (L2, 3, 53, 143, 153), even as he criticises the celibacy of Christian priests and monks as anti-natural (L113, 157–58). Usbek can send generous letters on the rationality of religious toleration (L82, cf. chapter 3), yet silently receive letters describing his wives' growing unease in his absence (L3, 6, 7), his eunuchs' killing of two men who dared to look upon the women (L47), and a young girl of seven being transported to the seraglio to be made to serve there, for the indefinite term of his good pleasure (L62). It is strongly suggested that even Roxana, the wife whom he claims to love the best, was not at first a consensual sexual partner. She "defended until its last gasp a dying virginity", he recalls, and for a long time thereafter regarded him "as an enemy who had outraged [her]", rather than her husband (L24, 34). When, towards the end of *PL*, Usbek hears news of his wives' rebellion at the seraglio, Usbek grants "unlimited power" to his first eunuch to use "fear and terror" to restore order (L140, 205–06). As a result of this tyranny, Roxana ends by taking her own life, having been discovered in the embraces of a lover (L149, 212). Her final letter to Usbek is a searing indictment of his hypocrisy:

> How could you think that I was such a weakling as to imagine there was nothing for me in the world but to worship your caprices; that while you indulged all your desires, you should have the right to thwart me in all mine? (L150, 213)

What then are we to make of Usbek's presence in *Persian Letters*? Is he there, as some commentators have suggested, to show the limits of the enlightenment Montesquieu supports, or perhaps even its impossibility?[16] Or is Usbek's hypocrisy meant to teach a pessimistic lesson about the unavoidability of despotism, and the emptiness of all appeals to liberty, equality, and the rest of the modern ideals? I don't think this is Montesquieu's intention, for reasons which will become clear soon enough. It seems to me much more likely, as well as more consistent with the rest of *Persian Letters*, that Usbek's failings are there to show us the *challenges* of enlightenment—if we take enlightenment to involve the ability to honestly, critically appraise oneself, despite all the counterweights of our epistemic (and wider) egoism and the Baconian idols of the mind (1.2).

Consider this striking passage from Locke's *Conduct of the Understanding*, §10. I think it gets to the heart of what is at play in Usbek's travails, as well as using the ground metaphor for the enlightenment itself (see chapter 2):

> Everyone declares against blindness, and yet who almost is not fond of that which dims his sight and keeps the clear light out of his mind, which should lead him into truth and knowledge? False or doubtful positions, relied upon as unquestionable maxims, keep those in the dark from truth who build on them. Such are usually the prejudices imbibed from education, party, reverence, fashion, interest, etc. This is the mote which everyone sees in his brother's eye, but never regards the beam in his own. For who is there almost that is ever brought fairly to examine his own principles and see whether they are such as will bear the trial? But yet this should be one of the first things everyone should set about and be scrupulous in, who would rightly conduct his understanding in the search of truth and knowledge.[17]

Enlightenment can only come when we are able to see the beam in our own eye, as well as decrying the motes in our brothers' or sisters'. So *we* as readers readily see how distant Usbek's own conduct is from the ideals he professes. But, then, the enlightening thing Montesquieu is arguably prompting us to do, through staging Usbek's hypocrisies, *is to turn the critical mirror around*. To what extent are we, too, like Usbek, after all? Can we really say that we are not prey to the same kinds of contradictions between saying and doing, ideals and actualities, which Montesquieu makes us see so clearly in this Other? Are the kinds of despotism he represents really only something "over there", a curiosity we can enjoy denouncing, without worrying that they may implicate us?

To develop this claim, we turn now to the more directly political dimensions at work in *Persian Letters*, and its seraglio.

THE THEOLOGICO-SEXUAL POLITICS OF DESPOTIC RULE

Judith Shklar, in her invaluable book on Montesquieu, proposes that *Persian Letters* is its own coded critique of emerging conceptions of the enlightened despot,[18] an idea on whose fires Voltaire and Diderot would both soon singe their hands. Shklar's suggestion has the merit of positioning *PL* in such a way as to square it with Montesquieu's larger *chef d'oeuvre*, *The Spirit of Laws* (*De l'esprit des lois*), published decades later, in 1749.[19] This text of systematic political theory has had an enormous influence, not least on the American founders. *The Spirit of Laws* is widely understood to involve a defence of the division of legislative, executive, and judicial functions of government. For large commercial societies like the modern European states, Montesquieu recommends constitutional government broadly along the lines of the English system following the revolution of 1689, and with it, the overthrow of the absolute monarchy. If we explore *The Spirit of Laws'* depiction of such autocratic forms of government, in fact, what becomes clear is that Usbek's Seraglio in *PL* is not just "over there", an exotic curiosity to spice things up. Like Shah Solimon's Persia in Letter 82 (see above), it is a further "Other scene" in whose injustices Montesquieu wants his Western readers to see the lineaments and dangers of all forms of absolute rule, including their own.

The Spirit of Laws gets its title from Montesquieu's claim that each system of government (monarchy, despotism, aristocracy, republic) has its own "spirit" (*esprit*). This spirit is the most general character of its subjects, which energizes and directs public life. The spirit of a people is shaped by any number of this-worldly factors: the climate, resources, size of the territory, and density of the population, as well as a polity's history, religion, customs, laws, and traditions. Monarchies are characterised by the predominance of public concern for honour, for instance. Virtue is the characteristic spirit of republics, as Usbek's fable of the Troglodytes in *Persian Letters* puts on show

(L12–13). Importantly, there is no "one size fits all" utopian scheme for perfect government, according to Montesquieu, any more than we will find one in Diderot or Voltaire. Rather, wise law-making should be adapted

> to the people for whom they are framed . . . , to the nature and principle of each government, . . . to the climate of each country, to the quality of its soil, to its situation and extent, to the principal occupation of the natives, whether husbandmen, huntsmen or shepherds: they should have relation to the degree of liberty which the constitution will bear; to the religion of the inhabitants, to their inclinations, riches, numbers, commerce, manners, and customs. In fine, they have relations to each other, as also to their origin, to the intent of the legislator, and to the order of things on which they are established; in all of which different lights they ought to be considered.[20]

But here's the thing: The spirit of despotic one-man rule is *fear*. Montesquieu is emphatic: "As virtue is necessary in a republic, and in a monarchy honor, so fear is necessary in a despotic government: with regard to virtue, there is no occasion for it, and honor would be extremely dangerous".[21] As the classical philosophers had seen, despotism (or tyranny) can only be founded by destroying those intermediary social forces between "the base" and the Throne which might provide resistance to the ruler's absolute control. Famously (and laconically), Montesquieu thus writes that "when the savages of Louisiana are desirous of fruit, they cut the tree to the root, and gather the fruit. This is an emblem of despotic government".[22] Maintaining such a regime is demanding, since it requires that the energies of the people be constantly "depressed", and any embers of independence be quickly "extinguished".[23] All presumption of innocence must be withdrawn from subjects; a correlative to the absolute law-making power of the sovereign. This creates a spirit of mutual suspicion and surveillance, as well as an internalized sense of always being guilty: "those laws in fine which find nobody innocent where one may happen to be guilty are made with a design to implant in the people a mutual distrust, and to make every man the inspector, witness, and judge of his neighbor's conduct".[24]

However great the power imagined for the sovereign in any ruler cult might be, it remains that a despot cannot prosecute his rule all on his own. He must recruit others whom he can trust unconditionally, and who as such must have demonstrated a willingness to renounce "setting a value upon themselves" which might present an obstacle to his diktats.[25] Moreover, being in possession of access to every pleasure and entertainment he demands, and being constantly flattered by his toadies that "he himself is everything and that his subjects are nothing", despots tend to become "lazy, voluptuous, and ignorant. In consequence of this, [they] neglect public affairs", or soon come to know very little about them beyond what their inner circle tells them.[26] (We might wish that many of our fellow citizens could read these passages from Montesquieu in 2022.)

The issue for the despot is *how* he can select individuals he can unconditionally trust, who will pose no possible threat to his imperium. In this light, Montesquieu observes, despots throughout history have favoured eunuchs as counsellors, as well as their own family members. For eunuchs, being castrated, are more "naturally attached to [the family] of another", since they can plan no rival dynasties in families of their own.[27] The *PL* reader's ears should already have been pricked up at this point.

The sections on despotism in *The Spirit of Laws*, remarkably, proceed to lay out a critique of the sexual politics of the "strong man"—another subject very much in the news in the era of Mr. Trump. If sex is power, at least in the minds of these *hommes de pouvoir*, then their prerogatives must extend from the boardroom to the bedroom. "Give me absolute control, over every living soul, and lie beside me, baby—that's an order", as the late Leonard Cohen sang. Montesquieu, for his part, writes a passage of *The Spirit of Laws* which he can only have penned whilst thinking back upon his earlier literary masterpiece:

> The princes of despotic governments have ever perverted the use of marriage. They generally take a great many wives, especially in that part of the world where absolute power is in some measure naturalized, namely, Asia. Hence, they come to have such a multitude of children that they can hardly have any great affection for them, nor the children for one another. The reigning family resembles the state; it is too weak itself, and its head too powerful; it seems very numerous and extensive, and yet is suddenly extinct.[28]

And so we are returned directly from *The Spirit of Laws* back to Usbek's seraglio at Ispahan. Its presiding spirit is one of fear. Mutual contempt and malice reigns between the eunuch-vizirs and Usbek's many wives; a kind of nightmare "ebb and flow" of humiliations (L9). The women and eunuchs over whom he rules, Usbek declares, exist "only to live under his laws" and "only insofar as they can obey" (L21, 29). In a well-run seraglio, the chief of the black eunuchs rejoins, "complete silence" must be jealously preserved (L62, 84). Everyone rises and retires at the same time. Spies and informants prevent any conspiracy or solidarity between the women, who are maintained in their stations as envious rivals for Usbek's favours. The master can then "captivate" their hearts, as we are told, since his impotent seconds have already "subdued their spirits" (L62, 85). The eunuchs report that they secretly enjoy exacting cruelty on the women, a substitute for their own lost virility. These castrated slaves also envy the sexual prerogatives of their master, whom they resent for having everything which he has taken from them (L9). But they, too, are kept in place by fear of Usbek, who promises a godlike "thunderbolt" will be visited upon them should they fail in their duties (L21, 29). Usbek's only response when reports of discontent and conspiracy begin to reach him, as we have said, is to call down more complete despotic horrors on his subjects. It is this terror which leads to revolt and the suicide of Roxana, as the last of *Persian Letters* reports (L150, 212–13).

Nor can we in fact assume that Montesquieu is only trying to show what happens in other places, far from the Catholic France of his early-eighteenth-century readers. As Sanford Kessler has written, when we reflect, we see that, uncannily:

> In many respects [Usbek] is like the theocratic despots such as the Czar of Russia and King Louis XIV of France whose empires extended to the life, property, and "very minds" of their subjects. Montesquieu also calls attention to similarities between Usbek's rule and that of the Pope. The "Head of the Christians", as our author describes him, "held a great country under his dominion", kept the entire Catholic world in spiritual bondage, and administered his power through a celibate priesthood which resembled the impotent army that carried out Usbek's commands.[29]

And there is more. When we think of who (or "Who", as it were) this Eastern ruler who rules absolutely over twelves wives might call to mind for an eighteenth-century European reader, there can only be one answer: *viz.* the God of the Bible, with the twelve tribes of Israel, or indeed, the Son, with his twelve apostles. The tyrant Usbek certainly shares a defining attribute with the "jealous God" of the Old Testament. As Shklar comments:

> Like any despot, and Montesquieu's God, Usbek is absent from his domain . . . Whether he pardons or threatens its inmates, he is never there. Unlike God he is however a despot because he is not bound by laws of any kind.[30]

It should not finally escape our attention just how oddly the seraglio, as it is depicted for us, presided over by joyless celibates, *resembles a Christian monastery or convent*—as we've indicated, one object of Usbek's projective criticisms, for the way these institutions denature men and women, and depopulate Europe (L108–18). With its separate rooms like cells, its strict code of silence, its daily regimens, its long abstinences, and its inevitable intrigues, Shklar again comments:

> The seraglio is a thinly veiled picture of a convent, with all its sexual repressions and its irrational discipline. The eunuchs, like the clergy, are celibate while the

women are wedded to an omnipotent and absent being and are kept in strict obedience by a mixture of blind faith and fear.[31]

Despotism, *The Spirit of Laws* tells us, "is productive of the most disastrous calamities to human nature, [and] the very evil that restrains it is beneficial to the subject".[32] Before *The Spirit of Laws*, Montesquieu's *Persian Letters* had already staged the inhuman calamities this form of government occasions. In a way which we need now to investigate further, it also singled out their specifically gendered dimensions for critical attention in a way which is especially remarkable for us today.

ZULEMA AND ANAIS, OR: WHAT IF GOD WERE A WOMAN?

What we call sexual politics is in fact never far from the shimmering surfaces of *Persian Letters*. This is a text in which some 55 of the 161 letters are by women (13), or to them (5 are by Usbek to his wives), or concern European women and sexual customs (12); with 3 letters taking as their subjects exemplary women (Anais, Zulema, Astarte), and no less than *20* concerning the women in the Persian seraglio, including the last 11 letters of the book. It is a text in which men's treatment of women is an ongoing consideration (L112–13, 155–59). Here as elsewhere, the visiting Persians are quickly able to discern the discontents which surround contemporary Western norms of monogamy: a central concern, as we'll see later, of Denis Diderot's (chapter 6). As far as Usbek can see, although Christian marriage is promoted as a defence against the sin of fornication, Christians "do not view it as consisting in sensual pleasure" (L113, 157). They instead "seem to want to banish sensual pleasure as far as they can" from the institution. "The prominent role women have in Montesquieu's scheme of things is a part of his attempt to free the female from her unjust subjection to men sanctioned, in his view, by the Biblical religion", Kessler writes: "while suggesting that women as a rule are physically weaker than men, he teaches that the sexes are equal in a decisive respect, namely, their capacity for virtue [Letters 88, 96]".[33]

The extent to which this extraordinary claim can be borne out will require us to look at what, for many contemporary readers, will be the most extraordinary Letter in the book. We mean Letter 135 (187–194), the longest in *Persian Letters*, which contains the fabulous stories of Zulema and Anais. It is Rica who tells these intersecting tales. Montesquieu presents them immediately before the real women at Ispahan are about to begin their revolt, to stress their significance.

The settings of both tales are in fact Persian seraglios. In the first seraglio lives Zulema, a woman whom we are told has achieved the highest peaks of religious understanding. During a discussion about the nature of heaven and the status of women in Islam, she is asked whether paradise is "made only for men" (L135, 188). Zulema answers by recourse to the Koran, in which woman are admitted into heaven. However, she boldly then goes on to protest that the teachers of her religion leave "nothing . . . undone to degrade our sex", and that the "Jewish nation . . . maintains by the authority of its sacred books, that we don't have a soul" (L135, 188). The source of these opinions, Zulema contends, is neither God nor nature. It is the overweening pride of men

> who wish to carry their superiority even beyond this life, forgetting that at the last day all creatures will appear before God as nothing, and that no one will have any advantage over another except that which virtue gives (L135, 188).

Next, Zulema tells the extraordinary story of Anais. She claims to have read this "fable within the fable" in an unnamed "Arab book" (L135, 189). It tells of another seraglio ruled by an "insufferably jealous" Lord whose name, Ibrahim, is transparently the Islamic version of Abraham, progenitor of all the biblical peoples. Like Usbek, Ibrahim runs his seraglio as a virtual convent, enforcing isolation and silence through fear. However, amongst his twelve wives, there is one, Anais, whose mind Zulema characterizes as "truly philosophical" (L135, 189). Refusing to suffer in silence, Anais uses her enforced solitude to enlighten herself, passing along "the tracks of human reason". She then rebels against Ibrahim, who has her executed. But as she goes to her death, she promises her friends: "My dear companions, if heaven has pity for my virtue, you will be avenged" (L135, 189).

What happens next is that Anais is taken up into heaven for her failed revolt against the Old Ibrahim, suggesting scandalous theological comparisons for Christian readers. But this is a new heaven, one in which "virtuous women" are sent to a "place of delights", separate from that of men, yet equal to theirs in all respects (L135, 188). The women are here provided with companions of the opposite sex. In a "superb palace" where "everything seemed to contribute to the delight of her senses", we are told that her male servants labour to provide Anais with the highest degrees of satisfaction, including sexually (L135, 188).

Anais herself is virtually deified. Like the biblical God, she commands and is obeyed. But like the God of the New Testament, she is moved by compassion at the memory of her former companions in the earthly Ibrahimic seraglio. So, remembering her dying promise, Anais orders one of her male companions to return to life, impersonate her former husband, and make himself master of the seraglio in his absence (L135, 192). The slave steals Ibrahim's keys, enters the seraglio, and proceeds to placate and court the women, treating the eunuchs with clemency. When Ibrahim returns and reasserts domination, he is deserted by his servants and his wives. He is then banished from the seraglio and would have suffered "death a thousand times" had the new master not generously spared his life (L135, 193–94).

After this theologico-sexual revolution, the New Ibrahim makes a New Covenant with the women, as Montesquieu continues to wax heretical. New Ibrahim promises to "take upon [himself] the duty of watching over [the women's] happiness" in return for their continued support. In response, they "swear eternal fidelity" to him (L135, 193). The New Ibrahim, like Anais his Goddess, is altogether humane and free from the jealousy which plagued his predecessor, which plagues Usbek, and which characterised the God of the Old Testament. He is trusting: "I shall know how to feel sure of you without embarrassing you. I have a good enough opinion of my worth to think you will be faithful to me" (L135, 193). Far from imposing his whims as a despot, he dismisses the guards, opens the seraglio to all, and disperses "with great liberality the fortune of the jealous Ibrahim" (L135, 194). He encourages the wives to cease veiling their faces. On feast days, he allows them to mingle freely with male guests. Finally, the New Ibrahim is wise enough to instruct his subjects on the workings of the tyranny they had formerly suffered. So, when the Old Ibrahim returns to make the seraglio great again, he is roundly rejected.

That Montesquieu included this extraordinary fable of women's liberation in a text published in 1721 beggars the imagination. Knowledge of it ought to have been enough to long ago quiet any suggestions of blanket androcentrism in the enlightenment (see chapter 6). The name "Zulema" appears to derive from the Hebrew word "Suleima", meaning "peace". "Anais" evokes the Greek, "of good will". Montesquieu could hardly have been clearer. What Rica's story of Zulema and Anais suggests is the justice of resistance, both against worldly tyranny and also against any religion that licenses the despotic repression of subjects' natural capacities. Since despotism has been championed by men wanting to dominate women (as well as each other), and since absolute rule has been sanctioned by revealed religions who posit a Father-God, Montesquieu suggests the need for striking religious reformation in Catholic France. Divorce should be legalised in cases of loveless unions (L112–13), celibacy and monasticism be discouraged, not sanctified (L113, 157–58)[34], and slavery should be forbidden (L114, 159; see chapter 5). Above all, women's equal capacities for freedom, intelligence, and virtue with men should be honoured (L88, 96, 135). It is with good reason, and in the name of a reason Montesquieu sees that women share, that the dying Roxana cajoles her distant, despotic master: "O, I have lived in slavery, and yet always retained my freedom: I have remodelled your laws upon those of nature; and my spirit has always remained independent" (L150, 213). As Shklar comments:

> [Montesquieu's] scepticism went so far that he could even question whether male domination over women was justifiable. The power of men stifles the talents of women in just the same way as despotism inhibits all its subjects, especially the most gifted among them. The dependence of women demoralizes them and reduces them to perpetual dissimulation. Rica notices that in the seraglio all the women are squeezed into a single mould and are forced to pretend that they are all alike [L63].[35]

FROM MONTESQUIEU TO VOLTAIRE, VIA THE VIEW FROM THE OTHER

Sanford Kessler seems to us right to have stressed that "the considerable attention Montesquieu devotes to sexual equality in *Persian Letters* makes this work an important philosophical source for the women's liberation movement".[36] We have also argued in this chapter that *Persian Letters*, this founding text of the French enlightenment, should be considered as a remarkable counter-document, whenever the wholesale racism or Eurocentrism of modern thought is mooted. Things are not so simple (see chapter 4). *Persian Letters*, not least, is a lasting document in the continuing struggle against political despotism, whose contemporary relevance is accordingly clear. Yet above all, we've tried to show how *PL*, with its artful mirror doublings, operates as a kind of literary engine pushing readers to see themselves through the eyes of non-Western Others, as well as to confront their own failings in the shortcomings of the Other. By setting up this literary practice of self-othering, our argument is that *PL* in effect sets up the decisive critical template for later enlightenment literature and thinking. Given the egoism and partiality of human beings, any more expanded and humane perspective on ourselves and others must start with the ability to "know thyself", and our own predilections towards hybris, error, despotism, and prejudice. But to achieve this, we need to be able to open our eyes to how others see us, how we appear to them, and how we very often enact and embody what we decry in those we criticise.

In Montesquieu's 1721 classic, it is visiting Persians who represent this foil, this mirror, and this source of critical self-estrangement. But the precedent *PL* so brilliantly set would soon be followed by Voltaire, in whose profuse work the cast of edifying others would grow, from the Quakers of the *Letters on the English*, to American Indians, Chinese, Babylonians, Brahmins, interstellar visitors from the planet Sirius, and a proverbially candid Westphalian youth.

NOTES

1. Montesquieu, *Persian Letters*, introduction by Andrew Kahn, trans. Margaret Mauldon (Oxford, UK: Oxford University Press, 2008). In-text bracketed letter numbers and pagination in this chapter refer to this text and edition.
2. Montesquieu, "Reflections on the *Persian Letters*" [1754], in *Persian Letters*, 227–29.
3. Montesquieu, "Reflections", 227.
4. Montesquieu, "Reflections", 228.
5. Montesquieu, "Reflections", 228.
6. Ira Wade, *Intellectual Foundations of the French Enlightenment*, 362. See Geoffrey Atkinson, *The Extraordinary Voyage in French Literature from 1680 to 1700* (New York: Columbia University Press, 1920); *The Extraordinary Voyage in French Literature from 1700–1720* (Paris: Champion, 1922). On Locke and travel writing, see Stephen Gaukroger, *The Collapse of Mechanism and the Rise of Sensibility: Science and the Shaping of Modernity, 1680–1760* (Oxford: Oxford University Press, 2011), 402–09.
7. Wade, *Intellectual Origins*, 364.
8. Wade, *Intellectual Origins*, 390.
9. See Sankar Muthu, *Enlightenment against Empire* (Princeton, NJ: Princeton University Press, 2003), 11–71.
10. Wade, *Intellectual Origins*, 373.
11. Wade, *Intellectual Origins*, 391; cf. Henry Vyverberg, *Human Nature, Cultural Diversity*.
12. Wade, *Intellectual Origins*, 391.
13. Leo Strauss, *Persecution and the Art of Writing* (Chicago: University of Chicago Press, 1948).
14. Lloyd, *Enlightenment Shadows*, 27; see Matthew Sharpe, "What of All the Others?", in Lloyd and Boucher, *Rethinking the Enlightenment*, 61–87.
15. On this philosophical exercise, see Hadot, "View from Above", in *Philosophy as a Way of Life*, 238–50.
16. Shklar, *Montesquieu*, 35, cf. 31–33.
17. Locke, *Conduct of the Understanding*, §10.
18. Judith Shklar, *Montesquieu*, (Oxford, UK: Oxford University Press, 1987), 33.
19. Montesquieu, *The Spirit of Laws*, trans. Thomas Nugent (Chicago: Britannica Great Books 38, 1952). References to this text will be by book, then chapter, then page number. Hereafter in notes SL.
20. SL I, 3 3.
21. SL III 9, 12
22. SL V 13, 26.
23. SL III 9, 13.
24. SL II 9, 13.
25. SL II 9, 13.
26. SL II 5, 8.
27. SL XV, 8, 111.

28. SL V 14, 27; cf. XV 8, 111.
29. Sanford Kessler, "Religion and Liberalism in Montesquieu's *Persian Letters*", *Polity* 15, no. 3 (Spring 1983), 385.
30. Shklar, *Montesquieu*, 34..
31. Shklar, *Montesquieu*, 44.
32. SL II 4, 8.
33. Kessler, "Religion and Liberalism", 390.
34. Kessler, "Religion and Liberalism", 384–90.
35. Shklar, *Montesquieu*, 42.
36. Kessler, "Religion and Liberalism", 390.

Chapter 3
Voltaire's Smiling Philosophy

AN IGNORANT PHILOSOPHER?

Voltaire's centrality to any account of the French enlightenment can hardly be disputed, even by scholars like Jonathan Israel who contest his exact significance. "Italy had its renaissance, Germany its reformation, France had Voltaire", comments Will Durant.[1] If there is one figure in which all of the threads informing the enlightenment came together in an unlikely synthesis— from libertine literature, travel writings, and the recovered classical philosophers to Lockean metaphysics, Baylean critical scepticism, biblical criticism, and Newtonian science—it was Voltaire.[2] Yet, where the enlightenment is spoken ill of today, this "patriarch" of the *philosophes* is often scarcely mentioned. The enlightenment is meanwhile slated with an unregenerate rationalism of the kind which Voltaire reviled, an optimism which he increasingly renounced, an intolerance he ceaselessly struggled against, and a closure to the ludic and playful in which he excelled.

It is not easy to pin Voltaire down. He began his career, and made his adopted name, as a poet and dramatist. His philosophical writings only began after his first exile (to England) at the behest of a *lettre de cachet* in 1726. In coming decades, he would write celebrated histories, romances, works proselytising Newtonian physics, philosophical *contes*, biblical criticism, encyclopedia entries, and portable philosophical dictionaries, as well as myriad pamphlets in the cause of religious toleration. There is also a voluminous correspondence with kings and commoners across Europe and the New World.

Voltaire's conception of being a philosopher, as we glimpsed in the introduction, is not ours today. In his entry for "Philosopher" in the *Philosophical Dictionary*, he makes clear his more ancient conception of this vocation, in which ethics and a concern to better human life are paramount:

Philosopher, "lover of wisdom," that is, "of truth." All philosophers have possessed this two-fold character; there is not one among those of antiquity who did not give examples of virtue to mankind, and lessons of moral truth.³

To write (*écrire*) for Voltaire was to act (*agir*). He could echo Epicurus's famous dictum that the words of philosophers that do not conduce to curing human woes are vain. As such, in "Philosopher", it is the ancients' ethical philosophies that he focuses upon as decisive in their search for wisdom, not their physics or metaphysics, which Voltaire considered Newton and others to have surpassed. Voltaire notably elevates the Chinese thinker, Confucius, to the highest status as "a sage of simple manners and character, without arrogance, who taught how to live happily six hundred years before our era".⁴ Plato is praised for a few passages which move us to "ardent love of generous actions". The philosopher-statesman Cicero is rated as "perhaps more valuable than all the philosophers of Greece", as much for his life as his writings.⁵ In the article "Dogmas", Epictetus and Marcus Aurelius, alongside Socrates, Montaigne, Bayle, and Spinoza, are listed as "great men who, having taught and practiced the virtues that God requires, seem to be the only persons possessing the right of pronouncing his decrees".⁶

Voltaire's use of a variety of media to reach, entertain, persuade, and move different audiences, reflects this old sense of philosophy as a moral or ethical calling. This is not to say that Voltaire had no doctrinal positions of his own, which he sought to explore and illustrate in these different ways. He wrote at least two philosophical treatises in his life, *The Treatise on Metaphysics* of 1736, and the tellingly titled *The Ignorant Philosopher* of 1764. Ira Wade is right to observe that, throughout his life, five metaphysical subjects which Voltaire already considered in the 1736 *Treatise* continued to focus his reflections: the natures of God, matter, and the soul, the question of free will, and the bases of morals (notably including the problem of evil).⁷ Nevertheless, as the title of his later treatise *The Ignorant Philosopher* suggests, Voltaire's positions on these subjects remained characterised by a scepticism deeply redolent of the philosophies of Locke, Bayle, and Montaigne. When he ironizes that his character Zadig knew as much as all of the wise men from any nations knew about metaphysics, which is to say, next to nothing, Voltaire is speaking for himself.⁸ Of God, Voltaire would claim that little more could be known than that it is most probable that a Creating, Ordering Principle exists. Of matter, he would quip that we remain like the women of Paris, who enjoy their ragouts, without knowing what goes into making them up.⁹ Of the soul, we can know even less:

> It would be a fine thing to see one's soul. *Know thyself* is an excellent precept . . . but it is only for God to put it into effect . . . we call "soul" that which

animates. We know little more about it, our intelligence being limited. Three quarters of mankind go no further, and do not worry about this thinking being: the remaining quarter seek the answer, nobody has or will ever find it.[10]

Whilst Voltaire initially defended free will, in his later work he moved closer to a guarded determinism, on grounds which reconcile his abiding Lockeanism with (despite Jonathan Israel) a growing sympathy for Spinoza.[11] Again, the lesson is one of humility, if not of learned ignorance:

> It is strange that men should not be content with this measure of liberty, that is to say, the power which they have received from nature of doing what they choose [but on the basis of ideas determined by experience]: the planets have it not; we possess it, and our pride makes us sometimes believe we possess still more.[12]

But all of the debates about these questions could, in Voltaire's view, be ultimately reduced back to *la morale* (chapter 3). Decades before Kant's better-known academic version, Voltaire propounded a "primacy of practical reason" to metaphysics.[13] Voltaire, this poet and wit, was above all fascinated with human nature, in the light of the discoveries of the previous centuries. Like Locke, Montesquieu, and Montaigne, he was struck by the sheer diversity of human things across cultures:

> Everything is different between them [the Chinese] and us: religion, policy, government, mores, food, clothing, and the manner of writing, expressing, and thinking. The way in which we bear the greatest resemblance to them is in our propensity to war, murder, and destruction.[14]

The *Treatise on Metaphysics* observes that "the majority of rules on good and evil vary as much as languages or clothes", when we take in the full sweep of global cultures.[15] Like Montesquieu, Voltaire is also unconvinced of the possibility of any one-size-fits-all form of legislation, given the overwhelming realities of difference. For laws should best be adapted to local conditions, histories, and customs. "The empire of custom is much vaster than that of nature", he writes, "it extends over all mores, over all usages; it spreads over the face of the universe . . . the soil is everywhere the same, but culture produces diverse fruits".[16]

Yet this principle of diversity is balanced by observations, rooted in his extensive historical studies, of underlying commonalities. Human nature is characterised everywhere by the same combination of vulnerability and capacity for good or evil:

> It needs twenty years to lead man from the plant state in which he is within his mother's womb, and the pure animal state which is the lot of his early childhood,

to the state when the maturity of the reason begins to appear. It has needed thirty centuries to learn a little about his structure. It would need eternity to learn something about his soul. It takes an instant to kill him.[17]

There is a common moral core at the basis of all societies: the golden and silver rules (do [not] do unto others as you would [not] have done unto you).[18] "Farmers, artisans, artists have not taken a course in morality", Voltaire writes:

> They have read neither Cicero's *De Finibus* nor Aristotle's *Ethics*, but as soon as they reflect, they are unwittingly Cicero's disciples. The Indian dyer, the Tartar shepherd, and the English sailor know justice and injustice. Confucius did not invent a system of morality as one constructs a system in natural philosophy. He found it in the hearts of all men.[19]

At the motivational basis of morality, kneaded into human nature, are what some of Voltaire's contemporaries were calling "moral sentiments": "We all have two sentiments which form the foundation of society: sympathy (*commiseration*) and justice".[20] At its principled basis, there is a natural law, giving all human beings a basic conscience for right and wrong. Differing customs are "mere laws of convention, arbitrary usages, transient modes"; Voltaire can hence write:

> What is essential remains ever the same. Point out to me any country where it would be deemed respectable or decent to plunder me of the fruits of my labour, to break a solemn promise, to tell an injurious lie, to slander, murder or poison, to be ungrateful to a benefactor, or to beat a father or mother presenting food to you.[21]

The virtues are for Voltaire every bit as real as they were for the ancient Eastern and Western ethicists he revered. Whilst we are born with potentials for courage, moderation, generosity, and justice, we need to cultivate these potentials as we grow. As for his near-contemporary David Hume, the virtues are all those ways of behaving which peoples have found useful, beneficent, or pleasing.[22] Yet, we should undertake virtuous actions for their own sake, never asking for rewards—for instance, in a theologically promised heaven of (oddly terrestrial) delights (see chapter 2). Remarkably, Voltaire will nevertheless insist that justice is the only true virtue. For it alone of the "cardinal virtues" directly serves others, as against wisdom, temperance, or courage. Significantly, for Voltaire, faith is neither a virtue nor a vice; "if that which you believe seems to you to be true, there is no merit in believing it; if it seems to you to be false, it is impossible for you to believe it."[23]

Yet even justice, as Voltaire sees things, is not complete. It too needs to be supplemented by *bienfaisance* (generosity or benevolence), if we are to treat others well. This is clearly a secularised species of Christian *charitas* (charity), or what Romans called *humanitas* (humanity), as Voltaire would not have denied. The great variety and unpredictability of human experience which Voltaire stages so comically in a *conte* like *Zadig* also recommends caution. *The Treatise on Metaphysics* makes clear that even laws against lying (to save a friend), incest (if there's only one family on Earth, for instance, just after the Fall), and murder (in cases of tyrannicide) admit of justifiable exceptions.[24]

With this much said concerning philosophical principles, let's turn to three of the patriarch's foremost productions, to see this ignorant philosopher putting his vast learning into action.

SETTING PARIS AQUAKE, FROM LONDON

After *Persian Letters*, Voltaire's twenty-four *Philosophical Letters*, or *Letters on the English*, is sometimes singled out as the decisive beginning of the French enlightenment.[25] Voltaire penned these letters on the basis of his exile in England between 1726 and 1729, after he had fallen foul of the Chevalier de Rohan and been forced to flee France. It was a *felix culpa* for the young man, and for the history of European ideas. Because of his enforced exile, Voltaire was exposed to the philosophies of Bacon, Locke, Isaac Newton, and the Deists, as well as to a system of limited or constitutional monarchy, in which there was far greater freedom of religion, inquiry, and publication than within his native, Catholic France. Voltaire became determined to champion these foreign intellectual and civic developments in his homeland.

The letters (again, noting this literary form) range widely. A kind of cultured travelogue, they describe different aspects of English life for Voltaire's French readers: the first 7 on religion, Letters 8 and 9 on government, Letter 10 on commerce, Letters 11 through 17 on philosophers, Letters 18 through 22 on poetry and the theatre, and Letters 23 and 24 on the regard the English show for their men of letters, the Royal Society, and other burgeoning natural-philosophical academies.

Like Montesquieu's before him, Voltaire's *Letters on the English* above all avail themselves of the self-othering or estranging effects we examined in chapter 2 in *Persian Letters*. As Rica in particular is a picture of naïveté when he arrives in Paris (chapter 2), so the narrative voice in Voltaire's early letters has an almost childlike innocence about it, as Voltaire encounters the exotic ideas and ways of these strange Englishmen and -women from the other side of the Channel. He opens by recounting his experiences with a figure his Catholic countrymen would be sure to find strangest of all, a Quaker:

> It seemed to me that the doctrine and the history of so extraordinary a group deserved investigation by some thoughtful person. To learn about them, I sought out one of the most famous Quakers in England, who, after thirty years in trade, knew how to set limits on his fortune and his desires, and had withdrawn to the countryside near London (L1, 1).

The first two letters recount Voltaire's conversation with this singular man, interspersed with Voltaire's expressions of wonder:

> I opened with that which good Catholics have more than once made to Huguenots. "My dear sir," said I, "were you never baptised?" "I never was", replied the Quaker, "nor any of my brethren." "Zounds!", say I to him, "you are not Christians then". "Friend," replies the old man in a soft tone of voice, "swear not; we are Christians, and endeavour to be good Christians, but we are not of opinion that the sprinkling water on a child's head makes him a Christian". "Heavens!", say I, shocked at his impiety, "you have then forgot that Christ was baptised by St. John". "Friend", replies the mild Quaker once again, "swear not: Christ indeed was baptised by St. John, but He himself never baptised anyone. We are the disciples of Christ, not of John" (L1, 1–2).

So, there is further uncanny surprise lurking in Voltaire's commentary. On one hand, playing to his audience's sense of what is right and sound, the narrator recounts and disparages the Quakers' bizarre customs, clothing, modes of address, selective use of scripture, lack of communion, and "quaking" when taken by the Holy Spirit, as well as the sect's unlikely foundation story and conception of its unique election as the only truly Christian sect in some 1,600 years of the religion (L2, 6; L3, 7–9). For Voltaire's Parisians, these curios will all have been as bizarre as their own practices were to Rica and Usbek in *Persian Letters*.

On the other hand, under the guise of reporting these enthusiasts' exoticisms, something unusual occurs. Unmistakably, amidst the absurdities, the Quakers are shown to be in many ways eminently humane and rational, "were it possible for mankind to respect virtue when revealed in a ridiculous light" (L4, 11). The Quakers have Holy Writ on their side, when they observe that Christ himself baptised no one with water, promising a new baptism in the Holy Spirit. Voltaire makes no comment of censure when he recounts the Quakers' tolerance towards anyone who believes in One God, no matter what their particular theology and rituals (L1, 2). He likewise indulges in no irony when the Quaker describes their custom of calling even the highest civil authorities "friends", addressing them as equals in dignity, if not in worldly power. When describing their strange, unadorned attire, the Quaker appeals directly to values Voltaire's Catholic French readers were bound to honour, at least in theory: "Others wear the badges and marks of their several dignities, and we those of Christian humility" (L1, 3). Then there is the Quakers' refusal to take up the sword against other human beings, which steals a march on Voltaire's own fierce denunciations of the senselessness of wars (see below):

> We never war or fight in any case; but . . . the reason of our not using the outward sword is that we are neither wolves, tigers, nor mastiffs, but men and Christians. Our God, who has commanded us to love our enemies, and to suffer without repining, would certainly not permit us to cross the seas, merely because murderers clothed in scarlet, and wearing caps two foot high, enlist citizens by a noise made with two little sticks on an ass's skin extended. And when, after a victory is gained, the whole city of London is illuminated; when the sky is in a blaze with fireworks, and a noise is heard in the air, of thanksgivings, . . . we groan in silence, . . . for the sad havoc which is the occasion of those public rejoicings (L1, 3–4).

In the guise of playing to his audience's curiosity, we see that Voltaire is quietly presenting critical countermodels to French mores, pretentions, and customs. This is what quickly saw the *Letters on the English* censored in France. Where Gallic pride might wish to flatter itself by itemising the absurdities of the inhabitants of the British Isles, Voltaire again and again suggests the varied superiorities over the French which the English have won from centuries of social struggle, and religious and political reform. "An Englishman, being a free man, may go to heaven by whatever path he chooses", Voltaire famously writes in Letter 5 (L5, 15). With Montesquieu, but this time using England, Voltaire then puts in a word for the merits of the religious toleration Louis XIV had extinguished in France:

> If one religion only were allowed in England, the Government would very possibly become arbitrary; if there were but two, the people would cut one another's throats; but as there are such a multitude, they all live happy and in peace. (L6, 20)

It is primarily in the philosophical realm that Voltaire's *Letters on the English* stakes out decisive intellectual ground in shaping the French enlightenment. The sequence on the English philosophers, Bacon, Locke, and Newton, begins with a letter on inoculation (vaccination) which, like so many enlightenment texts, reads in our time of pandemic as sadly prescient. "Upon a general calculation," Voltaire observes:

Sixty people in every hundred have the small-pox. Of these threescore, twenty die of it in the most favourable season of life, and as many more wear the disagreeable remains of it in their faces so long as they live. Thus, a fifth part of mankind either die or are disfigured by this distemper (L11, 35).

Yet, then as now, vaccination was refused by many. In France, it was prohibited on religious grounds, as an attempt to thwart the will of God. For Voltaire, this practice, which was developed by Lady Wortley Montagu, wife of the British attaché to Constantinople, represented a prime exemplar of the new kinds of inquiry and knowledges he wished to champion. For a start, it was a knowledge which ministered to human need, of the kind Francis Bacon (subject of the following letter, Letter 12) dreamed "that may in some degree subdue and overcome the necessities and miseries of humanity".[26] Secondly, it was the product of the careful observations and controlled experimentation which Lady Montagu undertook. Thirdly, it was a knowledge born of wide experience of the world (again, the Near East, and oddly, the experiences of young girls in a Circassian seraglio (chapter 2)), as well as sanctified by the experiences of other cultures. The French need only to have opened their parochial eyes to see this: "I am informed that the Chinese have practiced inoculation these hundred years, a circumstance that argues very much in [China's] favour, since they are thought to be the wisest and best governed people in the world" (L11, 35–36).[27]

In the letters on Locke and Newton, Voltaire then paves new philosophical ground, at least for his target home audience. Voltaire's account of these philosophers is set up by way of a direct contrast with the work of the French rationalist, René Descartes, whom pride would have recommended to his readers as surely superior:

> A Frenchman who arrives in London, will find philosophy, like everything else, very much changed there. He had left the world a plenum [Descartes' view], and he now finds it a vacuum [Newton]. At Paris the universe is seen composed of vortices of subtle matter [Descartes]; but nothing like it is seen in London (L14, 41).

Voltaire is on the side of the English. Descartes for him represents that "spirit of systems" which he above all abhors as an exercise in failing to lucidly account for our epistemic limits. "Our Descartes", he writes, "born to discover the errors of antiquity", proceeded "to substitute his own, . . . hurried away by that systematic spirit which throws a cloud over the minds of the greatest men" (L14, 42). Voltaire praises Descartes' sceptical questioning of established beliefs, as well as his contributions to the mathematical sciences. However, his own constructive rationalist philosophising built upon the innate ideas of the "natural light" of the *res cogitans* Voltaire deems little more than the product of the philosopher's "lively and strong imagination" (L14, 48):

> He at last abandoned this guide [geometry], and gave entirely into the humour of forming hypotheses; and then philosophy was no more than an ingenious romance . . . He admitted innate ideas, he invented new elements, he created a world; he made man according to his own fancy; and it is justly said, that the man of Descartes is, in fact, that of Descartes only, very different from the real one (L14, 50).

Given the academic myths about "enlightenment rationalism", let alone the supposed centrality of Descartes to everything "modern", we can probably never point enough times to these and myriad other passages in Voltaire, Diderot, and others, to underscore Gay's depiction of the enlightenment as above all involving the *critique* of rationalism.[28] For Voltaire, John Locke (chapter 1) is by far the superior analyst of the human soul to his countrymen. As we flagged in chapter 1, it is above all Locke's tentative, experience-based approach to forming inductions which Voltaire favours: "He sometimes presumes to speak affirmatively, but then he presumes to doubt. Instead of concluding at once what we know not, he examines gradually what we would know" (L13, 42). Then there is the implausibility of the rationalist notion, including in Descartes, that our soul is born imbued with innate ideas, which Voltaire has great fun mocking for the implication that we must then forget them when we leave the womb, and only ever after imperfectly recover them before dying. With mordant irony, Voltaire tells us that "he has the honour to be as stupid in this particular [the denial of innate ideas] as Mr. Locke", and we will see that Diderot shares this honour (L13, 42; cf. chapter 4).

Perhaps the most famous claim Voltaire makes in the letter on Locke, however, concerns his defence of the English philosopher's Socratic claim in *The Essay on Human Understanding* that, given the limits of human understanding, "we shall perhaps never be capable of knowing whether a being, purely material, thinks or not".[29] For Voltaire, the suggestions of pious clerics—that Locke was heretically claiming the soul is wholly material, in this proposition—are mistaken. They also completely miss the epistemic humility which for him singles out Locke's manner of philosophising as a model for enlightened inquiry:

> But why may not God, if He pleases, communicate to our more delicate organs, that faculty of feeling, perceiving, and thinking, which we call human reason? To whatever side you turn, you are forced to acknowledge your own ignorance, and the boundless power of the Creator . . . Human reason is so little able,

merely by its own strength, to demonstrate the immortality of the soul, that it was absolutely necessary religion should reveal it to us (L13, 45).

With this much said of Voltaire's first major venture in enlightenment self-othering, we turn to two of his famous philosophical tales.

MICROMÉGAS, OR THE VIEW FROM SIRIUS

"On one of the planets that orbits the star named Sirius there lived a spirited young man, who I had the honour of meeting on the last voyage he made to our little ant hill," Voltaire's *Micromégas* (published in 1754, drafted as early as 1738) begins. "He was called Micromégas, a fitting name for anyone so great. He was eight leagues tall, or 24,000 geometric paces of five feet each".[30] And so we open a further enlightenment travel tale, another clash of two worlds. Like Montesquieu's *Persian Letters*, *Micromégas* involves a comic play upon how we might appear to exotic others, and how they appear to us. In contrast to Montesquieu's Persians, the two travellers who visit "us" in this Voltairean fable are interstellar giants.

The childlike art of the text conceals its deep bases in the astronomical (and also microscopic) researches of the previous centuries, and the cosmic decentering of the premodern Western perspectives which they had achieved (chapter 1). Much of *Micromégas*'s comedy wrestles with the enormity of the universe modern research had uncovered, set against the smallness of human beings: a contrast condensed in the "small (*micro*)" and "great (*mégas*)" of the hero's name.[31] For added laughs, Voltaire makes the scale temporal, as well as spatial. Micromégas, we are told, "was not even 250 years old" when he studied at the most celebrated colleges on Sirius and managed through will alone to work out some fifty of Euclid's propositions, twenty more than Blaise Pascal—who, here as in the *Letters on the English*, is a Voltairean *bête noir* (120).[32] After having some of his work censored by a "mufti" on Sirius—a little like Usbek chased from Persian court to seek enlightenment in heathen lands (chapter 2)—Micromégas decided to travel as a philosophical exercise: "voyaging from planet to planet in order to develop his mind (*esprit*) and heart, as one says" (121).

In his travels, the Sirian giant meets an "academic" from Saturn, who is "only" about 6,000 feet tall, with a mere 72 senses, and lives for just "500 great revolutions around the sun [about 15,000 years, by our standards]" (123), all in mathematical proportions to the relative scale of his home planet compared to Earth. The cosmic travellers soon come upon our (for them) tiny planet. After rounding its surface, they cool their heels in the Baltic, glimpsing first a whale, then a ship. It is the vessel coming back from Lapland, which in 1736 had tested Isaac Newton's predictions on the arc of the terrestrial meridian near the poles (129–32).[33]

At first, neither giant can believe the humans could possess a soul or the ability to speak, because of their sheer tininess. After various technical operations make it possible for the giants to see and converse with the "animalcules", however, Micromégas addresses the expedition: "Invisible insects, that the hand of the Creator has caused to spring up in the abyss of the infinitely small . . . I offer you my protection" (137). A comic exchange ensues concerning human customs, science, nature, and the soul, featuring the Cartesian, Thomist, Malebranchean, and Lockean philosophers who happen to be on board (142–46). At its culmination, Micromégas generously promises that he will write them a book explaining "the fundament (*bout*) of things". Yet, the story concludes with another Voltairean proclamation of ignorance: "It was taken to the academy of science in Paris, but when the ancient secretary opened it, he saw nothing but blank pages" (146).

So, what is the meaning of this fable? On one hand, as in ancient philosophical imaginings of the "view from above" down upon human concerns, showing their insignificance, Voltaire wants to humble human's epistemic egoism.[34] When the humans first encounter the fabulous giants, who proceed to pick up their vessel as if it were a toothpick and address them, we see Bacon's idols of the tribe and cave played out in real time (chapter 1):

> If anyone has ever been surprised, it was the people who heard these words. They could not figure out where they were coming from. The chaplain of the vessel recited the exorcism prayers, the sailors swore, and the philosophers of the vessel constructed systems [*sic*], but no matter what systems they came up with, they could not figure out who was talking (135–36).

Like the ancient satirist Lucian, one of Voltaire's clear influences in *Micromégas*,[35] by introducing us to the view of human affairs from 24,000 feet, Voltaire wants to show how cosmically minute we—and our grand designs—truly are. *Micromégas*'s treatment of war, for instance, echoes that of Voltaire's Quaker in *Letters on the English* (as above). When the urbane giant inquires as to the cause of a conflict between two tribes of human ants he sees beneath him, a human philosopher instructs him:

> It is a matter . . . of some piles of mud as big as your heel [the Crimea]. It is not that any of these millions of men that slit each other's throats care about this pile of mud. It is only a matter of determining if it should belong to a certain man who we call "Sultan", or to another who we call, for whatever reason, "Czar". Neither one has ever seen nor will ever see the little piece of Earth, and almost none of these animals that kill each other have ever seen the animal for which they kill (140–41).

The Sirian is so outraged by this "maniacal rage" that he feels tempted "to take three steps and crush this whole anthill of ridiculous assassins" (141).[36]

As always for the French enlighteners, the *hybris* of theologians and systematic rationalist philosophers is in Voltaire's sights here. The discussion between the giants and humans turns to the nature of the soul. As in the *Letters on the English*, a Cartesian steps forwards, and his view of innate ideas is quickly reduced to absurdity. Then a scholastic "animalcule in a square hat" interrupts the others:

> He said that he knew the secret: that everything would be found in the *Summa* of Saint Thomas. He looked the two celestial inhabitants up and down. He argued that their people, their worlds, their suns, their stars, had all been made uniquely for mankind. (145)

In response to this Christian view, framing the entire Creation around the human *epos* of fall, incarnation, redemption, and judgement: "our two voyagers nearly fell over with that inextinguishable laughter which, according to Homer, is shared with the gods". In the depths of Micromégas's generous heart, our narrator tells us, he could not help being "a little angry that the infinitely small had an almost infinitely great pride" (145).

Fortunately, a little Lockean next addresses the cosmic travellers. And he fares rather better, from the cosmopolitan perspective Voltaire is asking readers to see through his sage Sirian giant:

> "I do not know", said [the Lockean], "how I think, but I know that I have only ever thought through my senses. That there are immaterial and intelligent substances I do not doubt, but that it is impossible for God to communicate thought to matter [cf. chapter 1 and above], I doubt very much. I revere the eternal power. It is not my place to limit it. I affirm nothing, and content myself with believing that many more things are possible than one would think" (144–45).

At this performance of Lockean humility, we are told that "the animal from Sirius smiled" (145).

Is Voltaire, this giant of the French enlightenment, so far then from being a naïve optimist concerning the scope of human progress as to be actually closer to a kind of Germanic cultural pessimist, after all? Not quite. It is significant that the little humans the two cosmic giants happen upon are returning from a pioneering scientific expedition (132, 141–42). They are at the cutting edge of the experimental knowledges of their day, built on the epistemic practices championed by Bacon, Locke, the Royal Society *virtuosi*, and others, in light of a heightened awareness of the fallibility and finitude of the human mind. When the Sirian and Saturnian question them on various physical and astronomical esoterica, they are nearly bowled over at the little humans' mathematical knowledge. The Saturnian, closer to we terrestrial humans than his Sirian fellow, both in space and in his propensity to be all-too-self-certain, "was tempted to accuse of witchcraft the same people he had refused a soul fifteen minutes earlier" (142). It is not, however, witchcraft at issue for Voltaire, any more than it is some kind of Cartesian project to become "master and possessor of nature".[37] What the scientific knowledge of the little humans shows is that we can become greater (*méga*), within limits. But, we can do this only to the extent that we recognise those limits, and learn to identify and tolerate, but correct against, the inveterate forms of parochialism, small-mindedness, and over-weening egoism that remain the *micro* dimensions of our natures.

CANDIDE, OR AGAINST RATIONALIST OPTIMISM

Then, in 1755, came the Lisbon earthquake, and with it the Europe-wide attempt to square such senseless suffering (tens of thousands, piled into the churches, were killed) with belief in a loving, just, all-powerful God. While theologians wrestled with "theodicy" (the attempt to explain God's justice to humans), Voltaire initially rattled off a despairing "Poem on the Lisbon Earthquake":

> Once did I sing, in less lugubrious tone, / The sunny ways of pleasure's general rule; / The times have changed, and, taught by growing age, / And sharing of the frailty of mankind, / Seeking a light amid the deepening gloom, / I can but suffer, and will not repine . . . / . . . the whole world in every member groans, / All born for torment and for mutual death. / And o'er this ghastly chaos you would say / The ills of each make up the good of all! / What blessedness! And as, with quaking voice, / Mortal and pitiful ye cry, "All's well". / The universe belies you, and your heart / Refutes a hundred times your mind's conceit.[38]

Voltaire's outrage was, however, not directed solely, or even primarily, at Christian theologians so much as at the German rationalist philosopher, Gottlieb Leibniz. Leibniz had been scandalized when Pierre Bayle (chapter 1), in his *Historical and Critical Dictionary* (1696), had dared to claim that the Manichean idea that the ways of the world are best explained by positing an eternal struggle between Good and Evil deities is more convincing than the idea that this world could be the product of an all-good, all-knowing, all-powerful God.[39] Leibniz responded by trying to show, *a priori*—that is, solely by rational thought—that such a Perfect God could only have created the best of all possible worlds.[40] It is just that people who lose their children in natural disasters, or who suffer heinous injustices, are unable to see the Whole. Voltaire saw such rationalism as profoundly irrational: a prime example of philosophers overvaluing human reason, in ways leading to the rationalisation of troubling inhumanity and avoidable suffering.

And so, *Candide* was born, this classic about the naïve Westphalian lad moved by an abiding love for his Cunégonde, and a childlike faith in the wisdom of his tutor, Pangloss, the vain, lustful, and absurd professor of "métaphysico-théologo-cosmolo-nigologie" who holds to his Leibnizian mantras,[41] despite all of the appalling sufferings to which he, Candide, Cunégonde, and their circle are soon subjected:

> "It is demonstrable," said he, "that things cannot be otherwise than as they are; for all being created for an end, all is necessarily for the best end. Observe, that the nose has been formed to bear spectacles—thus we have spectacles. Legs are visibly designed for stockings—and we have stockings. Stones were made to be hewn, and to construct castles—therefore my lord has a magnificent castle; for the greatest baron in the province ought to be the best lodged. Pigs were made to be eaten—therefore we eat pork all the year round. Consequently, they who assert that all is well have said a foolish thing, they should have said: all is for the best" (1, 4).

We cannot detail here all of Candide's travails, after he is booted unceremoniously from his youthful Eden in Westphalia for the "experiments in natural philosophy" (aka, canoodling) that he and Cunégonde are soon caught in the act of undertaking (1, 4–5). *Candide* is another enlightenment travel tale. But we must add the proviso that in it, our heroes are given a kind of express tour of the horrors Europeans' irrationality, prejudices, and greed were visiting both upon each other (they arrive in Lisbon in time for the recriminations after the 1755 earthquake), and upon the victims of colonial adventurism in the Americas. Candide's uncritical faith in the wisdom of Pangloss's Leibnizian "All is for the best", remarkably, is finally broken when he and his companions happen upon a crippled African slave to Dutch plantation owners in Surinam:

> "Yes, sir," said the negro, "it is the custom. [. . .] When we work at the sugarcanes, and the mill snatches hold of a finger, they cut off the hand; and when we attempt to run away, they cut off the leg; both cases have happened to me. This is the price at which you eat sugar in Europe . . . " "Oh, Pangloss!", cried Candide, "you had not guessed at this abomination; it is the end. I must at last renounce your optimism." "What is this optimism?" said Cacambo. "Alas!", said Candide, "it is the madness of maintaining that everything is right when it is wrong" (19, 44).

As well as another testament to how inaccurate claims that the enlightenment was univocally Eurocentric remain, this episode in *Candide* shows the heart of Voltaire's literary-philosophical procedure. In line with his Lockean predilections, it is all about putting fine and abstract ideas to the test of experience, like a kind of scientific experiment. "Broadly speaking", Roger Pearson writes:

> The typical Voltairean *conte* begins by introducing a theory, prejudice, or complacent assumption. Through the eyes and experience of an initially innocent observer, this "system" is juxtaposed with the facts of life, with the result that the observer's outlook is gradually transformed. In Voltaire's hands the *conte* is thus an instrument of demythification, of "defabulation", which inculcates a habit of mind more than it illustrates a series of aphoristic truths. Typically, his *contes* demonstrate that systems are an unwarranted and unsustainable imposition of false order on the facts of life, and they trace a coming to terms: with human ignorance, with the contingencies of living . . . with other people.[42]

In no tale is the absurd disjunction between philosophical speculation and real-world experience more vividly dramatized than in *Candide*. Often the characters are depicted as being so immersed in philosophising that real life, and the demands of moral decency, represents a kind of unwelcome intrusion. At one moment, as Candide goes to save a drowning man, Pangloss intervenes, "proving to him that the Bay of Lisbon was formed expressly for this Anabaptist to be drowned", and so he drowns indeed, due to Pangloss (6, 12). Candide himself, for all his love of Pangloss, undergoes a kind of "deconversion" from his master's systematic *délire*. But it is hardly an easy education, and Voltaire, by writing *Candide*, is clearly hoping for more bloodless cures:

> If this is the best of possible worlds, what then are the others? Well, if I had been only whipped I could put up with it, for I experienced that among the Bulgarians; but oh, my dear Pangloss! you greatest of philosophers, that I should have seen you hanged, without knowing for what! Oh, my dear Anabaptist, you best of men, that you should have been drowned in the very harbour! Oh, Miss Cunégonde, you pearl of girls! That you should have had thy belly ripped open (7, 15)!

Let's be clear again: If the enlightenment, as has been charged, championed a blind optimism in reason and social progress, *we should not be able to find at its very heart arguably the Western tradition's most acerbic criticism of the inhumanity such optimism can sanction*. We should also expect Voltaire, the enlightenment's principal and arguably most brilliant spokesman, to be an ally of metaphysical optimism, not its trenchant critic. We should expect Voltaire to have "reasoned away" the facts of evil, as well as the intercontinental injustices of European colonialism and the slave trade—for "all is well" (see chapter 5). But it is precisely such fatuous uses of reason as an instrument to rationalise needless human suffering that Voltaire opposed.

Jonathan Israel, a recent advocate for the enlightenment but critic of Voltaire, wants readers to position the latter as almost an anti-Baylean thinker whose importance has too often been overplayed.[43] Israel can only do so by suppressing the evident importance Bayle has in the "Poem on the Lisbon Disaster", and then, more cryptically, in *Candide* itself. Faced with the earthquake and the sufferings it occasioned, Voltaire tells us in his poem exactly that he turns above all "to learned Bayle", who "knows more" than those who would reason away these horrors:

> With the balance in his hands / Bayle teaches me to doubt / He, wise and great enough to need no system . . . / What is the verdict of our greatest mind? / Nothing: the book of fate is closed to us. / Man is stranger to himself.[44]

We can see this "greatest mind" shaping Voltaire's own acceptance of the reality of evil in the presence of a lesser-remarked character in *Candide*. This is Martin the Manichean, who Candide quickly takes to his side as one of very few honest men he meets (20, 47). When he asks Martin about his faith, Martin uncannily reproduces Bayle's heretical position in the *Historical and Critical Dictionary*—with the gallows humour being all Voltaire's own:

> "Sir," answered Martin, "our priests accused me of being a Socinian, but the real fact is I am a Manichean." "You jest," said Candide; "there are no longer Manicheans in the world." "I am one," said Martin. "I cannot help it; I know not how to think otherwise." "Surely you must be possessed by the devil," said Candide. "He is so deeply concerned in the affairs of this world," answered Martin, "that he may very well be in me, as well as in everybody else; but I own to you that when I cast an eye on this globe, or rather on this little ball, I cannot help thinking that God has abandoned it to some malignant being . . . " "There are, however, some things good," said Candide. "That may be," said Martin; "but I know them not" (21, 48).

VOLTAIRE AFTER BAYLE: BIBLICAL CRITICISM, DEISM, AND THE STRUGGLE FOR TOLERATION

The conclusion to *Candide*, as the world knows, is less dour, if more enigmatic, than Martin the Manichean's. Pangloss, unrepentant, continues to regale the chastened travellers about the hidden Reason behind all of their woes in their retreat outside Constantinople. Candide replies that "that is very well put . . . , but we must cultivate our garden" (30, 81). Just what that final line means continues to divide commentators. One thing is clear: Its reading as a call to sage Epicurean withdrawal from engagement in the broken world is contradicted by Voltaire's own later history, after *Candide*'s appearance in 1759.

In 1762, a young Protestant in Catholic Toulouse took his own life. The townspeople spread the slander that his father had killed him, to prevent his supposedly imminent conversion to Catholicism. The father, Jean Calas, was soon falsely imprisoned, tortured, and killed. The family, broken, fled to Ferney, seeking the aid of Voltaire, who would be animated by this injustice (then, the comparable case of La Barre in 1765) into the most extraordinary period of philosophical activism of his life.[45] Pamphlet after pamphlet, commentary, and dictionary entry now issued forth from his frenzied pen. To d'Alembert, one time co-editor of the *Encyclopédie*, Voltaire would write: "This is not a time for jesting; wit does not harmonize with massacres . . . is this the country of philosophy and pleasure? It is rather the country of the Massacre of Saint Bartholomew".[46] It is in this period that, aping the ancient statesman Cato's appeals to war against the Carthaginians, Voltaire famously took to signing all his letters with the injunction to *écrasez l'infâme*, or "destroy the infamy" of religious fanaticism. "Come brave Diderot, intrepid d'Alembert", Voltaire would muster the other *philosophes*:

> Overwhelm the fanatics and the knaves, destroy the insipid declamations, the miserable sophistries, the lying history, . . . the absurdities without number; do not let those who have sense be subjected to those who have none; and the generation which is being born will owe to us its reason and its liberty.[47]

If Voltaire's name still raises hairs on the backs of theologians (especially Catholic theologians), it is because of the writings he produced in this period: texts like *The Questions of Zapata, The Sermon to the Fifty, Letter to the Romans, The Homily on the New Testament, The Homily on the Old Testament,* as well as the *Philosophical Dictionary* in its rapidly proliferating editions, and the *Treatise on Toleration* itself.[48]

Voltaire himself was no simple unbeliever, and his morality is post- (and so, not anti-) Christian. He was trained in the Deism he had learned of in his travels in England (cf. L7). The English Deists, "free thinkers" like Collins, Blount, and Tolland, all writing between 1680 and 1720, had proposed (like Spinoza at the same time) that "reason is the only foundation of our certitude", and that the claims of biblical Christianity were not exempt from its scrutiny.[49] When applied to the Bible, however, these men had argued that God's book revealed itself to reason as a tissue of human contradictions. The biblical Creation story, including its claim that women were created from Adam's rib, the idea of inherited original sin, or Joshua's stopping of the sun, they found "irrational and repugnant to the nature of things".[50] Like Bayle in the latter's *Historical and Critical Dictionary*, they also pointed out how many of the behaviours seemingly sanctioned in the Old Testament (like David's various escapades, and Moses' slaughter of the Midianites), if read in anything like a literal way, seemed profoundly immoral.[51]

Voltaire instead aimed to divide what he deemed to be the superstitious shell of Christianity from its moral core. "There is no morality in superstition, [morality] is not in ceremonies," the *philosophe* maintained, "it has nothing in common with dogmas".[52] The problem comes when people, and authorities, seek to make morality depend upon metaphysical and theological dogmata, which Voltaire sees as beyond the scope of human verification. "Is Jesus word?", Voltaire asks rhetorically in the entry "Arius" of his *Philosophical Dictionary*:

> If he is word, did he emanate from god in time or before time? If he emanated from god is he coeternal and consubstantial with him or is he of a similar substance? Is he distinct from him or is he not? Was he made and not begotten? Can he beget in his turn? Has he paternity or the quality of production without paternity? Was the holy ghost made or begotten or produced or does he proceed from the father, from the son, or from both? Can he beget, can he produce? If his hypostasis is consubstantial with the hypostasis of the father and the son, how is it possible for him not to do the same things as these two persons who are himself . . . It was certainly necessary for these questions, so far above reason, to be determined by an infallible church.[53]

Voltaire insists that "it cannot be too often repeated that dogmas are different, and morality the same amongst all men who use reason." What follows, according to him, is that "morality comes from god like light; our superstitions are nothing but darkness."[54] The problem is that assertions concerning things which are at once mysterious, but invested with theological and political significance, too readily become the prompts for "curiosity, sophistic subtlety, acrimony, intrigue, fury to dominate, rage to persecute, blind and bloody fanaticism, barbarous credulity".[55] Like Montaigne, Bayle, and Locke before him, Voltaire supposes that, if theological issues could have been resolved like questions of geometry, with recourse to agreed-upon standards and evidences, agreement would long ago have been reached. But they have not.

The history of theological disputation, and the development of the Church, instead shows up for Voltaire as all too human, riven by "passions, intrigues, the lust for dispute, hatred, prejudice, [and] ignorance".[56] Voltaire is aware of, and gives fire to, the biblical criticism of his day questioning the "pious frauds" long accepted in Christendom concerning Jesus' fictive letters, Seneca's fictive letters to Paul, Paul's alleged Roman citizenship (no Jews were granted citizenship in Rome), the "interpolation" in Josephus concerning Jesus, the massacre of the innocents, the "Apostolic constitutions" establishing bishops, the impossible Pontificate of Peter, and the Donation of Constantine. Voltaire professes ironic shock that the "infallible" Church councils could have disagreed so often with each other: declaring Jesus consubstantial with the Father at Nicaea in 325 CE, only to deny him this same attribute at Rimini; making Mary mother of God at Ephesus in 431, then according Christ two natures there at 449, only to remove one of these in 451 at Chalcedon,[57] and so on.

Beliefs in invisible and unprovable deities are by themselves innocuous. Voltaire's own post-Lockean, post-Baylean perspective only recommends self-awareness, lest one's convictions bespeak "the caprices of the imagination, and the excesses of the passions".[58] Such dogmatism becomes politically and ethically problematic, for him as for Bayle, when peoples imagine themselves licensed to compel others to convert by fear, force, or fraud (see chapter 1). "Fanaticism is to superstition is what delirium is to fever, and what fury is to anger"; Voltaire specifies: "The man who has ecstasies and vision, who takes his dreams for realities, and his imaginings for prophecies, is an enthusiast. The man who backs his madness with murder is a fanatic".[59]

The only humane solution is not to persecute followers of different Gods. This solution involves toleration of anyone whose superstitions and enthusiasms, whatever their content, do not pass over into uncivil actions. "What is toleration?", Voltaire asks in *The Philosophical Dictionary*. He gives the Lockean-Baylean answer we by now can anticipate: "It is the appurtenance of humanity. We are all full of weakness and errors; let us mutually pardon each other our follies—this is the first law of nature".[60] Voltaire's defence of toleration is in fact his defining philosophical and political legacy, bringing together as it does all of the threads of his divergent arts and concerns.

Alongside this epistemic argument for toleration, there is the moral reciprocity of the golden and silver rules: We should not persecute others, since we do not wish to be persecuted for our convictions. To Christians, his principal audiences, Voltaire addresses an especial appeal: "Ours is no doubt the only good, the only true [religion], but we have done so much evil by means of it that we should be modest when we talk about other religions".[61] Toleration, Voltaire suggests, is a secular extension of charity to all neighbours, even those who happen to believe in different Gods to our own: "Of all the religions, the Christians ought to inspire the most toleration, although hitherto the Christians have been the most intolerant of all men".[62] The cultivation of toleration is also the necessary development of the ancient philosophical ambition to use reason to "civilize and soften the manners of men and prevent the access of the disease [of fanaticism] . . . for the effect of philosophy is to render the soul tranquil, and fanaticism and tranquillity are totally incompatible".[63]

BY WAY OF CONCLUDING

It is impossible for any single chapter, any single *book*, to take the measure of Voltaire's encyclopedic learning and his Herculean literary, historical, and philosophical labours.[64] It was not for nothing that the great nineteenth-century reactionaries, like Joseph de Maistre, reserved their especial vitriol for his sartorial, smiling philosophy.[65] Voltaire's work, like the classical texts he admired, is a chaos of clear ideas, the easy grace of whose style conceals the depths of his humanity, the immensity of his learning, and the subtleties of his art. (The scorn with which "serious" metaphysicians have always held him arguably only shames their notions of "seriousness" and "metaphysics".) The German poet-philosopher Goethe, Voltaire's near-contemporary, has given this peerless tribute:

> If you wish depth, genius, imagination, taste, reason, sensibility, philosophy, elevation, originality, nature, intellect, fancy, rectitude, facility, flexibility, precision, art, abundance, variety, fertility, warmth, magic, charm, grace, force, an eagle sweep of vision, vast understanding, instruction rich, tone excellent, urbanity, suavity, delicacy, correctness, purity, cleanness, eloquence, harmony, brilliancy, rapidity, gaiety, pathos, sublimity, and universality: perfection, indeed, behold Voltaire.[66]

Our aim here is to have shown how Voltaire carries forward the key enlightenment practices of critical self-othering modelled in Montesquieu's *Persian Letters*, grounded in his reception of the thought of Bacon, Locke, Bayle, the Deists, Montaigne, and many others. Taking aim at epistemic egoism, fallibility, prejudice, and conceits, Voltaire shows the French their limitations in the mirror of their English contemporaries, human beings' follies in the perspective of his fictional Sirian giant, and rationalists' hybris in the experiences and eventual recantation of the hapless Candide. Voltaire's post-Calasian campaign for religious toleration, and against religiously motivated violence, remains iconic. It represents the culmination of Voltaire's intellectual preoccupations, his conception of the philosopher, and his extraordinary energies. It also stakes out the heart of French enlightenment criticism, well-nigh as far from many of its more wholesale criticisms as Sirius is from our little planet.

NOTES

1. Will Durant, *The Story of Philosophy* (New York: Simon & Schuster, 1926), 201.
2. See Ira Wade, *Intellectual Development of Voltaire* (Princeton, NJ: Princeton University Press, 1969); Wade, *Esprit Revolutionnaire*, 27–28.
3. Voltaire, "Philosopher" in *Philosophical Dictionary*, ed. and trans. Thomas Besterman (London: Penguin, 2004), 334. As different editions produce different selections, we will use more than one edition of the text. Wherever possible, I will refer to this translation, and references to it will be abbreviated as *PD*.
4. Voltaire, "Philosopher", *PD*, 334.
5. Voltaire, "Philosopher", *PD*, 335.
6. Voltaire, "Dogmas", *PD*, 181.
7. Wade, *Esprit Philosophique*, 200–03.
8. Voltaire, "Zadig", in *Viking Portable Voltaire*, ed. Ben Ray Redman (London: Viking Penguin, 1977), 329.
9. Voltaire, "Matter", in *PD*, 158, 159.
10. Voltaire, "Soul", in *PD*, 21.
11. See Wade, *Intellectual Development*, 693–711.
12. Voltaire, *The Ignorant Philosopher*, in *The Complete Romances of Voltaire* (New York: Walter J. Black, 1927), 427.
13. To note the comparison is not to assert an identity. Voltaire would likely have had little sympathy with Kant's proposal to base metaphysical dogma on the alleged fact of noumenal human freedom attested by moral action.
14. Voltaire, *Essay on the Mores and Spirit of Nations*, at Rasmussen, *Pragmatic Enlightenment*, 70.
15. Voltaire, *Traité de métaphysique*, ed. W. H. Barber, in *The Complete Works of Voltaire, Volume 14* (Oxford, UK: Voltaire Foundation, [1736] 1989), 93.
16. Voltaire, at Rasmussen, *Pragmatic Enlightenment*, 71.
17. Voltaire, "General Reflection on Man", in *Philosophical Dictionary*, selected and trans. H. I. Woolf (New York: Dover), 203.
18. See Lester G. Crocker, *Nature and Culture: Ethical Thought in the French Enlightenment* (Baltimore, MD: John Hopkins University Press, 1963), 32–34.
19. Voltaire, "Morality", *PD*, 322; see Rasmussen, *Pragmatic Enlightenment*, 73. Such passages should be kept in mind when discussions of Voltaire's aristocratism are undertaken.
20. Voltaire, *Traité de métaphysique*, I intro. 7, 27. See Crocker, *Nature and Culture*, 299–300; Rasmussen, *Pragmatic Enlightenment*, 71–72.
21. Voltaire, "Law [Natural]", *The Works of Voltaire*, Vol. VI (Philosophical Dictionary Part 4) | Online Library of Liberty (libertyfund.org).
22. Crocker, *Nature and Culture*, 36.
23. Voltaire, "Virtue: Section I", The Works of Voltaire, Vol. VII (Philosophical Dictionary Part 5) | Online Library of Liberty (libertyfund.org).
24. See Rasmussen, *Pragmatic Enlightenment*, 76–77.
25. Voltaire, *Philosophical Letters, or Letters Regarding the English Nation*, ed. and with an introduction by John Leigh, trans. Prudence L. Steiner (Indianapolis/

Cambridge: Hackett Publishing Company, 2007). In-text letter and page references in this section refer to this text and edition.

26. Bacon, NO I.38.

27. On this letter in Voltaire, see the excellent commentary in Alan Charles Cors, *Voltaire and the Triumph of the Enlightenment*, available at https://www.thegreatcourses.com/courses/voltaire-and-the-triumph-of-the-enlightenment.html.

28. Gay, *The Rise of Modern Paganism*, 141.

29. Locke, *Essay on Human Understanding*, IV.3.

30. Voltaire, *Micromégas*, in I. Wade, ed., *Voltaire's Micromégas: A Study in the Fusion of Science, Myth, and Art* (Princeton, NJ: Princeton University Press, 1950), 119. In section 4.3, all unmarked numbers in brackets refer to the French text in this edition.

31. Pearson, *Fables of Reason*, 69–70.

32. Voltaire, *Letters on the English*, Letter 25.

33. Nicholas Cronk and J. L. Shank, "Introduction" to N. Cronk and J. L. Shank, eds., *Micromégas and Other Texts (1738–1742), Les oeuvres complèts de Voltaire, 20c* (Voltaire Foundation, Oxford, UK: Oxford University Press, 2017), 25–29; Pearson, *Fables of Reason*, 52.

34. See Hadot, "View from Above".

35. See Ralph Arthur Nablow, "Was Voltaire Influenced by Lucian in 'Micromégas'?", *Romance Notes* 22, no. 2 (1981): 186–91.

36. Cf. Nicholas Cronk, "The Voltairean Genre of the *Conte Philosophique*: Does It Exist?", *Enlightenment and Narrative: Essays in Honour of Richard A. Francis by Colleagues and Friends*, ed. P. Robinson, Nottingham French Studies, 48, no. 3 (2009), 61–73; 80–81; Cronk and Shank, "Introduction", 28–29.

37. René Descartes, *Discourse on Method*, trans. E. Haldane (Chicago: Britannica Great Books, 1952), VI.

38. Voltaire, "Poem on the Lisbon Disaster", trans. Joseph McCabe, in Toleration and other essays/Poem on the Lisbon Disaster - Wikisource, the free online library.

39. Bayle, *The Historical and Critical Dictionary: Selections*, 144–53; 166–93; 409–12 (the entries on "Manicheanism" and "Paulicians" specifically). M. Bayle and his "genius" (Leibniz 1951, 63) is mentioned nearly three hundred times in Leibniz's *Theodicy* (Gottlieb W. Leibniz, *Theodicy: Essays on the Goodness of God, the Freedom of Man and the Origin of Evil*, translated by E. G. Hubbard [London: Routledge & Kegan Paul, 1951]). He is the direct object of Leibniz's counterarguments at 57–123 and 172–373.

40. Leibniz, *Theodicy*, 57–123 and 172–373.

41. Voltaire, *Candide* 1, 4, trans. Robert M. Adems, ed. Nicholas Cronk (New York, London: W. W. Norton, 2016). Chapter and page numbers in brackets in this section refer to this text. On this text, see the canonical commentary by Ira Wade, *Voltaire's Candide: A Study in the Fusion of History, Art, and Philosophy* (Princeton, NJ: Princeton University Press, 1959), as well as the articles collected in the cited edition of *Candide*.

42. Pearson, *Fables of Reason*, 34.

43. For Israel's criticisms, which are political as well as metaphysical, see Israel, *Enlightenment Contested*, 360–61, 683, 751, 756–76.
44. Voltaire, "Poem on the Lisbon Disaster".
45. See Voltaire, *Treatise on Toleration*, trans. Desmond M. Clarke (London: Penguin, 2017), 1–5.
46. Voltaire, at Durant, *Story of Philosophy*, 306.
47. Voltaire, at Durant, *Story of Philosophy*, 307.
48. For a collection of these texts, see Voltaire, *Selected Works of Voltaire*, trans. J. McCabe (London: C. A. Watts & Co., 1948).
49. See Jeffrey W. Wigelsworth, *Deism in Enlightenment England* (Manchester, UK: Manchester University Press, 2009).
50. Tolland at Will and Ariel Durant, *The Age of Louis XIV* (New York: Simon & Schuster, 1935), 567–68.
51. Cf. eg Voltaire, "David", *PD*, 168–71; "Moses", *PD*, 317–21.
52. Voltaire, "Morality", *PD*, 322.
53. Voltaire, "Arius", *PD*, 47.
54. Voltaire, "Morality", *PD*, 322.
55. Voltaire, "Councils", *PD*, 147–48.
56. Voltaire, "Councils", *PD*, 147–48.
57. Voltaire, "Councils", *PD*, 147–48.
58. Voltaire, "Fanaticism", *PD*, 200.
59. Voltaire, "Fanaticism", *PD*, 200–01.
60. Voltaire, "Tolerance", *PD*, 394.
61. Voltaire, "Tolerance", *PD*, 394.
62. Voltaire, "Tolerance", *PD*, 394.
63. Voltaire, "Fanaticism", *PD*, 200–01.
64. Cf. Wade, *Intellectual Development*; *Esprit Revolutionnaire*, 7–66.
65. See Will Durant, *Story of Philosophy*, 201.
66. Goethe, in Joseph M. Wheeler, "Tributes to Voltaire", in *The Sincere Huron, Pupil of Nature* (Musaicum Books, 2017), 150.

Chapter 4

Eyesight from the Blind

Diderot, Saunderson, and Humans Born Blind

FROM VOLTAIRE TO DIDEROT

It is scarcely credible, but by passing from Voltaire to Denis Diderot, we meet another thinker of scarcely less Protean scope and energies. Here is a figure, dubbed by his friends simply "the *philosophe*", who was most famous in his lifetime for co-editing, and then editing, the massive *Encyclopédie, ou Dictionnaire raisonné des sciences, des arts, et des métiers* (*Encyclopedia, or Reasoned Dictionary of the Sciences, Arts, and Professions*). But Diderot also wrote plays, novels, aesthetic criticism, philosophical letters, and essays. The fullness of time, and the recovery of his many unpublished manuscripts, has revealed Diderot to posterity as also the author of transgressive philosophical novels and dialogues, and of the radically anti-colonialist interpolations into the Abbe Raynal's *Histoire des deux indes* that we will consider in chapter 5.[1] It is arguably even more difficult to find an "organic unity" in Diderot's work (and sheer *élan*) as in the near one hundred volumes of Voltaire's *oeuvre*.[2] Diderot's opening paragraph of the entry on "Eclecticism" in the *Encyclopédie*, which also steals the march on Immanuel Kant's better-known declarations in "What is Enlightenment?", seems as close a first approximation as we can venture:

> The eclectic is a philosopher who, riding roughshod over prejudice, tradition, antiquity, universal consent, authority, in a word, everything that subjugates the mass of minds, dares to think for himself, goes back to the most clear and general principles, examines them, discusses them, allowing only that which can

be demonstrated from his experience and reason; and having analyzed all philosophical systems without any deference or partiality, he constructs a personal and domestic one that belongs to him.[3]

By the time Diderot published his first philosophical works in the 1740s, Voltaire was over fifty. Voltaire admired the younger man, championing his cause and that of the *Encyclopédie* when they were subject to ecclesiastical and political censorship. But Voltaire is, as it were, classical, Diderot, more baroque. Voltaire's style condenses his passion for the causes of enlightenment into understated ironies, with occasional lightning flashes. Diderot (here more like his friend-turned-enemy Jean-Jacques Rousseau) is more Ciceronian. He wears his affects, even his tears, on his rhetorical sleeve.

Diderot's first works, starting with his translation and commentary on Lord Shaftesbury's theory of moral sentiments, share Voltaire's Deism (a belief in an ordering, moral deity discoverable by reason). However, in the later 1740s Diderot underwent a conversion to atheism which Voltaire would never take. It would be the literary expression of this atheism in our focal text in this chapter, his 1749 "Letter on the Blind, for the Use of Those Who See" ("*Lettre dur les aveugles, à l'usage de ceux qui voient*"), that would land Diderot for some months in Vincennes jail, touted by authorities as a dangerous figure, and warned that any similar publications would lead to a more terminal sentence.[4] At around the same time, Diderot began to engage far more closely than Voltaire ever did with the emerging biological writings of figures like John Needham, Georges-Louis Leclerc, Comte de Buffon, Pierre Louis Maupertuis, and Guillaume-François Rouelle, many of whose discoveries he saw as calling into question biblical and providential understandings of the natural world (see ch. 5).[5] We might say that Diderot's engagement with the emergent "life sciences", and their wider implications, played as significant a role in his philosophical formation as had Newtonian physics in that of his great predecessor.

With this much said, we approach the influential position of Jonathan Israel, and it is right to say a few words in this connection. In his monumental series on the enlightenment, Israel claims that the passage from Voltaire to Diderot marks the transition between a "moderate", Lockean and a "radical", Spinozist stream of the French enlightenment. The first was metaphysically Deistic and Newtonian, inclined to accept the argument from design for God's existence.[6] Politically, Israel suggests all "moderates" were reformist and aristocratic, rather than revolutionary and democratic; monarchist, rather than republican; and inclined to shy away from the revolutionary implications of enlightenment anti-clericalism and attacks on the theological bases of the *ancien régime*. By contrast, the radicals were led in France by Diderot and later by his friend and co-author, the Baron d'Holbach. After 1750, they transformed Voltaire and others' "anti-scripturalism, *tolérantisme*, and critique of ecclesiastical authority" into "overt antimonarchism, egalitarianism, and attack on privilege."[7]

The monumental sweep of Israel's work, as well as its larger aim to re-establish the progressive significance of the enlightenment despite its many detractors, deserve great honor. However, critics have questioned whether the extraordinary intellectual ferment of this period makes it susceptible to such a clean division into just the two streams he envisages.[8] Exceptions to his division of thinkers into either moderate or radical camps have been multiplied. In this book, we have seen, for instance, that Montesquieu was radical on gender, whilst defending constitutional monarchy in politics. Voltaire was surely radical on toleration, his own hesitations about the moral credentials or implications of atheism notwithstanding. He was radical in his opposition to torture and capital punishment, issues on which Diderot and d'Holbach were more ambivalent.[9] Again, we can find warm statements about the educability of the public in Voltaire, alongside the snobbish dismissals of the *canaille* Israel cites.[10] But we can equally find passages in Diderot wherein he questions the public's intelligence, and wonders whether *éclaircissement* might ever spread beyond the suburbs.[11] Diderot's last work, his sprawling commentary on the life and work of the ancient Stoic, Seneca, is meanwhile far from denouncing his great predecessor's compromises and conservatism, as Israel suggests. The aging Diderot in fact praises Voltaire as perhaps the greatest man who ever lived.[12]

We can wonder especially whether a defence of democracy, the equal dignity of the races and sexes, and the spread of secular education, freed from the clutches of the churches, requires a specific—and specifically Spinozist, systematic—metaphysics, as Israel supposes. We've seen Montesquieu's and Voltaire's patented scepticism concerning such systematizing thinkers as Descartes, Spinoza's great rationalist predecessor. Similar hostility to the "spirit of systems" is present in Diderot and d'Alembert's *Encyclopédie* (see introduction above), as well as in Diderot's own works, as we'll see. In chapter 1, we commented on how John Locke's emphasis on the shaping importance of experience in what individuals can know points him in several passages towards political critique. Many people are prevented from developing their natural capacities by their inability to access education, a situation which could be changed. Of course, Locke himself was no radical. Yet this empiricist argument in Claude Adrien Helvétius, and even in Baron d'Holbach, forms a key basis for their politically radical claims about the need for the far-reaching transformation of the sources of inequalities between the experiences of different groups within European societies and around the world.[13]

So, let us suspend here any commitment to identifying Diderot as wholly a radical or a moderate *lumière*. That he was Diderot provides challenges enough. We focus in this chapter on one key text, the "Letter on the Blind, for the Use of Those Who See", which caused Diderot such problems in 1749, and that carries forward our developing conception of the self-estranging other enlightenment.

BLINDNESS AND THE OPENING OF EYES

Diderot's "Letter on the Blind" [hereafter "the Letter"],[14] like Montesquieu's *Persian Letters*, represents another seeming enlightenment palimpsest or collection of paratactically (that is, obscurely) connected elements, albeit here in a single epistle. Diderot doesn't deny the text's apparent disorder. He advertises it, like the essayist Michel de Montaigne, whom he evokes in the Letter's conclusion: "You may blame my continual digressions, but digressions are of the essence of this treatise" (133).[15] The Letter concludes with a series of questions regarding the limited state of human knowledge, closing on a Voltairean note of enlightened scepticism:

> Alas! Madam, when we weigh our human knowledge in [Michel de] Montaigne's scale, we are almost reduced to adopting his motto. For what do we know? What of the nature of matter? Nothing. What of the nature of spirit and thought? Still less. What of the nature of movement, space and duration? Absolutely nothing. . . . [W]e scarce know anything, yet what numbers of books there are whose authors have all pretended to knowledge? I cannot think why the world is not tired of reading so much and learning nothing, unless it be for the very same reason that I have been talking to you for two hours, without being tired and without telling you anything. Yours etc. (141).

Our thread out of the labyrinth is the so-called "Molyneux's problem", with which the Letter opens and closes. Would a person born blind, who had known three-dimensional objects and geometric figures hitherto only by reading, listening, and the sense of touch, be instantly able to recognize them once their eyes had been restored to vision? The Letter's opening recounts that René Antoine Ferchault de Réamur is visiting Paris, promising to give eyesight to a blind young girl, the daughter of an engraver who has a cataract preventing her vision (70–71). Diderot, or his narrator "***",[16] has asked to be present to witness the opening of the girl's eyes. But this request has been denied, for reasons *** clearly suspects (70–71; cf. 135–36).

It is remarkable that Molyneux's problem, which frames the Letter, was of interest not only to Diderot in this period. Before him, John Locke, Étienne

Bonnot de Condillac, and Voltaire, amongst others, had all considered it.[17] Whether blind people, when restored to sight, could understand what they were seeing seems a curious question for philosophers to have been preoccupied with. But then we recall the wider, post-Lockean epistemological debates in which Diderot and the enlighteners were participating, concerning the origins, nature, and limits of human knowledge (ch. 1, ch. 3). Locke himself had included a discussion of Molyneux's problem in response to the latter's correspondence, in later editions of *Essay on Human Understanding*. It promises what Francis Bacon had called "an instance of the fingerpost" (a decisive, potentially falsifying experiment) to test the rationalist hypothesis of Descartes and others which the Englishman opposed.[18] According to that hypothesis, which we have seen Voltaire playing with (chapter 3), individuals' minds are furnished with the natural light (*lumen naturale*) of innate ideas. They should be equipped from birth even with the more abstract ideas, like "color", involved in visual perception. The issue that Molyneux's problem suggests for the rationalists, as the philosopher Gassendi curtly informed Descartes, is that experience does not bear the hypothesis out:

> I once knew a man who was blind from birth and studied philosophy under the same professor as me. I remember more than once putting various colors before him, in daylight as well as in the shade, and asking him to notice if there was any difference between them, but he never could. If you don't believe it, do the experiment.[19]

Readers may also have picked up, however, that this idea of a person born blind, restored to sight, has telling metaphorical echoes—not least for an intellectual period which was coming to know itself as one of "en-light-enment". The metaphorical associations between light, the sense of sight, and knowledge go deep in Western thought, and cut across sectarian boundaries. For Christians, those who refuse revelation are "refusing to see the light". Then there are the "blind" forces of nature, uninformed by Providence. Yet God is invisible to the human eye. There are also biblical echoes in an oculist visiting Paris, promising to give eyesight to the blind: Christ gave eyesight to the blind, as one of the signs of his Divinity. For philosophers, by contrast, tradition and hearsay have always been "blindnesses", compared to sound reasoning, based on calm observation. For them, many people with physical sight remain "blinded" by prejudice and ignorance. For "free thinkers", it is faith which is "blind", as perhaps are the "ways of God" that consign the innocent to suffer, and "turn a blind eye" to the perversions of the wicked (see chapter 3). As Locke, Bayle, or Voltaire would insist, we are surely effectively like the "blind", fumbling around in darkness, when we speculate on things we cannot know. For empirical philosophers in the Baconian lineage, after all, the rationalist drawing out deductions based on axioms furnished him by his "natural light" (innate or God-given reason) is akin to a blind man (see below).[20] Our very language can be "blind", when we pronounce on things which do not exist, based on illusion or hearsay, or speak unclearly or inaccurately of real things.

The enlightenment itself can be depicted, in the best ambitions of its leading thinkers, as trying to open the eyes of Europeans blinded by their epistemic egoism, parochialisms, residual superstitions, and the mastery of the Churches over education and public culture. A sighted man forced to live in a land of the blind, Diderot digresses at one point in the Letter, would hence be not unlike Diderot himself, and the other *philosophes*, facing censorship and persecution in Louis XV's France:

> poor wretches who discovered truth in the dark ages and were rash enough to reveal it to their blind contemporaries, and found their bitterest enemies were those from their circumstances and education [who] would have seemed most likely to receive it willingly (87).

In one of its registers, this is to say, Diderot's "Letter on the Blind" represents an allegory for enlightenment itself, a thought we'll return to later in this chapter. But it is also one more exercise in this difficult business.

A TRAVELOGUE FROM THE LAND OF THE BLIND

***'s inability to witness the wondrous spectacle of Réamur opening a person-born-blind's eyes (70–71) turns out to be another enlightenment *felix culpa*. It sends our correspondent to Puiseaux to speak directly to a man-born-blind of his life and experiences. In this way, exiting a Paris in which the most basic request for "enlightenment" concerning Molyneux's problem has been denied, the Letter sets up another philosophical travelogue.[21] Its exotic setting we might dub the land of the blind.

As critics have examined, Diderot was fascinated by what one of his heroes, Francis Bacon (chapter 1), called "deviating instances".[22] In the Letter, Diderot will use the word *écart* (difference, gap, disparity, space, or distance) to describe the blinds' place in nature.[23] These are examples of nature operating in unusual ways, even producing "monsters", whose attentive study Bacon thought could cast peculiar lights upon nature's "normal" course, and its hidden mechanisms. *The Novum Organum* explains that "he who is acquainted with the paths of nature, will more readily observe her deviations; and *vice versa*, he who has learnt her deviations, will be able more accurately to describe her paths".[24] On such a view, closely related to the principal enlightenment exercises of self-othering we have been examining, what is other (seemingly "unnatural") is positioned as being not unrelated to us, or beneath our concerns. The blind can provide another self-estranging mirror to we sighted.

So it is that the opening exchanges with the man-born-blind from Puiseaux mostly flatter the sighted. *** and his companions ask for the man's opinions on optical devices like the mirror, of which he can have had no experience (71–72).[25] As Bacon, Locke, or Voltaire would lead us to expect, the blind man describes these devices in his own terms, representing sight as if it were a species of touch (71). The eyes, he tells his visitors, are organs on which the air has the same effect as a stick has on his hand. So, if he places his hand between our eyes and the object, we can only see his hand, "and the object is absent. The same thing happens when I reach for one thing with my stick and come across another" (73). The mirror puzzles the man-born-blind. For he knows that it is an object which, "irrationally" by his lights, separates an object's untouchable image from its tangible source. He is likewise unable to clearly grasp the referents to many of our words, like those describing different facial expressions (80). In this light, there emerges the suggestion that the blind must be less compassionate than the sighted. They cannot, after all, hear the difference between the spilling of blood and the passing of water, or see the suffering expressed on others' faces. "I have no high thought of their humanity", *** says arrogantly, with these considerations in view (81). But his words are unwise, as will soon become clear.

Just as in Voltaire's account of the Quakers in *Letters on the English* (chapter 3), very soon this easy conceit about the lesser capacities of the blind is qualified—or, today, we might say "deconstructed". The narrator expresses admiration for the blind man's account of sight as a species of touch. This, he points out, closely mirrors the philosopher René Descartes' depiction of sight in the latter's *Dioptics* (76). And we soon learn that man-born-blind does very well for himself. He is intelligent, tidy, and skilled at needlework and the lathe. He is much more haptically (touch) and audially sensitive than we are. He has a better sense of duration (79), and senses atmospheric changes which are lost on most of the sighted. He has an exacting sense of space, and in his youth accurately cast a stone at a bully. He is very good at weighing things, another very "scientific" attribute, useful (the narrator underscores this) in statics (76–77). The man-born-blind has a subtle appreciation of music, and a strong memory for sounds (79, 75–76). *** also suggests that his heightened sense of touch gives him certain advantages in the act of love, which is after all not nothing (106–08): "a smooth skin, fine flesh, an elegant shape, sweet breath, charm of voice and graceful pronunciation are qualities he prizes very highly" (107–08). Finally, like Voltaire's Quaker, his blindness gives him an advantage in not being overawed by the imposing finery of civil authorities, like most sighted are. How, after all, could he fear imprisonment or even death, given that for twenty-five years he has been deprived of his eyesight by God or Nature (77–78)? Our narrator is especially impressed by this philosophical impassability, as someone who is "fond of moralizing" (78).[26]

In any case, by the end of the exchange, things have been turned on their heads. It is the man-born-blind who is mocking his sighted visitors for their vanity and inability to imagine what it is like to be blind, and what the blind are capable of. He tells *** that:

> he should think of himself a pitiable object in wanting those objects which we enjoy, and that he should have been inclined to consider us superior beings *had he not a hundred times found us very inferior to him in other respects* (76 [emphasis added]).

We are next treated to a classical sceptical argument, hearkening back to Sextus Empiricus, but renovated by Diderot.[27] We sighted can "see" how much of our experience is unavailable to the blind. But then, how much of the world might we be missing by having just five senses, which a being with six or more senses (like the Saturnian in Voltaire's *Micromégas*, whom we remember had *seventy-two* [chapter 3]) could apprehend? In fact, we sighted are blind at night, relative to owls, and our scientific instruments can "see" everything, from bands of light we cannot ordinarily see to radiation and microwaves. What if our very enjoyment of sight might, as it were, close the eyes of our minds to "what is possible" (113) for people with different capacities than our own? "I perceive, gentlemen, that you are not blind", the man-born-blind thus advises his visitors. "You are astonished at what I do, and why not as much at my speaking?" (79)

THE MORAL AND METAPHYSICAL ENLIGHTENMENT OF THE BLIND

The Letter turns next to the morals and metaphysics of the blind (80 ff.). These are striking subjects! For morals and metaphysics have traditionally been considered by philosophers to be universal in scope, and far more elevated as subjects than anything that might be affected by different peoples' sensory capacities. Metaphysical principles are after all immaterial and could seemingly have no connection with our mere senses. Moral laws are usually taken to apply to everyone. They are blind (as we say) to differences of race, language, tradition, and ways of life. So, what follows for these subjects if we jettison the rationalist assumption that the mind might be wholly non-material, and take seriously the Lockean claim that knowledge is based on experience, given the massive differences between the sensory experiences of the blind (or the deaf . . .) and those of us with our five senses? In the "Letter", *** disarmingly expresses his post-Lockean orientation: "Ah madam, how different the morality of the blind is from ours!", he exclaims:

> As to me, it has always been very clear that the state of our organs and our senses has a great influence on our metaphysics and our morality, and that those ideas which seem purely intellectual are closely dependent on the conformation of our bodies (80).

Nevertheless, his evidence here seems obviously unconvincing, at least concerning morals. Men-born-blind fear being cuckolded by lovers who can make signs to their beloveds which they cannot see. So, they are very strong on prohibiting adultery (78, 80–81). But this is hardly a preoccupation unique to the blind. The blind hate theft and dishonesty, for the same reasons. Yet this does not again seem really different from "our" values (81). True, *** recounts how the blind, as it were, out-philosophize or "out-Cynicize" the ancient Cynic Diogenes, who walked around in rags, in their disregard for what people wear, and whether or not we conceal our privates (81). Yet, it is unclear that Diderot sees these as points against them, given his own clear admiration for the Cynics, on which critics have widely remarked (see chapter 6).[28] As for the claim that the blind, lacking our ability to see others' faces, must be less capable of "moral sentiments", *** actually turns this around into a point to *our* moral limitations, which are little different from those of the blind:

> Do not we ourselves cease to be compassionate when distance or the smallness of the objects produces on us the same effect as deprivation of sight upon the blind? So much do our virtues depend upon the sensations we receive, and the degree by which we are affected by external things (81).

We sighted are after all often blinded to others' sufferings by nothing more principled than our physical distance from them, or perhaps their skin color (which for the blind is nothing), perhaps their differing attire, or religious profession. If it was not for fear of the laws, *** reflects in a way which resonates in the age of drone warfare:

> Many people would find it less disagreeable to kill a man at a distance at which he would appear no bigger than a swallow, than to cut an ox's throat with their own hands. We pity a horse in pain, and we make nothing of crushing an ant; and is it not by the same principle that we are moved? (81–82)[29]

With this much on comparative morality, Diderot next tells us that the metaphysics of the blind "agrees no better" with ours than their morals allegedly do (82). But again, there are reasons to suspect some irony here. There have been many blind men who have excelled in the most abstract sciences of all, those of the mathematics.[30] The blind's perceptions of physical objects, without sight, is always already a good deal more "abstract", if not "metaphysical", than our own, or so we sighted might suppose. The blind are far more dependent on touch than we are, both for experience, and as such, in the operations of their imaginations and memory. A blind person can only remember objects in space through the impressions these objects have made on their touch.[31] In any case, metaphysics involves abstracting general explanatory principles (God, nature, gravity) from particular experiences. Metaphysicians vocationally posit such principles which are imperceptible by the senses, and can only be "seen" by the eye of understanding: an eye which the blind share. In this field, that of purely speculative questions, we therefore have little reason to suppose that the blind could be at any disadvantage, even compared to our sighted sages, like Plato or Pythagoras (cf. 88). "Blindness" in this field might above all consist in empty speculations, imagining entities and principles which do not exist, and taking one's own Ideas to be more real than what we can physically see, hear, smell, or touch. "Those philosophers are termed idealists who, conscious of their own existence and of a succession of external sensations, do not admit anything else", *** hence reflects, calling this philosophy:

> an extravagant system which should to my thinking have been the offspring of blindness itself; and yet, to the disgrace of the human mind and philosophy, it is the most difficult to combat, though the most absurd (114).

The most infamous part of the Letter follows this critique of metaphysical philosophies. It confirms that if Diderot thinks the blind might have different metaphysical predilections to ours, this is no reason for complacency on our side. The pages in question consider at length the achievements and character of the blind mathematician, Nicholas Saunderson. This blind savant, a model of enlightenment and ingenuity, invented his own means of arithmetic and geometric calculation by touch alone. Amazingly, he even taught optics at Cambridge University, holding the chair since occupied by Stephen Hawking (101).

There are good reasons to suspect that Saunderson, as *** presents him, is more ideal or fictitious than real. But the Diderotian fiction is educational. *** is repetitively drawn to compare Saunderson with the ancient pagan wise men or sages, heroes of the enlighteners, as we glimpsed in chapter 3:

I might add to this account of Saunderson and the blind man of Puiseaux, Didymus of Alexandria, Eusebius the Asiatic, and Nicaise of Mechlin, and some other people who, though lacking one sense, seemed so far above the level of the rest of mankind that the poets might without exaggeration have feigned the jealous gods to have deprived them of it, for fear lest mortals should equal them (108).

Saunderson speaks with great elegance. But he uses a predominance of tactile analogies based on his experience that seem quaint to us. Diderot hence comments that, to listen to his discourse is like hearing a foreigner (perhaps a Persian or Englishman?) speaking a second language:

> It is evident that in these cases, Saunderson, with all his intelligence, was not aware of the full force of the terms he employed, since he only realized half of the ideas attached to these terms. But does not this happen to all of us at times? (100)

Above all, despite ***'s unsustainable denigration of the moral character of the blind, Saunderson is represented to us as "blessed" with a "purity of life and uprightness" which Diderot suggests is rarely found in people possessing five senses (114–15). *** does not baulk at comparing Saunderson directly to Socrates (115)—an especially meaningful comparison for Diderot, who would console himself in Vincennes prison by translating Plato's *Apology of Socrates*.[32]

The decisive metaphysical arguments of the Letter come in the account, or rather two accounts, Diderot gives of the death and last words of this blind enlightenment sage. The second account given by *** is based on a fictional biography of Saunderson by one "Inchcliff" (115–16). Throughout his life, *** tells us, Saunderson had never knowingly harmed another person: the very pith of Plato's recommendations in the *Gorgias*. Like Socrates, Saunderson's last concerns were accordingly not for himself, but for others' grief at his passing:

> "I am going," he told them, "where we all go. Spare me your distress, which I feel moved by. The signs of pain that escape your lips only make me more sensitive to the ones that elude my grasp. I feel no sorrow at leaving a life that has been nothing more to me than one long deprivation and endless yearning. Live as virtuously as I have and more happily and learn to die as peacefully" (116).[33]

To recall chapter 1, Diderot presents in this part of the Letter as a reality the prospect Bayle's *Various Thoughts on the Occasion of a Comet* was condemned for evoking: that of the virtuous atheist. It is above all the first account of Saunderson's death which *** recounts to us that makes this scandalizing atheism clear. When it was evident that Saunderson was soon going to die, we are told, a clergyman "of great ability", Mr Gervase Holmes, was called to his side. Holmes began to "harangue" the blind man on the beauty of the cosmos (108–09)—the key basis of what is called the argument from design for God's existence (cf. 82). Saunderson protests:

> "Don't talk to me of that magnificent spectacle, which it has never been my lot to enjoy. I have been condemned to live my life in darkness, and you cite wonders I can't understand and which are proof only for you and those who see as you do" (109).

For Saunderson to believe in God, he tells us, he would need to be able to touch him. But he cannot, any more than we can see Him.

There are high stakes to this deathbed discussion (109). Voltaire for one abided by the argument from Design for the existence of God, animated by a sense of wonder at the order and beauty of the world. Diderot's "Letter on the Blind" is far more sceptical, although it appeals to the same value of epistemic humility at the heart of Voltaire's conception of enlightenment. "If we think a phenomenon is beyond man, we immediately say it's God's work", Saunderson protests, "our vanity will accept nothing less, but could we be a bit less vain and a bit more philosophical in what we say?" (109–10) The same acknowledgement of enlightened ignorance greets the argument for the necessity of a first cause or unmoved mover:

> If nature presents us with a problem that is difficult to unravel, let's leave it as it is and not try to undo it with the help of a being who then offers us a new problem, more insoluble than the first. Ask an Indian how the world stays up in the air, and he'll tell you that an elephant is carrying it on its back; and the elephant, what's he standing on? A tortoise. And that tortoise, what's keeping him up? . . . To you, that Indian is pitiful, yet one could say the same of you as you say of him. So, Mr Holmes, my friend, start by confessing your ignorance, and let's do without the elephant and the tortoise (109–10).

If we accept, as Holmes does, the authority of thinkers like Isaac Newton and Samuel Clarke about the rational order of the universe *right now*, Saunderson next asks, who is to say that the order we presently admire is stable and unchanging? Might it not change, and be itself the product of endless, earlier changes? What follows is Saunderson's scandalous positing of an "epigenetic", proto-evolutionary hypothesis. This looks back in classical thought to the Epicurean philosopher, Lucretius's poem, *De rerum natura*, but sideways at contemporary research in the biological sciences, and the study of microscopic organisms.[34] "Who told you all, you, Leibniz, Clarke, and Newton, that when animals first came into being, there weren't some with no heads and others with no feet?", Saunderson queries his interlocutor (111). To wonder at the present natural order is to overlook how, at every moment in natural history, what we would see as "monsters" and evolving creatures have taken their place besides more apparently finished products. Saunderson can speak with authority on this matter, he assures Holmes. For he is himself a speaking, tangible proof that what people standardly take to be "monstrous" is every bit as natural as what is more normative at any moment in natural history. "Look me in the face, Mr Holmes", he enjoins. "I have no eyes" (112).

We come close at this point of the Letter to the problem of evil which inspired Voltaire's *Candide* (chapter 3). How could a world created by an all-powerful, benevolent deity include seemingly unjustifiable suffering? In response, Voltaire hesitates. Diderot crosses the atheistic Rubicon. "What have we done to God, you and I, such that one of us has that organ, and the other is deprived of it?", Saunderson challenges Holmes (112). As Tunstall has noted, his question echoes one the disciples asked Jesus about a person-born-blind: "Who did sin, this man, or his parents, that he was born blind?"[35] In his dying moments, Saunderson ascends to a kind of oneiric "view from above" which we met in Voltaire in the imaginary figure of Micromégas, the enlightened 24,000-foot-tall giant from the heavens:

> "What is this world, Mr Holmes, but a complex, subject to cycles of change, all of which show a continual tendency to destruction; a rapid succession of beings that appear one by one, flourish and disappear; a merely transitory symmetry and momentary appearance of order?" (113)

The problem Saunderson targets is precisely that which we have called epistemic egoism and seen to be pivotal for each of the enlightenment thinkers. People take their present perspectives as the measure of all things, in time as well as space. Once we step back, outside of what most immediately strikes us, the Whole appears differently:

> You judge the phases of the world's existence [like] the ephemeral insect of yours [which you disregard]. The world seems to you eternal, just as you seem eternal to the creatures of a day; and the insect is more reasonable than you . . . Yet we shall all pass away without a possibility of denoting the real extent which we took up, or the precise time of our duration. Time, matter, and space are perhaps but a point (114).

After this philosophical outpouring, Saunderson is said to have passed into a fever lasting several hours. He awoke only to cry out, "O thou God of Clarke and Newton, have mercy on me!", then pass away (114). When we remember that the God of Clarke and Newton is not the biblical God of judgement who might forgive anyone, Diderot's daring here is patent.

WHAT THE BLIND CAN TEACH THE SIGHTED, THAT THE SIGHTED MIGHTN'T OTHERWISE SEE

The extravagant melodrama of Saunderson's death scene(s), as well as their boldness in giving voice to a neo-Epicurean, epigenetic understanding of nature as a dynamic evolving totality, have understandably dominated the reception of Diderot's "Letter on the Blind". It is these passages, above all, that secured the philosopher's temporary lodgings in Vincennes jail. Diderot would never again publish anything so bold in his own name, in his own lifetime. Yet these episodes with Saunderson are not the last word of the Letter. An entire, extensive final section follows this dramatic climax of the text's action, in which Saunderson does not feature (117 ff.). In this section, Diderot returns to Molyneux's problem, with whose consideration the Letter opens. Diderot now plays out a consideration of this experiment—how to conduct it, and what it reveals—in the light of his virtual travels in the land of the blind. This final section of the Letter, too often overlooked, is actually vital to grasping Diderot's *constructive* vision of enlightenment, as well as appreciating his *destructive* intelligence and wit.

In one of the few things we learn about "Madame", the addressee of the Letter, we are told that "she likes method" (134). Which method does Diderot intend? In the *philosophe*'s near-contemporary, erotic-comic novel, *The Indiscreet Jewels*, there is a famous philosophical dream which I think points our way. It is the dream of one "Mangogul", set in the vast ancient temple of speculative "hypothesis", in which metaphysical philosophers worship. But then "experience" arrives, embodied in evolving human form:

> While he was uttering these words, I saw at a distance a child walking towards us in a slow but sure pace. He had a little head, slender body, weak arms and short legs: but all these parts increased in all dimensions, according as he came forward. In the progress of his successive growth, he appeared to me under a hundred different forms; I saw him directing a long telescope towards the heavens, estimating the fall of bodies by means of a pendulum, determining the weight of the air by a tube filled with quicksilver, and discomposing light with a prism. He was now become an enormous Colossus: his head touched the heavens, his feet were lost in the abyss, and his arms reached from one to the other pole. With his right hand he brandished a torch, whose light spread a vast way in the sky, enlightened even the bottom of the waters, and penetrated into the entrails of the earth. I asked Plato, what that gigantic figure was, that was coming towards us. "It is experience," said he. Scarcely had he made me this short answer, when I saw experience draw near, and the columns of the portico of hypotheses began to shake, its arches to sink in, and its pavement to crack under our feet. "Let us fly," said Plato, "let us fly: this edifice has but a moment

to stand." At these words he departs, and I follow him. The Colossus arrives, strikes the portico, it tumbles down with a frightful noise, and I awake.[36]

Only two years after the publication of "Letter on the Blind", Diderot would publish the famous "*Discours préliminaire*" ("Preliminary Discourse") to the *Encyclopédie*; co-authored with his friend, Jean le Rond d'Alembert. This text lays out the program for the entire *Encyclopédie*, this extraordinary collective publication at the heart of the enlightenment, which aimed to bring together experts in every extant body of knowledge. In this "*Discours*", Francis Bacon, the father of methodical experimental philosophy and inspiration for the British Royal Society, is credited not simply for the division of knowledges that shapes the *Encyclopédie*'s structuring classification, but as "the greatest, the most universal, the most eloquent of philosophers" (see chapter 1).[37]

Diderot's own deep debts to post-Baconian natural philosophy are perhaps clearest in his 1754 text, *Pensées sur l'interprétation de la nature* (*Thoughts on the Interpretation of Nature*).[38] The text's early sections set out an opposition between "rationalist" and "empirical" ways of philosophizing (§22). In a way which casts further doubt on readings of Diderot as a Spinozist, *Pensées* makes clear his allegiance to empiricism. It is easier to "commune" with our own thoughts than patiently to observe, profoundly to reflect upon, and carefully to test our ideas concerning external nature (§10, §15). As a result, far too much energy has hitherto been given to the "abstract" sciences. As Bacon had lamented, "words have proliferated endlessly and knowledge of things has lagged behind" (§17). Rationalist philosophers deductively synthesize and systematize data that has already been granted, rather than enabling us to discover new things (§20).

Yet all of the systematic edifices erected by rationalist philosophers, like the Temple of Hypothesis in *Indiscreet Jewels*, will eventually be undermined by the patient accumulation of observations and inductive generalizations. These sooner or later discover exceptions or monsters, like Saunderson (§21). Like Voltaire in *Letters on the English*, Diderot as such can commend the sublime imagination and, in some cases, "great eloquence" of great systematic philosophers (§21). But he looks to empirical philosophy as the way forward for enlightened inquiry (§21, 23). In a key passage hearkening back to the "Letter on the Blind", Diderot praises such empiricism exactly for being like a person who is "blind-folded", "always groping its way, grasping everything which comes to hand and finally encountering precious things" (§23).

In the light of *Thoughts on the Interpretation of Nature*, the final section of the Letter should be seen as an exercise in Diderot practicing what he preaches. This last section of the text undertakes what Diderot's hero Bacon calls an "initiative" presentation of experimental philosophy in action.

*** may not directly do the Molyneux experiment, as Gassendi advised Descartes, but he thinks through its conditions, its possible variations, and how it could yield the most telling findings for understanding the bases of human knowing, in an impeccably post-Baconian manner.[39] Hence:

- *** begins with a survey of existing opinions on Molyneux's problem (119–20);
- then come considerations concerning the lighting conditions which could make the experiment decisive, including allowing time for subjects' newly opened eyes to adapt to their new condition (120–21; cf. 126–27; 129–31);
- next, Diderot examines how, and whether, the newly sighted person will be able, by recourse to what he has previously touched or been told by others, to identify different objects or attributes:
  - firstly, geometric shapes like a sphere (122–35, 138–39);
  - secondly, three-dimensional perspective in paintings (125–26);
  - thirdly, colours (129–30).[40]
- There follow reflections on the different qualifications of potential subjects and observers for the experiment and the likely responses to becoming sighted of a "dullard", an intermediary class of educated men and mathematicians, then a true "metaphysician" (134–36);
- Diderot then entertains a reflective comparison between someone who has always seen an object, not knowing its use, as against someone who has always known its use, but never seen it (the latter, Diderot argues, will be more likely to fare better upon a first practical encounter with the thing [138]);
- this comparison is succeeded by reflections on how a *man born sighted without the sense of touch* might fare, *if this sense of touch* were suddenly awakened in him (139), as compared to the neo-sighted person-born-blind;
- the "experimental" sequence closes by imaginative reflections on whether someone whose different senses did not operate interdependently could ever reliably learn anything of the external world, and which sense they would end by trusting to get around in the world— Diderot suggesting *touch* (140).

There is a sheer curiosity at work in this part of the "Letter on the Blind", reflecting the effervescent intellectual energy that characterises everything Diderot did. Diderot revels in thinking through every conceivable aspect and modulation of Molyneux's problem, as well as indulging in his passion for pointed digressions. But there is post-Baconian method to this Diderotian madness. And there is something else going on, captured in the work's subtitle:

"Letter on the Blind *for the Use of Those Who See*" (emphasis added).[41] In this chapter, we have already seen several such "uses". Conversing with the man-born-blind has challenged ***'s—and our—complacent "sighted" superiority over the blind. Reflection on the putative weakness of the blind's capacity for empathy has prompted enlightening reflections on the dependency of our morality on the limitations of the senses (there are motes in our eyes, although they can see). Saunderson's feats have showed us that the blind are in no way beneath us in their capacity for abstract pursuits like mathematics, or, indeed, metaphysics and theology. The blind sage's final reflections, as himself a deviation from nature's usual order, have advertised then-still-emergent theories in the life sciences, and allowed Diderot to give voice to a growing challenge to Christian and Deistic conceptions of Nature in which species would be unchanging, and humans at the privileged centre of a static divine design. It is as if Saunderson died in the light, Diderot muses, where we sighted mostly "lead the life of the blind" (115).

We commented earlier on how Francis Bacon had advertised the study of deviating instances like blindness in human beings as a means to cast new light on "the ordinary", how it works, and what we might miss by taking the way things usually appear for granted. In this perspective, the "Letter on the Blind" effectively rejoins, we should take a second look at the workings of sight, and its role in the ways we form our knowledge-claims about the world. Sight's powers in shaping how people experience the world are ordinarily experienced in conjunction with the workings of our four other senses: hearing, touch, taste, and smell. When philosophers reflect epistemologically, moreover, we usually presuppose the normative condition of a "fully-five-sensed-adult" (82). (It is just as if there were not people-born-blind, and all adults were not previously infants.) The ways that our predominant optical sense might interact with, and depend upon, the testimony of other senses, are ordinarily overlooked. Likewise, we typically do not consider the ways our visual understanding *must have developed* to its present capabilities. To consider the "deviating instance" of the blind, exactly *by contrast*, is to also gain new perspectives on these subjects, and as such, on the makeup of our regular sighted condition.

We sighted folk can easily, for instance, look down upon the blind's dependency on touch to establish object constancy (the fact that an object remains present before them) as curious and unfortunate. As ever, Diderot turns this observation around. *Yes*, Diderot effectively responds, *but how, after all, could the sighted have ever established "object constancy" without checking what their eyes reported with the sense of touch, which allows us repeatedly to "bump up against" things we have seen, to know they are substantial* (122–25, 135)? The sighteds' development of three-dimensional depth perception must likewise historically rely upon our sense of touch. For without the haptic sense, we could never have been able to "see" that closer objects, those we can presently bump into, appear larger than more distant objects, even when wider experience shows that they are not truly so?

Again, we sighted can pity how dependent the blind are on hearsay to shape their beliefs, taking what others have said on blind trust. *Yes*, Diderot effectively replies: *but what then should we say concerning the extent to which all of us necessarily depend on others' testimony in shaping our worldviews?* We cannot, after all, have even learned the very names of the things we see and discuss except by relying on others' spoken (that is, *heard*) confirmations: "That's right . . . " (This is what the philosopher Donald Davidson calls "triangulation".) Secondly, we could never have come to comprehend anything about immaterial realities like mathematical relations, let alone metaphysical sublimities, without trusting the authority and reliability of what our teachers have told us, at least in the beginning.

If Diderot is right, that is, perhaps the greatest use of discoursing with the blind other(s), for those of us able to see, is to be reminded of the ways in which we all began life like people-born-blind. It is to be made to see also that we remain not a little like the blind, every time we uncritically accept what we read and hear, without thinking for ourselves, and testing our ideas against external reality. We all began life as children, dependent on touch to certify what our eyes suggested, and above all on our own first others (parents, siblings, teachers) to establish any knowledge about the things of the world, and competence to navigate around it (124, 126).

We might also think here of Immanuel Kant's later description of the enlightenment as humankind's emergence from its self-incurred infancy,[42] as well as Diderot's earlier comparison in the "Letter on the Blind", of a sighted man in a land of the blind with a thinker persecuted for discovering the truth in an age of censorious darkness (86). To emerge from cultural blindness, the blindness of pre- or anti-enlightenment, is to submit to reasoned doubt and critical consideration all traditions and superstitions conveyed to us by hearsay and sanctioned by worldly powers. It is to seek out the truth, beginning by "frankly admitting 'I do not know' ", rather than "to keep babbling on and covering oneself with embarrassment by endeavouring to find explanations for everything", as *Thoughts on the Interpretation of Nature* puts it (§10). One can only achieve such enlightenment by proceeding slowly, as if blindfolded, and feeling one's way, step by step (*Thoughts*, §23)—which is to say, aware of our inveterate tendencies to error and hybris, awake to the sensible preconditions of our understanding, and careful before we leap to dogmatic conclusions which we try to impose on others.

So, someone might ask, who then could the ideal subject for the Molyneux experiment be, according to Diderot? We already know the answer. S/he would be a subject very much like Saunderson, learned and philosophical, but aware of how much s/he does not know.[43] And what would such an iconically enlightenment person-born-blind or prejudiced say, when her sight was restored? Diderot's and Voltaire's many differences aside, this new sage's discourse would closely echo the learned ignorance of the Lockean in *Micromégas* on the soul (chapter 3):

I am v*ery much inclined* to think that this is the body which I have always called a circle, and that again what I named a square, *but will not assert it to be really so. What is to prevent* their disappearance if I were to touch them? *How am I to know* whether the bodies I see are also meant to be touched? *I do not know* whether visible things are palpable; but *were I assured* of this, and did *I take the word of those about me* that what I see is really what I have touched . . . "Gentlemen", would [I] conclude, "this body *appears to be* the square, that the circle; but that they are the same to touch as to sight *I have no certain knowledge of*" (135 [emphasis added]).[44]

NOTES

1. See Curran, *Diderot and the Art of Thinking Freely*, 1–7.
2. See Wade, *Esprit Revolutionnaire*, 67–118.
3. Diderot, "Eclecticism", in Denis Diderot, *The Encyclopedia*, ed. and trans. Stephen J. Gendzier (New York: Harper, 1967), 86.
4. Curran, *Diderot and the Art of Thinking Freely*, 79–87.
5. See Charles T. Wolfe, "Epigenesis and/as Spinozism in Diderot's Biological Project", *The Life Sciences in Early Modern Philosophy*, eds. Ohad Nachtomy and Justin E. H. Smith (Oxford, UK: Oxford University Press, 2014).
6. Israel, *Democratic Enlightenment*, 7–11, gives a good synopsis of the wider position. But see *Radical Enlightenment*, 331–41; *Enlightenment Contested*, 87, 92–93, 148, 388, 413, 426, 456, 528, 538.
7. Jonathan Israel, "Enlightenment, The", *The Encyclopedia of Political Thought*, Wiley Online Library (2014), Enlightenment, The - Israel - - Major Reference Works - Wiley Online Library.
8. See Harvey Chisick, "Looking for Enlightenment", *History of European Ideas* 34, no. 4 (2008): 576, 579; Anthony J. La Vopa, "A New Intellectual History? Jonathan Israel's Enlightenment ", *Historical Journal*, 52, no. 3 (2009): 717–38; Thomas Muenck, "The Enlightenment as Modernity: Jonathan Israel's Interpretation Across Two Decades," *Reviews in History*, 15 (December 2016); Michael Mosher, "Reviewed Work(s): Radical Enlightenment: Philosophy and the Making of Modernity 1650–1750 by Jonathan I. Israel", *Political Theory* 32, no. 3 (Jun., 2004): 427–31; Eric Schleisser, "Jonathan Israel, Democratic Enlightenment: Philosophy, Revolution,

and Human Rights, 1750–1790," *Oeconomica: History, Methodology, Philosophy* 4, no. 4 (2014); Samuel Moyn, "Mind the Enlightenment", *The Nation*, May 12, 2010; "A Response to Jonathan Israel", *History News Network, HNN Special: Debating the Enlightenment*, URL https://historynewsnetwork.org/article/128433; Antoine Litti, "Comment écrit-on l'histoire intellectuelle des Lumières? Spinozisme, radicalisme et philosophie," *Annales HSS* 1 (janvier–février 2009): 171–206.

9. See Haydn Mason, "Crime and Punishment: Voltaire (1694–1778), *Commentaire sur le livre des délits et des peines* (1766)", in *French Writers and Their Society, 1715–1800* (London: Palgrave Macmillan, 1982).

10. See, e.g., Israel, *Revolution of the Mind*, 6; *Enlightenment Contested*, 547; *Democratic Enlightenment*, 122, 658.

11. See Gay, *Science of Freedom*, 517–28.

12. Denis Diderot, *Essai sur les règnes de Claude et de Néron et sur la vie et les écrits de Sénèque pour servir d'introduction à la lecture de ce philosophe* (Paris: L'Imprimerie de J. J. Smith et al., 1792 [orig. 1782]).

13. See David Wootton, "Helvétius: From Radical Enlightenment to Revolution", *Political Theory* 28, no. 3 (June 2000): 307–33; Stanley E. Ballinger, "The Idea of Social Progress through Education in the French Enlightenment Period: Helvétius and Condorcet", *History of Education Journal*, vol. 10, no. 1/4, Tenth Anniversary Issue (1959): 88–99.

14. Denis Diderot, "Letter on the Blind for the Use of Those Who See", in Margaret Jourdain ed. and trans., *Diderot, the Early Philosophical Works* (Chicago and London: Open Court Publishing, 1916). Bracketed page numbers in the remainder of chapter 4 refer to this text and edition.

15. The text also has a number of intriguing paratextual features. Enthusiasts may wonder that the narrator's "name", "***", can be tapped out, but not spoken or heard, corresponding to the way we are told that that the blind "imagines" and remembers sensations of external things. It is almost as if Diderot wants the narrator's unsayable name to signify an ellipse in the text, as it is suggested the blind are a seeming ellipse in the providential order. But we digress.

16. See previous note.

17. See Katherine Tunstall, *Blindness and Enlightenment*.

18. Locke, *Essay*, II 8. See Michael Bruno and Eric Mandelbaum, "Locke's Answer to Molyneux's Thought Experiment", *History of Philosophy Quarterly* 27, no. 2 (2010): 165–80.

19. Gassendi at Tunstall, *Blindness*, 62 (emphasis added).

20. Diderot, *Thoughts on the Interpretation of Nature*, §10.

21. See Daniel Brewer, *The Discourse of Enlightenment in Eighteenth-Century France: Diderot and the Art of Philosophising* (Cambridge, UK: Cambridge University Press, 2006), 101–02.

22. Bacon, *Novum Organum*, II 29. See Brewer, *Discourse of Enlightenment*, 98–99, 105–06.

23. See G. Norman Laidlaw, "Diderot's Teratology", *Diderot Studies* 4 (1963), 105–29; Andrew Curran and Patrick Graille, "The Faces of Eighteenth-Century Monstrosity", *Eighteenth-Century Life* 21, no. 2 (1997): 1–12.

24. Bacon, *Novum Organum*, II 29.
25. They also ask concerning his views on the micro- and telescope, defining instruments of the new learning, at 72–74.
26. And well might Diderot have been, as someone soon to experience time on the inside for the "Letter" itself.
27. See Tunstall, *Blindness*, 78–79, and Montaigne, "The Apology of Raymond Sebond".
28. See Louisa Shea, *The Cynic Enlightenment: Diogenes in the Salon* (Baltimore, MD: John Hopkins University Press, 2010).
29. For a being with superior senses to ours, *** then asks, how spotty and inferior would our morality have to appear? Surely, little better than *** had himself initially taken that of the blind to be is what is implied.
30. Sciences which Plato, for instance, had praised precisely for teaching people pure thought, without sensible contents at all (Plato, *Republic*, Bk. VII), in a conception which would decisively shape Western pedagogy into the middle ages.
31. Reflecting on this curious insight, *** cannot resist another dig at Descartes, suggesting that if a blind philosopher constructed a man as the great rationalist had, his soul would be located at the end of his fingers (87).
32. Curran, *Diderot and the Art of Thinking Freely*, 98; cf. Russell Goulbourne, "Diderot and the Ancients", in *New Essays on Diderot*, ed. James Fowler (Cambridge, UK: Cambridge University Press, 2014).
33. Cf. Tunstall, *Blindness*, 125.
34. See Tunstall, *Blindness*, 115; also Wolfe, "Epigenesis and/as Spinozism in Diderot's Biological Project".
35. Tunstall, *Blindness*, 111. Saunderson cannot see it. But Holmes's eyes fill with tears in response to this query, as if to momentarily blind him (112–13).
36. Denis Diderot, *Indiscreet Jewels* (Project Gutenberg e-book), online at https://www.gutenberg.org/files/54672/54672-h/54672-h.htm, ch. XXIX, "Mangogul's Dream, or a Voyage into the Region of Hypotheses".
37. Diderot and d'Alembert, "Preliminary Discourse".
38. Bracketed section numbers in this section 4.5 refer to this text.
39. For comparison, see Francis Bacon, "Preparative towards a Natural and Experimental History [*Parasceve*]", in *The Works of Francis Bacon, Volume VIII, Translations of the Philosophical Works*, trans. J. Spedding et al. (Boston: Houghton Mifflin, c. 1900), 351–72.
40. A loaded digression follows, looking back to Saunderson's touching laments to Mr Holmes (4.4), in which pain's relationship to pleasure is distinguished from the interdependency of "light and darkness". (For a man born in pain will still, according to ***, imagine himself miserable or "guilty", although he has never known pleasure [132–33]. This suggests that Christians are blind, to the extent they believe in original sin).
41. Cf. Brewer, *Discourse of Enlightenment*, 100–01.
42. Immanuel Kant, "An Answer to the Question: What is Enlightenment?", in *Political Writings*, ed. H. S. Reid (Cambridge, UK: Cambridge University Press, 1991), 54.

43. Here we directly contest Brewer's claim at *Discourse of Enlightenment*, 106–07.

44. See *Thoughts on Interpretation of Nature*, §10.

Chapter 5

Enlightenment, Race, Slavery, and Anti-Colonialism

POSING THE QUESTION: WAS THE ENLIGHTENMENT (UNIVOCALLY) RACIST?

When it is discussed publicly today, critics often contend that "the enlightenment" *tout court* had a "race problem".[1] John Locke, so vital in pre-shaping the French enlightenment (chapter 1), wrote the *Fundamental Constitution of Carolina* (1669). The document explicitly supports hereditary nobility in the colony, including the "absolute power" of colonists over their African slaves.[2] Passages from enlightenment philosophers like the Scottish philosopher, David Hume, express dark racial prejudices:

> I am apt to suspect that negroes, and in general other species of men, to be naturally inferior to the whites. There never was any civilized nation of any other completion than white, nor even any individual eminent in action of speculation.[3]

Even the moralistic Immanuel Kant could in his early writings declaim that "the negroes of Africa have by nature no feeling that rises above the trifling", and we can find similar remarks in his *oeuvre* about the proverbially idle "South Sea Islanders".[4] No person of colour who has come to Europe, Kant would write, "has accomplished something great in art or science or shown any other praiseworthy quality".[5]

Such racially prejudicial passages (and others can be cited) raise serious questions about how we should understand the enlightenment's normative credentials. Some on the "Alt-Right" of course welcome such declarations, happy to co-opt whatever elements of "the enlightenment" they can to prosecute their anti-liberal aims. For some on the postmodernist New Left, on the other hand, such passages would wholly delegitimise "the enlightenment" *tout court*. Enlightenment ideals of rationality, it is suggested, were responsible for colonialism's destruction of indigenous peoples' life-worlds. They paved the objectifying, scientising way towards the biological racism that would darken the twentieth century. Many critics go further and claim that all of "Western civilization" has been characterised by a racism which white thinkers have come only after 1960 to acknowledge and are still yet to fully face.[6]

It is one of the ironies of the postmodern period that the key shaping influencers of the latter grand narrative are the great German reactionary philosophers, Friedrich Nietzsche, who remains a staple of the transatlantic Far Right, and Martin Heidegger, who we now know to have been an unrepentant National Socialist.[7] This irony is not necessarily a happy one. By accepting these thinkers' grand narratives of civilisational decline—while asymmetrically challenging any *grand récit* of social progress—liberal critics may be blinded to many key intellectual sources of the progressive values that inform their positions. It is also possible to entertain doubts about the plausibility (and lasting results) of accepting the premises of thinkers like Nietzsche or Heidegger, who renounced the ideals of scientific reason, liberty, equality, and cosmopolitan solidarity, while hoping to invert their conclusions to face in progressive directions.[8]

All parties to the culture wars can agree that it is important to try to cut reality at the joints, to use a Platonic metaphor: that is, to try to understand the texts, ideas, and issues in dispute clearly, steadily, accurately, and thoroughly. No one wishes to tilt at windmills or take flight from scarecrows. In this chapter, drawing on original texts and too widely neglected scholarship on the enlighteners, we will show that the idea that "the enlightenment" spoke with one voice on race, slavery, and colonialism, is unsustainable. The striking instances of enlighteners expressing deep racial prejudices we opened by citing license our censure. But they cannot support wholesale generations about this entire period of intellectual history, and much less about all of Western civilisation reaching back to Homer, Moses, Socrates, Plato, or Christ.

Of course, in the language of social media, the kind of enlightened suspension of judgement carefully examining the historical record on these issues involves is unlikely to "go viral", with its myriad "yes, but"-s, "and, yet"-s, and "actually, no"-s. With that said, perhaps the greatest value of applying the kinds of critical inquiring whose seventeenth- and eighteenth-century proponents we have been examining *to the enlightenment itself* lies in presenting one small challenge to the culture of strident, one-sided assessments which too often define our present state.

COLONIALISM, THE SLAVE TRADE, AND RACISM, BEFORE THE *LUMIÈRES*

It bears stressing from the start in these debates that the enlightenment thinkers, and their arguments in favour of the newly experimental, self-limiting, and self-othering forms of inquiry which we have been seeing, postdated European colonialism's beginnings, and the transatlantic slave trade, by several centuries.[9] To recall some of the most salient pre-enlightenment facts and figures:[10]

- 1441 CE was the year in which the first slaves from Mauritania were brought to Europe by the Portuguese;
- in 1452, the Pope, Nicholas V, issued the *Dum Diversas* bull, granting Alfonso V of Portugal the right to reduce "Saracens, pagans and any other unbelievers" to hereditary slavery, a "right" reaffirmed by the *Romanus Pontifex* bull of 1455;
- in 1492, the same year the Jews were expelled from Catholic Spain, Columbus discovered the "New World", and the Treaty of Tordesillas two years later (1494) divided the Americas between Spain and Portugal (it goes without saying, without representatives of the territories at issue present);
- in 1501, the first African slaves were transported to the Americas by the Spanish;
- in 1519, Hernán Cortes and the Pizarros began the genocidal conquest of the Incas, Aztecs, and Mayans;
- in 1529, the Treaty of Zaragoza generously divided the entire globe up for exploration and colonisation between Spain and Portugal;
- in 1542, the Spanish monarchy banned slavery in Spain itself, although slavery continued in Spanish Cuba and Puerto Rico (pre-eminently for the production of sugar) until 1873;
- by 1552, the extent of the transportation of African slaves to Portugal was such that they constituted about 10 percent of the population of the capital, Lisbon;
- by 1619, there were more than 250,000 African slaves in Spanish and Portuguese colonies alone;
- in the British empire, slavery remained a legal institution in the thirteen American colonies throughout the seventeenth and eighteenth centuries. It accounted for about 5 percent of the economy of the United Kingdom at the start of the nineteenth century.

In the second half of the sixteenth century, the focus of the European slave trade shifted from importing slaves to Europe to brokering slave transports directly to American colonies for the extraction of sugar and other commodities (amongst the Portuguese, Dutch, and Spanish). The Christian countries around this date also overtook the Islamic countries as the chief slave exporters from Africa. The numbers are staggering:

- By the 1660s, over 20,000 African slaves per year were being transported by European powers to the Americas and "West Indies" (the Caribbean);
- by 1700, this number had doubled, whilst in the 1720s, when *Persian Letters* created such a sensation, and Voltaire was exiled to England, over 60,000 African slaves per year were being transported by Europeans;
- by 1789, the year of the French Revolution, around 90,000 Africans each year were being transported in slavery across the Atlantic.[11]

The effects on the indigenous peoples who fell under the yoke of European colonialism between 1492 and 1945 were overwhelmingly devastating. Pre-colonisation, there were perhaps around 70 million Native American inhabitants. By 1900, this population had declined by more than 80 percent, decimated by smallpox, measles, cholera, drink, and violence. Some 12.5 million African men, women, and children were enslaved between 1501 and 1866 by the European nations, to either die in transit[12] or be used and disposed of by their colonial masters, "as the price at which you buy sugar in Europe", to evoke Voltaire's *Candide* (chapter 3).[13]

It is true that the writings of the enlighteners, or their social advocacy, did not immediately end colonialism, or the race-based slave trade. The former survived into the twentieth century, with Nazi Germany seeking to introduce colonialism and slavery into Europe itself. Slavery was abolished in Denmark in 1792 by Charles VI, under the influence of the pro-enlightenment advisor Johann Friedrich Struensee. It was briefly abolished in the French colonies under revolutionary rule in 1794. "What [the Assembly] will say to the blacks, what it will say to the planters, what it will tell to the whole of Europe," Honoré Gabriel de Requit proclaimed:

is that there are not and cannot be, either in France or in any territory subject to French laws, any men other than free men, other than men equal to each other, and that any man who keeps another in involuntary servitude acts against the law.[14]

But Napoleon restored slavery in Guadeloupe and Martinique in 1804, following the successful slave revolt in Haiti which fulfilled Diderot's call for a new "Black Spartacus" to rise up and overthrow the European oppressors (see below, and chapter 6). The British Abolition Act came only in 1834. In France, slavery was once more prohibited in 1847. In the United States, the rhetoric of the Founders concerning the equality of "all men" notwithstanding, the Civil War of 1862–1865 would be needed to end chattel slavery. Slavery by European powers would finally finish in the colonies only in 1888, and on the high seas in 1890, with the Brussels Conference Act.

How was any of this justified, if it was not by appeal to the "superior rationality" of the Europeans, which we have seen Hume and Kant underscoring? In truth, political potentates, colonial adventurers, and avaricious slave traders in pre-1700 Europe hardly wanted for ideological rationalisations. The philosopher Aristotle, central to medieval university curricula, had posited the existence of "natural slaves". Above all, as we have glimpsed, Christian thought never definitively opposed slavery, at least outside of Europe, despite its central doctrine of the equality of souls before God. For some Christian theologians, one could still enslave others' bodies, leaving their souls to Divine care. For others, the very absence of knowledge of the Redeemer in the non-European worlds was grounds "to bring civilization and God's words to the benighted natives", if only at the point of the sword. The *Code Noir* of Louis XIV, passed in the same year as the Revocation of the Edict of Nantes (1685 [see chapters 1 and 2]), appealed to monarchical, aristocratic, and theological ideas to restrict the activities of free people of colour, mandate the conversion of all slaves throughout the French empire to Roman Catholicism, define the punishments which could be meted out to slaves, and expel the Jews from France's colonies.[15]

As for the manifestly racist bases for imperialism and slavery, and Europeans' sense of their "civilizing mission": racist prejudices were as long-established in eighteenth-century Europe as elsewhere.[16] Like Christian anti-Semitism, they were also caught up in biblical and theological ideas. Writing in 1578, the explorer George Best opined that the dark pigmentation of Africans' skin must result from "some naturall infection of the first inhabitants of that Countrey [Africa], and so all the whole progenie of them descended, are still polluted with the same blot of infection."[17] The original infection, he reasoned, stemmed from God's biblical damnation of Ham (*Genesis* 9:22–25) for his sexual incontinency, rendering his descendants "so blacke & lothsome, that it might remaine a spectacle of disobedience to all the World." Some decades later, in 1615, Reverend Thomas Cooper expressed the view that "this cursed race of Ham [should be] scattered towards the South, in Africa."[18] The missionary Morgan Godwin, touring Barbados in the 1670s, reports that he frequently met with this protest from Europeans: "What, those black dogs be made Christians?"[19]

Now, the enlightenment thinkers, as everyone agrees, were the first generation of European intellectuals for nearly 1,500 years to be openly critical of biblical Christianity, both for its metaphysical-theological postulations, and its use to sanction oppressive socio-political realities. In chapter 4, we saw in Voltaire the kinds of anti-clerical and biblical-critical arguments which would fill pamphlet after pamphlet after 1760 in France[20] from more openly atheistic thinkers like the Baron d'Holbach: protests against the immorality of biblical figures, even kings, long held up as exemplary; denunciations of "Holy forgeries" in the history of the Church; growing scepticism about the historicity of miracles, and their inconsistency with modern understandings of nature; critiques of the irrationality of monastic and priestly vows of chastity; questions about the plausibility of Christian theodicy and doctrines of a benevolent Providence (chapters 3 and 4); doubts about the cosmic centrality of the human drama in an infinitely large cosmos; and above all, concerns that the Churches' elevating of pledged faith in select theological dogmata to the putative basis for morality and group-inclusion was a continuing recipe for sectarian hatred.[21]

When we recall the centrality to enlightenment thought of this anti-clerical, anti-theological rebellion, our expectations concerning the supposed pro-colonialist Eurocentrism of the *lumières* begin to shift. By calling into question the metaphysical and moral credentials of Christianity, they were also pulling at the ideological rug that had undergirded European imperialism and racial slavery. For Voltaire, Diderot, and many other lesser *lumières*, as we might say, European religion, culture, and society was in such urgent need of its own reforms that it was in no fit condition to be exported anywhere else.

ENLIGHTENMENT DIVIDED: POLYGENISM, MONOGENISM, AND ABOLITIONISM

"The enlightenment", therefore, certainly did not *cause* the kinds of racial and theological prejudices called upon by European imperialists and slave masters in the centuries which had the good fortune to predate it. At most, we might maintain that the enlightenment thinkers transformed these earlier baleful prejudices, giving them new philosophical or perhaps proto-scientific grounds, whilst scuttling their previous, Christian scaffolding. This remains a very serious charge. Looking back from the other side of the horrors of the twentieth century, it is imperative to establish if, and how, enlightenment thought might be considered as intellectually antecedent to the emergence after 1850 of forms of pseudo-scientific racism and social Darwinism in the works of figures like Arthur Gobineau and Houston Stewart Chamberlain.[22]

To repeat (see Introduction), the deepest problem with blanket claims for or against "the enlightenment" is the Olympian level of generality at which they operate. The moniker "the enlightenment", with its definite article, posits that kind of unified cultural bloc which there is every reason to doubt has ever existed. It certainly did not exist in the France (or Potsdam, Ferney, or Geneva) of Montesquieu, Voltaire, Diderot, Jean-Jacques Rousseau, and the other *philosophes*. Two specifications need therefore to be proffered, before we can proceed further.

Firstly, however we may adjudge different *lumières*, it needs to be remembered that almost all Europeans outside of philosophical circles, at home and abroad, during the middle decades of the eighteenth century, assumed European civilisation and the Christian religion to be superior to those of all others. When enlighteners like Voltaire, Hume, or Kant expressed racist convictions, they were speaking in accord with sanctioned majority opinion. By contrast, when we find enlightenment *philosophes* elsewhere (as we shall) speaking out directly and vigorously *against* slavery, racial supremacism, and colonialism, as well as Christianity's sense of being the Universal Faith, we need to recall that they were speaking as a minority within Europe, risking censorship and persecution. To treat "the enlightenment" as spun from one dark cloth (or indeed, one light cloth) with the forces of Throne and Altar who opposed the *philosophes* on these issues is to anachronistically forget the theologico-political *divisions* riving this period.

Secondly, as we glimpsed in chapter 4, the period of Voltaire and Diderot saw the beginnings of what we call the modern life sciences. In the studies of figures like the Comte de Buffon, Joseph Needham, Carl Linnaeus, and Johannes Blumenbach, new conceptions and classifications of botanical, animal, and human life were generated, in *relative independence* from the thought of the *philosophes*.[23] In chapter 3, we saw how, for Voltaire, it was his encounter with Newtonian physics and cosmology which profoundly shaped his philosophy—not the other way around. In chapter 4, we saw how Diderot comparably *responded* philosophically in works like "The Letter on the Blind" (but also "D'Alembert's Dream" and others) to the kinds of transformist, epigenetic, and even hylozoic hypotheses about living creatures which Needham's, Buffon's, and these other eighteenth-century naturalists' studies had begun to suggest.[24] Nevertheless, anyone today who would try to paint with one brush the latest advances in the life sciences or particle physics as "the same" as the works of Alain Badiou, Gilles Deleuze, Wilfrid Sellars, Martha Nussbaum, Bernard Williams, etc., would not be taken too seriously. In the same way, we need to distinguish in the enlightenment era between the thought of the *philosophes*, with their epistemological, metaphysical, socio-political, and normative concerns, and those of the naturalists in whose works the first attempts to systematically classify different human groups were ventured.

We saw in chapter 2 that the increasing European exposure to non-European worlds after 1492 had introduced a debate between what Ira Wade called the "principle of unity" and "the principle of diversity".[25] At the most basic level, was the "human race" one species, hailing from a single stock before dispersing across the globe? Or are the human groups, so evidently physically and culturally divergent, as it were, "different all the way down", looking back to their prehistorical beginnings?

When we examine the primary literature and its scholarship, what we see is that neither all of the enlightenment-era philosophers (whom we will consider in this section), nor all of the enlightenment-era naturalists, were of one voice on these questions.[26] On one side of the debates were the "monogenists". These thinkers maintained that the human species was fundamentally one, springing from one ("mono") origin ("genesis"). Monogenists amongst the *philosophes* included the Abbé Raynal and Denis Diderot, as well as several other of Jonathan Israel's radicals. For these figures, since the fundamental biological and historical unity of the human species was given, it was the apparent physical, technological, and cultural differences between human groups that need explanation. As we shall see, they presented broadly post-Lockean assessments of these differences as hailing from divergences in empirical, historical experiences.

On the other side of the enlightenment debates, we find "polygenists" like Voltaire, Kames, Hume, and other of Israel's moderates. For these enlightenment-era *philosophes*, the different human groups hailed from many ("poly") biological origins. So, it is their apparent, common attributes, propensities, and institutions which are in need of explanation. Voltaire's polygenism informs his remarks about Africans in the 1735 *Treatise on Metaphysics* as having not "descended from the same man" as Europeans.[27] This comment reads for us as simply reprehensible. It is worth recalling that in the eighteenth century, the polygenetic position had a political-theological subversiveness, given the position of the Churches, based in Genesis, that all human beings are descended from Adam.[28]

For many of us raised in the postmodernist era, it may seem that the polygenists in this period had things unequivocally right. Cultural difference goes all the way down, doesn't it? It is precisely any erroneous postulate of unity or an "essentialist" human nature that licenses the suppression of difference, if not forms of imperialism and totalitarian control. However, in the enlightenment period, more or less the opposite was the case. Certainly, it would be monogenists led by Diderot and the other authors of the *History of the Two Indies* (see below) who would lead the intellectual charge against the injustices of European colonialism. And they would do so precisely by appealing

Enlightenment, Race, Slavery, and Anti-Colonialism 117

to a universal morality, rooted in common human nature, as against a prioritisation of physiological or cultural differences between peoples.

There are as ever complications in the kinds of alignments we might expect here. At a semantic level, table 5.1 shows how both monogenist and polygenist positions can license respect for other peoples, and also be appealed to in order to justify their oppression.

Table 5.1. Monogenism and Polygenism: Ethico-Political Pros and Cons

	If we take unity to be basic	*If we take diversity to be basic*
Positives	Stressing human unity means affording equal dignity to all people(s), regardless of differences.	Recognising multiplicity recommends fostering diversity as an end in itself.
Negatives	We can maintain that all peoples are equal by nature, but by history and knowledge, that "we" are "more equal" than others.	We can maintain that different races are inferior or superior, and that superior races have the "burden" of dominating others, who can only benefit from this.

In fact as in principle, leading enlightenment polygenists were, contra Jonathan Israel, highly progressive on the abolition of race-based slavery, the most abhorrent feature of the era's imperialism. Take Montesquieu. He was a polygenist, and we have seen that a plurality of experiential factors he proposes differentiates the experiences of societies, and should inform wise legislation (chapter 2). Yet, Montesquieu was stridently *anti*-slavery, capable of scathingly mocking the absurdities of European justifications of the slave trade, since "sugar would be too expensive if the plant which produced it were not cultivated by slaves, or if one treated them with some humanity".[29] The opening chapter of Book XV of *Spirit of the Laws* issues a famous, unequivocal condemnation of slavery:

> Slavery, properly so called, is the establishment of a right which gives to one man such a power over another as renders him absolute master of his life and fortune. The state of slavery is in its own nature bad. It is neither useful to the master nor to the slave; not to the slave, because he can do nothing through a motive of virtue; nor to the master, because by having an unlimited authority over his slaves he insensibly accustoms himself to the want of all moral virtues, and thence becomes fierce, hasty, severe, choleric, voluptuous, and cruel.[30]

Voltaire too was a polygenist, as we have said. Yet, whilst Voltaire's ethos as a historian meant that he could hardly deny that slavery seems to be nigh as old as humanity itself, his ethos as a *philosophe* found it unconscionable. We saw this in our analysis of *Candide*, and the famous episode of the African slave whose torture at the hands of his Dutch master draws forth from

Voltaire's hero a tearful recantation of cosmic optimism (chapter 4). "We have enjoyed this right for six hundred years; why then despoil us of it?", Voltaire imagines a slaveholder asking indignantly, in his entry on "Slaves" in his *Philosophical Dictionary*. Voltaire's reply is trenchant:

> We may humbly rejoin, that for these thirty or forty thousand years, the weasels have been in the habit of sucking the blood of our pullets; yet we assume to ourselves the right of destroying them when we can catch them.[31]

As for the idea of the Natural Law theorist Samuel von Pufendorf, that slavery can be entered into by voluntary contract (an idea Montesquieu believed historical), Voltaire here is of one voice with Jean-Jacques Rousseau:

> Pufendorf says that slavery has been established "by the free consent of the opposing parties." I will believe Pufendorf, when he shows me the original contract . . . the author of *The Spirit of Laws* adds, that according to Captain Dampier, "everybody sells himself in the kingdom of Achem." This would be a singular species of commerce, and I have seen nothing in the "Voyage" of Dampier which conveys such a notion. It is a pity that a man so replete with wit should hazard so many crudities and quote so badly.[32]

What then of the *Encyclopédie*, on many accounts the definitive time capsule documenting the leading thinking of the French enlightenment? It suffices to read Louis de Jaucourt's opening lines on "*Traite des nègres*" to underscore how widespread opposition to race-based slavery was amongst the enlightenment *philosophes* by the 1750s:

> The slave trade is the purchase of Negroes made by Europeans on the coasts of Africa, who then employ these unfortunate men as slaves in their colonies. This purchase of Negroes to reduce them into slavery is a negotiation that violates all religion, morals, natural law, and human rights . . . the Negroes did not become slaves by any right of war; nor did they voluntarily sacrifice themselves to slavery. Therefore, their children are not born as slaves. Everyone knows that Negroes are being purchased from their princes, who believe they have the right to own their freedom. Everybody is also aware that merchants transport these Negroes as if they were merchandise, either to their colonies or to America, where they are put on display to be sold.[33]

If the enlightenment had a race problem, we are compelled to concede that this problem did not affect the leading French *philosophes*' principled opposition to African slavery. Even divergent views on whether the human race hailed from one or plural sources did not affect this shared philosophical opposition. It would seem difficult for the sternest critic of the enlightenment to *imagine* a more strident denunciation of the unconscionable business than Jaucourt's continuation in the *Encyclopédie*:

> If a trade of this kind can be justified by a moral principle, then there is absolutely no crime, however atrocious, that cannot be legitimized. Kings, princes, and magistrates are not owners of their subjects; therefore, they are not entitled to their subjects' freedom, nor do they have the right to sell anyone into slavery. Moreover, nobody has the right to buy these subjects or to call himself their master. Men and their freedom are not objects of commerce; they can be neither sold, nor purchased, nor bought at any price. Thus, a man must blame only himself if his slave escapes. He paid money for illicit merchandise, even though all laws of humanity and equity forbid him to do so.[34]

THE RISE OF THE LIFE SCIENCES AND THE EMERGING CONCEPTIONS OF "RACE"

If we still hold to the claim that "the enlightenment" had a race problem, we are accordingly forced to specify that this problem must have been found less in the minds and hearts of its key *philosophes* than in the naturalistic, physiological, and biological authors they were reading, who were revolutionising biblical and Aristotelian understandings of the natural world (chapter 1). However, the picture is not as clear as we might anticipate, even here.

The work of Swedish botanist Carl Linnaeus was on any reckoning decisive in reshaping eighteenth-century understandings of the forms of life. Linnaeus's *Systema Naturae* first appeared in 1735, but such was its popularity that ten editions had been published by 1758.[35] The *Systema Naturae* sets out to systematically describe and classify animals and plants for the first time in a distinctly modern, observational fashion. The different species of flora and fauna, as Linnaeus conceives of them, consist of similar individuals sharing the same defining attributes, although to what extent he should be thought of as an "essentialist" is now disputed.[36] The species are in any event unchanging ("species fixism"), remaining as created by God in the beginning. Human beings are to be categorised, in Linnaeus's system, alongside *Homo nocturnes*, the higher apes. *Homo sapiens* is to be understood as one species of *Homo diurnes*, alongside two species of "monstrous", almost-humans one can imagine Diderot would have been interested to engage with, like dwarves.[37]

Decisive for us here is that Linnaeus divided the human species itself into four racial groups: *Americanus* (American Indians), *Europaeus* (Europeans), *Asiaticus* (Asians), and *Africanus* (Africans).

It is not difficult to see that this was a prejudicial categorisation, tying physical observations to contemporary racial stereotypy, with geopolitical implications. *Europaeus*, for instance, is described by Linnaeus as "white, serious, strong. Hair blond, flowing. Eyes blue. Active, very smart, inventive. Covered by tight clothing. Ruled by laws". *Africanus*, on the contrary, was "black, impassive, lazy. Hair kinked. Skin silky. Nose flat. Lips thick. Women with genital flap, breasts large. Crafty, slow, foolish. Anoints himself with grease. Ruled by caprice."[38]

Yet, Linnaeus's was neither the last nor the simply authoritative voice in enlightenment-era naturalism, and the period's attempts to categorize humans into racial groups.[39] Already in his *Histoire naturelle, générale et particulière*, published in thirty-six volumes between 1746 and 1788, the Comte de Buffon posited not four but *six* "races": adding the Lapps or "Polar" group, and the "Tartars" or Mongolians to Linnaeus's European, American, Asian, and African races.[40] Nevertheless, by contrast to Linnaeus, Buffon was a monogenist. That couplings between members of different races produce fertile offspring for him shows the common nature of all humans. The apparent physiological and cultural differences between the human races should hence be explained by divergent environmental factors. The descendants of a "negro" living in Europe for two hundred years, Buffon argued, would become paler-skinned and attain to all of the civilisational achievements of the whites.[41] "Every circumstance", Buffon wrote, "concurs in proving, that mankind are not composed of species essentially different from each other". On the contrary: "there was originally but one species, who, after multiplying and spreading over the whole surface of the earth, have undergone various changes by the influence of climate, food, mode of living, epidemic diseases, and the mixture of dissimilar individuals".[42]

After Buffon, there is Johann Friedrich Blumenbach's work in *On the Unity of Mankind* (1795). Blumenbach divides the human species based on analyses of skin pigmentation, hair colourings, physiognomy, and dental and cranial morphology. For him, there are *five* groups: Caucasians, Mongolians (East Asians), "Ethiopians" (sub-Saharan Africans), "Americans"; and "Malays", the peoples of "Oceania".[43] Like Buffon, and in contrast to Linnaeus, *On the Unity of Mankind* presents post-Lockean environmental considerations as the causes of the differing physical and other attributes of the races. But the "many varieties of man as are at present known", Blumenbach agrees with Buffon, are "one and the same species":

> Although there seems to be so great a distance between widely separate nations, that you might easily take the inhabitants of the Cape of Good Hope, the Greenlanders and the Circassians for so many different species of man, *yet when the matter is thoroughly considered, you see that all do so run into one another,*

that one variety of mankind does so sensibly pass into another, that you cannot mark out the limits between them.[44]

Furthermore, Blumenbach challenges the prejudices still found in Linnaeus and many others:

> I am of the opinion . . . after all the numerous instances I have brought together of negroes of capacity, that there is no so-called savage nation known under the sun which has so much distinguished itself by such examples of perfectibility and original capacity for scientific culture, and therefore attached itself so closely to the most civilized nations of the earth, as the Negro.[45]

Where then do we find our inquiry, at this point? Any alleged connection between enlightenment-era naturalistic categorisations of the different races, and the advent of the hateful, racist pseudo-sciences of the second half of the nineteenth century, is clearly far from simple, direct, or incontestable. At most, it can be said that the eighteenth-century categorisations of different "races", notably that of the polygenist Linnaeus, anticipated these theories in their attempts to account for human diversity by distinguishing, in an objectifying lens, the *physical* differences between racial groups. Nevertheless, in the monogenist works of Buffon and Blumenbach (but Stanhope Smith and others could be cited[46]), the aetiology of such diversity is considered to be environmental. The works of many of these enlightenment-era naturalists in no way point to fundamentally different, unchanging "essences" of specific races, the appeal to which could license specific historical missions or imperial prerogatives. On the contrary.

To therefore assign responsibility to enlightenment-era works in natural history for later pseudo-scientific racism, with its hierarchies of essentially different racial groups, is highly contentious. To blame "the enlightenment" *tout court* for "leading to" (a wonderful phrase) Arthur Gobineau, Houston Stewart Chamberlain, and those who drew upon their racist and eugenicist visions to overthrow the liberal and socialist traditions' commitments to human equality, is to approach what the philosopher Ludwig Wittgenstein called a senseless claim.

ENLIGHTENMENT ANTI-COLONIALISM AND ABBÉ RAYNAL'S *HISTORY OF THE TWO INDIES*

We arrive now at the book that "made a world revolution", according to Jonathan Israel: the *Histoire philosophique et politique des établissements et du commerce des Européens dans les deux Indes*, or simply *Histoire des deux Indes* (*History of the Two Indies*) of 1770. The work, commissioned by Guillaume-Thomas, the abbé de Raynal, addresses European relations with the "East Indies" (everywhere East of Persia and South of Russia) and the "West Indies" (the Americas and Africa). Eventually spanning nineteen volumes, this mostly forgotten tome created a sensation in its day, running to thirty editions between 1770 and 1787 in France, with over fifty editions internationally. "Among enlightenment publications none provide a more challenging general outlook or had a greater effect on both sides of the Atlantic and the rest of the world", Israel claims.[47] Like Diderot and d'Alembert's *Encyclopédie*, it was also a collective work, penned by a cast of anonymous authors, including radical *philosophes* like Jacques-André Naigeon and the Baron d'Holbach. Anthony Pagden calls *History of the Two Indies* a "mini-Encyclopedia of all the evils European colonisation had visited upon the world."[48]

In 1776, Raynal made the fateful decision to commission Denis Diderot "to correct the style" of the earlier editions. As he might well have predicted, the result was that, in the next four years, Diderot added around a *third* more content (some seven hundred pages). Diderot's new content included highly charged declamations on the barbarism of slavery, the inhumanity of the colonialists, the promise of the newly founded republican United States, and the justice of slave revolts against the European oppressors. Diderot would call the resulting 1780 edition of *History of the Two Indies* "the book that I love, and which Kings and courtesans detest, the book which will give birth to Brutus".[49]

At the same time, Diderot would declare that it was a work of history which had been written "with eyes full of tears" (VII, 1). "O Barbaric Europeans!", he cries out:

> I have not been dazzled by the splendour of your deeds. Their success has not obscured their injustice . . . if I cease for one moment to see you as so many flocks of cruel and ravenous vultures, with as little morality and conscience as those birds of prey, may this work and my memory . . . become objects of the utmost contempt and execration (I, 24).[50]

As a historical record, indeed, *History of the Two Indies* presents a grim chronicle. It is far from whitewashing Europeans' savagery on the global stage. "Settlements have been formed and subverted; ruins have been heaped on ruins; countries that were well peopled have become deserted; ports that were full of buildings have been abandoned" (IV, 3; cf. VII, 1).[51] *History of the Two Indies* pitifully documents the Spanish *conquistadores'* destruction of the Incas' religion, institutions, and social order; the enslavement of most of their men; and the dispersion of liquor amongst the rest, who have as such "fallen into the most degraded and brutal state" (VII, 27).[52] As for the Spanish decision to turn to the African slave trade after 1501, Diderot is similarly clear-sighted: "This mode of substitution which was dictated by the refinements of European barbarity, was more prejudicial to Africa than useful to the country of the Inca" (XII, 27).[53]

These proclamations by the leading *philosophe* of his generation need to be cited, given what is said of "the enlightenment" in some places, often in ignorance of *History of the Two Indies*. Nevertheless, it is important to stress, with Sankar Muthu, that these Diderotian statements in the later editions of the text are more than the admirable, passionate responses of an individual, uninformed by principled philosophical developments.[54] Our contention in this book is that such defences of non-Europeans against the *philosophes*' own countrymen's crimes in fact represent one perfectly logical culmination of enlightenment philosophizing, on a par with criticisms of the acts of inhumanity performed by peoples of any races or times. As we have shown, this philosophizing principally turned around the practice of learning to look at oneself (and one's group) and "our" actions from the perspective of the Other, as well as fostering the ability to see ourselves in others, whose plights might otherwise attract only our indifference, our fear, or our hatred. In *History of the Two Indies*, enlightenment self-othering reaches its apogee, transcending the field of edifying fictions and calling out "the evil genius that speaks our several languages, and which diffuses the same disasters in all parts": the evil genius of imperialism (IV, 33).[55]

To lay claim to a vast empire, whether on secular or theological grounds, Diderot declares is a "great evil" and "contrary to nature" (XIII, 1).[56] Human beings are raised into particular national cultures and characters—what Montesquieu called a "spirit of laws" (see chapter 2). *History of the Two Indies* describes this as a "mask" of custom that restrains peoples' darker potentials, and which can ennoble them. By contrast, Diderot writes, in a thought which anticipates Hannah Arendt's denunciations of the demoralising effects of colonial adventurism in *The Origins of Totalitarianism*:

> the greater the distance from the capital, the looser the mask become. At the frontiers, it falls off. Going from one hemisphere to another, what does it become? Nothing . . . Beyond the equator a man is neither English, Dutch, French, Spanish, nor Portuguese. He retains only those principles and prejudices of his native country which justify and excuse his conduct . . . he is a domestic tiger returning to the forest, the thirst of blood takes hold of him once more (IX, 1).[57]

Men who might, in metropolitan Paris or Berlin, have lived lives restrained by social law and ordered by elementary morality, are in the colonies drawn to act "contrary to all humanity, to their interest, to their safety, and to the first dawnings of reason". Indeed, they "become more barbarous than the savage" (X, 1), whose putative lack of civilisation is adduced as the reason for their oppression. In plain truth, the colonies are forms of despotic government of the kind which Montesquieu had warned (chapter 2) were destructive of everything best in people. This despotism is visited on undeserving populations whose only "crime" was their being unable to expel the invaders, or too willing to trust in their good faith. As Diderot addresses the colonists and their apologists:

> You hold the system of Hobbes in abhorrence, and yet you practice at a distance this fatal system which makes strength the supreme law. After having become thieves and assassins, nothing remains to complete your character, but that you should become, as you really are, a set of execrable sophists (XIII, 13).

The virtual "creed of the colonist" which Diderot puts in the mouth of a European sounds like the nihilistic declaration of a venture capitalist today, anticipating the famed "Greed is good" speech of Gordon Gekko:

> Let my country perish, let the region perish also; perish the citizen and the foreigner; perish my associates, provided that I enrich myself with the spoils. All parts of the universe are alike to me. When I have laid waste, exhausted, and impoverished our country, I shall always find another, to which I can carry my gold (III, 41).

European colonialists for Diderot evince that "coloniality of power" which Amy Allen has charged against the enlightenment itself, in *The End of Progress: Decolonising the Normative Foundations of Critical Theory*.[58] The colonialists assessed the others by our own lights, coding difference as inferiority, and eschewing all moral sympathy and reciprocity. "Savage Europeans!", Diderot hence cries out again: "you doubted at first whether the inhabitants of the regions you had just discovered were not animals which you might slay without remorse because they were black, and you were white" (VII, 22).[59] Such a lack of moral imagination, and of basic humanity

> carried to an excess of infatuation beyond example, would have inclined [the Spanish conquistadors] to consider Athens in the same contemptuous light as they did Tlaxcala. They would have treated the Chinese as brutes, and have everywhere left marks of outrage, oppression, and devastation (VI, 9).[60]

History of the Two Indies, readers can see, stands as the clearest, most radical refutation imaginable of all totalising claims about the alleged, unruffled Eurocentrism of the enlightenment *simpliciter*. As Israel and Pagden have stressed, this book embodies the radical enlightenment as *critique* of Eurocentrism.[61] Far from being ignored, *History of the Two Indies* ought to have been celebrated in later modern progressive understandings of the prehistories of later modern anti-imperialist struggles and postcolonial criticism. Against the criminality of colonialism and savagery of the slave trade, Diderot's interpolations posit sacred laws of hospitality which, far from encoding European prerogatives, he again and again reviles the Europeans for desecrating. If a territory is unoccupied, it may be freely occupied. If it is part-occupied, including by nomadic peoples, the presently unoccupied parts may be occupied, with the uncoerced consent of the previous inhabitants. If the land is occupied, then the stranger must ask and submit to the hospitality of the hosts, no matter from whence s/he may hail, and whatever putative Revelation s/he might bring. Beyond this:

> with reason . . . and with no offence against the laws of humanity and justice, the people could expel and kill me if I seized women, children and property; if I infringed its civil liberty; if I restricted its religious opinions; if I claimed to give it law; if I wished to make it my slave. Then I would be only one more wild animal in its vicinity, and no more pity would be due to me than to a tiger (XIII, I).[62]

Enlightenment criticism of colonialism could surely go no farther, short of the call Diderot duly makes in the same work for a "black Spartacus" to rise up and expel "the Spaniards, Portuguese, English, French, Dutch", "all their tyrants", with "arms and flames".[63]

THE *PHILOSOPHES* AS HISTORIANS, NOT PHILOSOPHERS OF HISTORY

We have seen that claims about a race problem facing the enlightenment can be sustained neither concerning all of the *philosophes*, nor concerning all the eighteenth-century naturalists in whose works the first modern understandings of "race" were developed. Some of these thinkers were monogenists, others, polygenists. Yet all of the *philosophes* we have considered, led by Montesquieu, Voltaire, and Diderot, were opposed to slavery as an affront to morality and human dignity. Far from sanctioning the imperialist adventures of the European powers since the fifteenth century, the enlighteners' fierce anti-clericalism targeted the theological bases justifying the "civilizing mission" of the white nations in the "two Indies". Far from being single-mindedly Eurocentric, by the time of *History of the Two Indies*, the *philosophes* surrounding Diderot were loudly decrying the cruelty and atrocities European colonialism was visiting upon non-Europeans. If all human beings have the capacities for reason and virtue, and if all peoples can better themselves through experience, reflection, and education, then there can be no legitimate basis for one people tyrannising over others. The fact that the imperialism has been "ours" is a source of shame.

Yet, in more sophisticated criticisms of the alleged Eurocentrism of the enlightenment, like Amy Allen's work, *The End of Progress?*, one last trumping argument is presented, with whose consideration we will close this chapter. Allen points out that eighteenth-century thinkers like Adam Smith developed a "stadial" vision of history, postulating four progressive stages of human development.[64] The stages are based on economic-material-technological features: firstly, nomadic hunters and gatherers; secondly, semi-nomadic pastoralists; thirdly, settled agricultural communities; and fourthly, commercial-civic societies like those of the eighteenth-century European monarchies. The issue Allen identifies with this account of history is that it sets up a single, crypto-teleological set of assumptions about how *all* societies either have, or *should*, develop. In its light, peoples who have remained nomadic, or pastoralists, even agriculturalists, can be looked down upon, from a position of more advanced European civilisational achievement, which is taken for granted as normative. Given the stadial, progressive view of history, "all non-Europeans could be considered as pre-Europeans", not simply as different, with their own intrinsic values and dignity.[65]

As with the claims concerning a wholesale race problem, for this identification of the stadial philosophy of history sketched in Smith—but also in Turgot and Condorcet amongst the French, and Robertson, Millar, Ferguson, and Kames on the British Isles—to succeed as a criticism of the enlightenment *tout court*, we would need to establish that all of (at least the leading) enlighteners held to this progressive, stadial philosophy of history. But this cannot be established. As works like Henri Vyverberg's *Historical Pessimism in the French Enlightenment* or J. B. Bury's *The Idea of Progress* instead document, "history was in general a gloomy panorama before the eighteenth-century eye, and for many writers past and future were clearly discontinuous".[66] Whether in aesthetics, morality, philosophy, or politics—any areas outside of the natural philosophies—there was robust debate amongst the *philosophes* as to whether any progress was discernible, possible, and whether (as such) the eighteenth century was not a period of decadence and decline.[67] From Montesquieu's first study on the decline and fall of Rome, the weight of testimony amongst the *philosophes* instead points, if anywhere, towards a revival of the cyclical philosophy of history propounded by the ancients whom they greatly admired, as against a linear, post-Christian conception such as would later be propounded in Hegel, Comte, and others.

"After raising itself for a time from one bog, the world falls back into another; an age of barbarism follows an age of refinement," Voltaire writes in

"Miracles" in *The Philosophical Dictionary*: "This barbarism is in turn dispersed, and then reappears; it is a continual alternation of day and night."[68] In Jaucourt's article on "Government" in the *Encyclopédie*, the organic analogy, so often associated with this ancient "cyclical" view of history, is developed: "The best constituted governments, like the best formed animal bodies, bear within themselves the principle of their destruction . . . after their early growth, all states tend towards decadence and disintegration".[69] Diderot himself entertains hesitations as to the irrefutability of Rousseau's wholly pessimistic account of progress, and the superior felicity of "noble savages" (ch. 6). Even as he expressed his great hopes for the new American republic in the final years of his life, he would still intone dourly that "the destiny that rules the world wills everything to pass. The happiest condition of man, of a State, has its term. Everything carries within it the secret germ of its destruction."[70]

We should be careful, with this much said, of claiming that the "rise of modern paganism"[71] in the enlightenment period saw all the enlighteners embracing this cyclical philosophy of history either—or indeed, that they were all convinced that *any* philosophical or theological principle could drive and explain human history. The very idea of a "philosophy of history", as we find it sanctified above all in the nineteenth-century German thinker, W. G. F. Hegel, could only look to the kind of sceptical, self-limiting thinking of *philosophes* like Voltaire or Diderot as every bit like a secularisation of the theological idea of Providence they had each by the 1750s become exceedingly dubious about.[72] Voltaire, Montesquieu, and Diderot were philosophers who wrote history. But this is a different, far less august, and contentious calling than claiming to espy a single philosophical meaning in and beyond human historical experiences, as both optimistic (Hegel) and pessimistic (Heidegger) nineteenth- and twentieth-century philosophers of history have claimed to do.

When we look at enlightenment-era, philosophical reflections on historiography, the study of history, what we tend to find are neither progressive-stadial, nor pagan-cyclical theorisations of the whole. What we do find are much more modest statements, tying history to the post-Lockean, self-limiting empiricism we met in chapter 1. To study history "teaches us facts and shows us the happy and unhappy events which were their outcome", Du Marsais hence writes in "Experience" in the *Encyclopedia*.[73] "I consider history to be a collection of observations offering to the citizens of all classes the truths relative to them", Condillac similarly reflects: "if we learn to draw upon those elements useful to us we shall become more wise through the experience of past ages."[74] We are a long way from Hegel's claims about a world-Spirit (*Geist*), traversing its inevitable, triumphantly blood-stained way behind the backs of historical actors towards a single nineteenth-century Prussian terminus. We are also a long way from denigrations of the dignity of other or earlier cultures' historical experiences, by recourse to claims about the historical inevitability or unshakable superiority of our own. In historiography as elsewhere, it is rather the case that the leading enlighteners aspired to a cosmopolitan impartiality perhaps stated best already by Pierre Bayle in his *Historical and Critical Dictionary* (ch. 1):

> All those who know the laws of history will agree that a historian who wishes to fulfil his tasks faithfully must free himself from the spirit of flattery and slander. He must, as far as possible, adopt the state of mind of the Stoic who is moved by no passion. Impervious to all else, he must heed solely the interests of the truth to which he must sacrifice resentment aroused by an injustice as well as recollection of favours—even his love for his country. He must forget that he belongs to a particular country, that he belongs to a particular faith.[75]

NOTES

1. Justin E. H. Smith, "The Enlightenment's 'Race' Problem, and Ours", *New York Times*, February 13, 2013; see David Theo Goldberg, *Racist Culture: Philosophy and the Politics of Meaning* (London: Wiley-Blackwell, 1993).

2. John Locke, *Fundamental Constitution of Carolina*, online at Fundamental Constitutions| Ncpedia, as cited in Smith, "The Enlightenment's 'Race' Problem".

3. See Emmanuel C. Eze, "Hume, Race, and Human Nature", *Journal of the History of Ideas* vol. 61, no. 4 (October 2000): 691–98; Xander Richards, "Was David Hume Racist? Here's the Scottish Philosopher's Racist Comment in Full", *The National*, September 14, 2020.

4. Kant, at Muthu, *Enlightenment against Empire*, 183.

5. Immanuel Kant, cited at Ronald Judy, "Kant and the Negro", *Surfaces* 1 (1991) https://doi.org/10.7202/1065256a, 3.

6. For extensive consideration of these questions, see Robert Bernasconi and T. Lott, eds., *The Idea of Race* (Indianapolis, IN: Hackett, 2000); Robert Bernasconi and S. Cook, eds., *Race and Racism in Continental Philosophy* (Bloomington: Indiana University Press, 2003).

7. See Beiner, *Nietzsche, Heidegger and the Far Right*; Losurdo, *Friedrich Nietzsche: Aristocratic Rebel*; Faye, *Heidegger, Introduction of Nazism into Philosophy*; Don Dombowsky, *Nietzsche and the German Autumn* (2020), online at (16) (PDF) Friedrich Nietzsche and The German Autumn Don Dombowsky ©2020 (researchgate.net).

8. This is not to argue that all those who accept the radical criticisms of "modernity" we find in both their works do not hold to values of equality and some conception(s) of freedom and flourishing. But these thinkers' premises work to sideline or discredit all traditional bases of these concepts, which is why Nietzsche and Heidegger advertised their works as radical "overcomings" of JudaeoChristian civilisation, "Jewish rationality", "Western metaphysics", etc. One is left firstly with the delicate exercise

of at once declaring oneself a superior interpreter of these thinkers' works than the authors themselves, who one at the same time is exalting as superior sources of insight, to for example enlightenment authors. One is left secondly, having accepted a wholly negative account of Western history as a long decline reaching back to "the Greeks", with a decision in favour of progressive causes, that is arguably admirable but normatively groundless, or else with the kinds of opaque, uncommitted or anti-nomic messianism we find in Derrida, Agamben, Nancy, etc.

9. Slavery was common in the ancient world, and never entirely disappeared from the European mainland, or the Islamic world, before the modern period. Neither the New Testament nor the Old Testament condemn this institution, any more than the ancient pagan philosophies had done. Moreover, its inhumanity was resurrected within Europe by the Nazis on a grand scale and has not been entirely ended, even in the Europe of the twenty-first century. See https://www.thenewfederalist.eu/the-reality-of-modern-slavery-in-europe?lang=fr.

10. I draw in the historical section which follows on Jeremy Black, *A Brief History of Slavery* (New York: Little, Brown Book Group, 2011); Susanne Keegan, *History of Slavery* (UK: Grange Books, 1997).

11. Aaron O'Neill, "Slaves Brought from Africa to the Americas", *Statista*, at https://www.statista.com/statistics/1143207/slaves-brought-from-africa-to-americas-1501-1866/.

12. We get an idea of the conditions of these hateful transports when we note that between 10 percent and 20 percent of those shipped throughout this period did not disembark alive. *Ibid.*

13. Aaron O'Neill, "Number of Slaves Taken from Africa by Region, Country", *Statista*, at https://www.statista.com/statistics/1150475/number-slaves-taken-from-africa-by-region-century/.

14. At Jeremy D. Popkin, *You Are All Free: The Haitian Revolution and the Abolition of Slavery* (Cambridge, UK: Cambridge University Press, 2010), 32.

15. Israel, *Enlightenment Contested*, 606.

16. Christian anti-Semitism dated back at least as far as the Crusades. The Jews had by the eighteenth century for nearly a millennia been blamed for the death of Christ, the Black Death, and other misfortunes, as well as accused (topically, in our period of "QAnon") of conducting various barbarous, unholy rituals, sometimes involving children. The fifteenth and sixteenth centuries saw pogroms and expulsions, with hundreds of thousands of Jews forcibly converted.

17. George Best, at Brooke N. Newman, *Dark Inheritance: Blood, Race, and Sex in Colonial Jamaica* (New Haven and London: Yale University Press, 2018), 80.

18. Cited at Jonathan Schorsch, *Jews and Blacks in the Early Modern World* (New York: Cambridge University Press, 2004), 157.

19. Schorsch, *Jews and Blacks*, 157.

20. See Durant and Durant, *Age of Voltaire*, 680–754.

21. See Frank E. Manuel, *The Eighteenth Century Confronts the Gods* (Cambridge, MA: Harvard University Press, 1959).

22. See Losurdo, *Nietzsche,* 612, 733, 739, 743–46, 763, 772–74, 781, 816, 1004–05, 1008; Gyorgy Lukacs, *Destruction of Reason,* trans. Peter Palmer (India: Askar Books, 2017), 669–713.

23. See esp. Stephen Gaukroger, *The Collapse of Mechanism* and *The Natural and the Human* (Oxford, UK: Oxford University Press, 2016), for exhaustive accounts of the development of the scientific culture in the eighteenth century, in its interactions with the *philosophes,* and for itself.

24. See Kurt Ballstadt, *Diderot: Natural Philosopher* (Oxford, UK: Voltaire Foundation, 2008); Calas Duflo, *Diderot, Philosophe* (Paris: Honoré Champion, 2003), 65–270 ("Le Vrai"); and John Hope Mason, *Irresistible Diderot* (London and New York: Quartet, 1982), 219–63.

25. Wade, *Intellectual Foundations,* 391–93.

26. See Kenin Malik, "On the Enlightenment's 'Race Problem'" | Pandaemonium (kenanmalik).

27. Voltaire, *Treatise on Metaphysics,* chapter 1, "What is a Man?".

28. It was only in the nineteenth century, in Herder and the Romantics, that anything like what we might term a "cultural essentialism" developed, which hypostasised the differences between peoples based on their different histories. But such cultural essentialism shares with enlightenment-period polygenism the sense of that what divides peoples is more real than what unites them—a position which we know from the twentieth century can also be used to license forms of racism.

29. Montesquieu, SL XV, 5; Gay, *Science of Freedom,* 412.

30. In a monarchical government, Montesquieu specified, "where it is of the utmost importance that human nature should not be debased or dispirited", there should be no slavery. In democracies, where equality is governing spirit, and likewise "in aristocracies, where the laws ought to use their utmost endeavours to procure as great an equality as the nature of the government will permit, slavery is contrary to the spirit of the constitution: it only contributes to give a power and luxury to the citizens which they ought not to have" (SL XV, 1). Yet, at other points, which Voltaire duly attacks, Montesquieu seems to believe on good faith stories of people willingly selling themselves into slavery: "This is the true and rational origin of that mild law of slavery which obtains in some countries: and mild it ought to be, as founded on the free choice a man makes of a master, for his own benefit; which forms a mutual convention between the two parties" (SL XV 6). As we will see, Voltaire pillories his predecessor for this position.

31. Voltaire, "Slaves", in *Philosophical Dictionary, Volume 9,* The Project Gutenberg eBook of A Philosophical Dictionary, by Voltaire.

32. Voltaire, "Slaves".

33. Jaucourt, "Slave Trade", in *Encyclopedia,* at Slave trade (umich.edu).

34. Jaucourt, "Slave Trade".

35. See Gaukroger, *The Natural and the Human.*

36. Joeri Witteveen, "Linnaeus, the Essentialism Story, and the Question of Types", *TAXON* 69, no. 6 (2020): 1141–49.

37. Gaukroger, *The Natural and the Human,* 240–41

38. For the previous paragraph, see Malik, "On the Enlightenment's 'Race Problem' ".

39. See Gaukroger, *The Natural and the Human*, 221–36.

40. See Claude-Olivier Doron, "Race and Genealogy: Buffon and the Formation of the Concept of 'Race' ", *Humana Mente: Journal of Philosophical Studies* 22 (2012): 75–109; Gaukroger, *The Collapse of Mechanism*, 379–83, 194–96. In his work, also, we see the lineaments of an epigenetic understanding of life, including the evolution and transformation of species, as well as the beginnings of increasing challenges to the biblical chronology then still regnant, arguing for a 6,000-year-old Earth. See Gaukroger, *The Natural and the Human*, 219; Devin Vartija, "Revisiting Enlightenment Racial Classification: Time and the Question of Human Diversity", *Intellectual History Review* (2020), DOI: 10.1080/17496977.2020.1794161.

41. See Amon Andereggen, "The Image of the African in the French Collective Psyche", *Peuples Noirs, Peuples Africains* no. 59–62 (1988): 135.

42. Buffon at Malik, "On the Enlightenment's 'Race Problem' ".

43. See Thomas Junker, "Blumenbach's Theory of Human Races and the Natural Unity of Humankind", in *Johann Blumenbach* (London: Routledge, 2018); Kenneth E. Barber, Johann Blumenbach and the Classification of Human Races | Encyclopedia.com; "Historical Race Concepts", *World Heritage Encyclopaedia*, Historical race concepts | Project Gutenberg Self-Publishing - eBooks | Read eBooks online.

44. Blumenbach, at Malik, "On the Enlightenment's 'Race Problem' " (emphasis added). Samuel Stanhope Smith, in his 1810 *Essay on the Causes of the Variety of Complexion and Figure in the Human Species*, concurred that "it is impossible to draw the line precisely between the various races of men, or even to enumerate them with certainty; and that it is itself a useless labour to attempt it." For Walter Tench, writing on Australian Aborigines in 1793, two years before Blumenbach's opus, it was "by the fortuitous advantage of birth alone do Europeans possess superiority . . . untaught, unaccommodated man, is the same in Pall Mall, as in the wilderness of New South Wales."

45. Blumenbach, at "Historical Race Concepts".

46. See Malik, "Enlightenment's 'Race Problem'"

47. Israel, *Democratic Enlightenment*, 413.

48. Pagden, *Enlightenment*, 169.

49. Pagden, *Enlightenment*, 169; Muthu, *Enlightenment against Empire*, 73. All citations to the *L'Histoire* in this section will proceed by book number, then chapter number, and are drawn from Muthu's text at indicated pages unless otherwise indicated.

50. Raynal, *L'Histoire*, I, 24, cited at P. Jimack, "Introduction" to *A History of the Two Indies: A Translated Selection of Writings from Raynal*, ed. and selected by P. Jimack (London: Routledge, 2006), 22.

51. Muthu, *Enlightenment against Empire*, 87, 91.

52. At Muthu, *Enlightenment against Empire*, 91.

53. At Muthu, *Enlightenment against Empire*, 81.

54. Muthu, *Enlightenment against Empire*. As Voltaire would write around the same time of his old *bête noir*, the idea that "all is well" in this best of all possible

worlds: "If you would say "all is well", say the word, if you dare, in connection with [Pope] Alexander VI and Julius II, say it amid twelve millions of Americans who are being assassinated in twelve million ways, to punish them for not being able to understand in Latin a papal bull that monks have read to them". Voltaire, "We Must Take Sides", in *Selected Works of Voltaire*, trans. J. McCabe (London: C. A. Watts & Co., 1948), 30.

55. Cf. Muthu, *Enlightenment against Empire*, 87.

56. At Muthu, *Enlightenment against Empire*, 94.

57. At Muthu, *Enlightenment against Empire*, 74. Then there is the element of self-selection of colonial adventurers: "distant posts are never filled, except by indigent, rapacious men, without talents or morals, strangers to all sentiments of honour, and to every idea of equity, the refuse of the higher ranks of the state" (X, 1). Then, the changed circumstances, the "absence of witnesses and judges of our actions" (XIII, 1, at Muthu, *Enlightenment*, 95), as well as laws which recognise the humanity of the natives, license the worst in these people.

58. Allen, *The End of Progress*, 25.

59. See Muthu, *Enlightenment against Empire*, 93.

60. At Muthu, *Enlightenment against Empire*, 81.

61. Israel, *Democratic Enlightenment*, 413–15; Pagden, *Enlightenment*, 169ff.

62. At Muthu, *Enlightenment against Empire*, 75.

63. Raynal, *L'Histoire*, XI, 24. See C. L. R. James, *The Black Jacobins: Toussaint L'Ouverture and the San Domingo Revolution*, 2nd rev. ed. (New York: Vintage, 1963), 24–25, 171, 250; see Y. Benot, *Diderot: De l'athéisme à l'anticolonialisme* (Paris: François Maspero, 1970), 212–15; Susan Buck-Morss, *Hegel, Haiti, and Universal History* (Pittsburgh: University of Pittsburgh Press, 2009).

64. Amy Allen, *End of Progress*, 7–9, 19–20.

65. Quijano, cited at Allen, *End of Progress*, 21. At page 20, Gurminder Bhambra concurs that "the chronological (and evaluative) relationship established between different types of culture emerged out of a hierarchical ranking of contemporary cultures", encoding Eurocentric geopolitical valuations into a philosophy of history.

66. Henri Vyverberg, *Historical Pessimism in the French Enlightenment* (Cambridge, MA: Harvard University Press, 1958), 105.

67. See J. B. Bury, *The Idea of Progress* (2010), online at The Idea of Progress, by J. B. Bury (gutenberg.org), ch. 4, 7–9.

68. Voltaire, "Miracles", in *Philosophical Dictionary*, at Vyverberg, *Historical Pessimism*, 184.

69. Jaucourt, "Government" in *Encyclopedia*, at Government [abridged] (umich.edu).

70. Diderot, *Salon de 1767*, cited in Whitney Mannies, "Denis Diderot and the Politics of Materialist Skepticism", in *Skepticism and Political Thought in the Seventeenth and Eighteenth Centuries*, ed. John C. Laursen and Gianni Paganini (Toronto: University of Toronto Press, 2015), 187; see Matthew Sharpe, "Camus and Diderot: Modern Rebellion, Before the Terror", in Matthew Sharpe et al., eds., *Camus Amongst the Philosophers* (Leiden, Netherlands: Brill, 2019), 111–12.

71. See, i.e., cf. Gay, *Rise of Modern Paganism*.

72. See Hans Blumenberg, *The Legitimacy of the Modern Age*, trans. Robert M. Wallace (Cambridge: Massachusetts Institute of Technology Press, 1983).
73. At Vyverberg, *Historical Pessimism*, 106.
74. Condillac, "Discours Préliminaire in his *Course d'études pour l'instruction du Prince de Parme*, at Vyverberg, *Historical Pessimism*, 106. Compare d'Alembert's *Elements of Philosophy*, as cited at Cassirer, *Philosophy of the Enlightenment*, 204, for another statement of this broadly empiricist sense of history's utility for human beings.
75. Pierre Bayle, at Cassirer, *Philosophy of the Enlightenment*, 207–08.

Chapter 6

The Enlightenment, Sexuality, and Gender

WOMEN, SEXUALITY, AND THE ENLIGHTENMENT

To be a woman in the France of the later *ancien régime* was to inhabit a world we can scarcely imagine.[1] Here as elsewhere, women had few social or legal—and no political—rights. They couldn't retain a lawyer, sign contracts, or inherit property. Marriage and child-rearing were considered their highest callings. By entering into holy matrimony, they lost whatever semblance of legal independence was left to them:

> The husband and wife are one person in law; that is, the very being or legal existence of the woman is suspended during the marriage or at least is incorporated and consolidated into that of the husband: under whose wing, protection and cover, she performs everything.[2]

In the middle and upper classes, girls' education was mostly carried out at home by governesses, then by tutors, and finally by dancing masters. Its aim was to teach the arts of sitting, standing, walking, talking, and gesturing, with courtesy and grace. Some girls of more liberal-minded parents received private lessons in Latin. Nearly all girls except the very poor learned to sing and play the harpsichord. The higher education of girls, such as it was, was carried on in convents, where they progressed in religion, embroidery, music, dancing, and the proper conduct of a young woman and a wife.[3]

In the middle classes, Christianity remained widely intact, supporting paternal authority as the basis of social order. Marriage remained a matter of property and status. As Diderot for one was to find out, unsuitable matches from this perspective were unlikely to garner parental support.[4] As one *paterfamilias* is said to have told his daughter, proverbially, "chance is less blind than love." Love marriages, without parental consent, were nevertheless increasing in number and in the literature of the day. They were recognized as legal if sworn to before a notary, and the male was over thirty. The great majority of marriages were still arranged by the parents as a union of properties and family names rather than as a union of hearts.

Despite the reputation of the French, adultery seems to have been rare in middle and lower classes, and far rarer outside of Paris than within it. ("Those who live a hundred leagues from the capital," said Duclos, "are a hundred years away from it in ways of conduct and thought.")[5] No social stigma attached to adultery amongst the aristocracy. The king, of course, had known mistresses. In this, at least, a measure of sexual egalitarianism had been achieved amongst the elites:

> The double standard, which had sought to protect the inheritance of property by making the infidelity of the wife a far graver offense than that of the husband, was left behind when the wife came to Paris or Versailles; there the wife who confined her favours to her husband was considered old-fashioned.[6]

Many aristocratic couples lived separate lives. Some lived openly with their lovers, the arrangement being gracefully not talked about, so long as, in the woman's case, it was confined to one man at a time. The Duc de Lauzun is supposed to have answered gallantly that, if after a decade without seeing his wife, she sent him word that she was expecting a child, "I would write and tell her that I was delighted that Heaven had blessed our union; be careful of your health; I will call and pay my respects this evening."[7]

Child-rearing was women's business in the lower and middle strata of French society. The bourgeois wife was expected to be a paragon of industry, modest virtue, and piety. Amongst the peasantry, from a young age, boys would help their father on the farm, and girls, *maman* within the home. In the nobility, children were treated quite openly as burdens, sent off as soon as possible to wet nurses, governesses, and tutors. Intimacy between aristocrats of either gender with their children was exceptional. The son addressed his father as "Monsieur"; the daughter with equal formality kissed her mother's hand upon greeting. When the children grew up, they were sent off to the army, to the Church, or to a nunnery, the oldest son alone inheriting the paternal title.

Convents continued to operate, and they served several secular as well as sacred functions. The well-to-do used them as havens for surplus daughters. Even lower-class families, like Suzanne's family in Diderot's *The Nun* (*La religieuse*), used them to deposit unwanted children, or girls born from uncertain paternity. As Diderot's novel dramatizes, these nunneries were not always houses of austerity, simple piety, and devotion to the Holy life.[8]

Homosexuality, in France as everywhere else, was considered unholy, and prohibited as illegal. Such was the opprobrium surrounding this "unnatural" act that offenses were punishable with burning at the stake, albeit that this law was mostly enforced only upon the poor. The Abbé Pierre François Guyot Desfontaines, who had taught in a Jesuit college for fifteen years, was arrested on charges of homosexuality in 1725. It was Voltaire's intercession alone, despite his career-long ironies at the abbé's expense, which persuaded André-Hercule de Fleury and Madame de Prie to secure a pardon. Attitudes towards masturbation were likewise, by present standards, extremely backwards, although increasingly the subject was being broached by mid-century, as in the third dialogue of Diderot's *D'Alembert's Dream*.[9] Prostitution was widespread and democratic, patronised by members of all classes, and effectively forced upon many young women to supplement their daily wages. Estimates place the number of prostitutes in Paris in mid-century at around forty to sixty thousand, and public opinion was widely lenient to such women.

Nevertheless, unlike in the Greek enlightenment, unlike in the Roman golden or silver ages, unlike even in the Italian Renaissance, aristocratic women were central to the French enlightenment. It would be women to whom many of the great works of the enlightenment were addressed, as we have seen with Diderot's "Letter on the Blind" (chapter 4), or who would feature in these works as interlocutors and heroines, like Roxana in *Persian Letters*, Julie de L'Espinasse in *D'Alembert's Dream*, or Suzanne Simonin, the heroine of Diderot's *The Nun*. The new philosophy, as we know, was not restricted to the male-only universities, and the new *philosophes* were themselves increasingly either free-thinking aristocrats, like Montesquieu and d'Holbach, or authors who made their money by their wits, like Diderot. (Voltaire, middle-class but soon independently wealthy, is somewhere in between.) The culture which developed in Paris, in which the most liberal ideas were discussed, was however a highly feminised elite culture, as Jean-Jacques Rousseau would for his part complain:

> It was a brilliant age because the women in it were brilliant, combining brains with beauty beyond any precedent. It was because of them that French writers warmed thought with feeling and graced philosophy with wit. How could Voltaire have become Voltaire without them? Even blunt and cloudy Diderot confessed: "Women accustom us to discuss with charm and clearness the driest and thorniest subjects. We talk to them unceasingly; we wish them to listen; we are afraid of tiring or boring them. Hence, we develop a particular method of explaining ourselves easily, and this method passes from conversation into style."[10]

If the enlightenment in Paris is identified with any one social form, it is with the famous *salons*. Many of the most renowned salons were run by decorated, highly refined women, famed for their skill in the conversational arts, or hosting and directing conversation. In these convivial surrounds, savants gave lectures, authors read aloud their forthcoming books, and the latest works and subjects were discussed, all amidst wine and fine dining. From the time of the regency, the Marquise de Lambert every Tuesday entertained scientists and aristocrats; every Wednesday, she hosted writers, artists, and scholars, including Fontenelle, Montesquieu, and Marivaux. In the following decades, Madame de Tencin would be *salonière* to Fontenelle, Montesquieu, Marivaux, Helvétius, Marmontel, Duclos, Mably, Condorcet, and other *philosophes*. From 1739, Madame du Deffand's salon would entertain Henault, Montesquieu, Voltaire, and Emilie du Châtelet, as well as Diderot, d'Alembert, Marmontel, and Madame de Staal. Later, equally famed salons would be hosted by Mademoiselle de l'Espinasse and Madame Geoffrin, as well as Madame d'Epinay.[11]

Several of these extraordinary enlightenment women were also patronesses, and some of the leading correspondents of the period. After Voltaire fled from Paris following the public burning of *Letters on the English*, Madame de Deffand began a correspondence in 1736 with him which is itself a classic of French literature. Then there was Diderot's Sophie, Louise Henriette Volland, with whom he would maintain a correspondence and love spanning the last three decades of his life. "Ah, Grimm, what a woman!", he could declare to Baron Friedrich Melchior von Grimm, the famous chronicler of the French enlightenment:

> How tender she is, how sweet, how honest, delicate, sensible! . . . We don't know any more than she does in customs, morals, feelings, in an infinity of important things. She has her judgment, views, ideas, her own way of thinking, formed according to reason, truth, and common sense; neither public opinion nor authorities, nor anything, can subjugate them.[12]

Finally, many of these enlightenment women were authors in their own right. Claudine Alexandrine Guérin de Tencin's pseudonymous *Mémoires du comte de Comminge* was published in 1735, garnering both critical and popular acclaim.[13] No account of the enlightenment can omit Émilie du Châtelet, an extraordinary thinker who translated Mandeville and Newton, corresponded with leading mathematicians, wrote scientific works led by her *Essai sur l'optique* (1737), her *Dissertation sur la nature et la propagation du feu* (1737), and her 1740 *Institutions de Physique*, and undertook critical biblical readings with Voltaire.[14]

Sexuality and gender were in fact coming to the forefront of philosophical debate and cultural concern. It is important to stress at this juncture just how "sexy" the literature of the enlightenment was.[15] The new philosophy was itself distributed as contraband, like pornography, in brown paper bags, or else smuggled into France illicitly, having been published by necessity beyond the borders. From early on, moreover, many of the flood of philosophical tales of the period had highly sexualised content. Diderot's *Indiscreet Jewels*, one episode of which we met in chapter 4, takes as its premise that female genitalia can speak, and can be heard by way of a Congan Sultan's magic ring. But many enlightenment novels, like Diderot's *The Nun*, focus on female heroines and their educational and sexual awakenings. We already know how radical was Zulema's tale of Anais in *Persian Letters*, positioning a heroine as Christ or God Herself, and celebrating Persian women's overthrow of a seraglio so as to establish a new covenant between the sexes (ch. 2).

But take *Thérèse philosophe* (*Thérèse the Philosopher*), by Jean-Baptiste de Boyer, Marquis d'Argens, for another topical example.[16] The title, with its female philosopher, is already eye-opening. Thérèse, from solid bourgeois stock, becomes a student of Father Dirrag, a Jesuit who secretly teaches her materialist philosophy. Thérèse spies on Dirrag in the act of counselling her fellow student, Mademoiselle Eradice, and observes him using her spiritual ambitions, and the "holy rod" on her buttocks, to seduce her. Thérèse is placed in a convent, where she ails through abstinence and boredom. She is rescued by Madame C. and Abbé T., on whom she once again spies as they discuss libertine philosophy in between lovemaking. She is then seduced by Madame Bois-Laurier, an experienced prostitute, before finally meeting an unnamed count who desires her for his mistress. The count makes a bet with her: If she can last two weeks in a room full of erotic books and paintings without masturbating, he will not pursue her further. Our philosopher loses this bet and becomes the count's mistress.

On the basis of novels like *Thérèse philosophe*, it is easy to agree with Philipp Blom that passion, desire, and moral sympathy were more important than "reason" to the enlightenment.[17] Some authors for this reason indeed designate the enlightenment as the "age of sensibility".[18] It was also, as we will now consider, an age of growing philosophical calls for sexual liberation, marriage reform, and revised understandings of the relations between the sexes. The calling into question of Christianity, which we have everywhere seen; the calling into question of the Cartesian mind–body dualism, which we saw in chapters 3 and 4; as well as the defence of human dignity and educability, independent of creed or nationality, which we saw in chapter 5—all of these threads came together in the enlightenment to create the cultural climate out of which, in due course, feminism would emerge by the time of the French Revolution.

WHAT TAHITIANS CAN TEACH EUROPEANS ABOUT LOVE, SEX, AND MARRIAGE

Denis Diderot loved women, and his attraction to defying and baiting the authorities also drew him towards his own *érudit libertinage*. For Diderot, a man of great passions, the old link Plato had established between the *eros* for letters, and sexual *eros*, was very real. His increasingly open materialism committed him to the position that the rational or "spiritual" must be one with the bodily, including the sexual.[19] Perhaps the most comical, but deadly serious, example of this is in the passage in *D'Alembert's Dream*, wherein the dreaming philosopher-mathematician relates a fevered cosmic vision of the transformation of all species to his lover, Julie de l'Espinasse whose climax is, well, a climax:

> "Who knows the races of animals which came before us? Who knows the races of animals which will come after ours? Everything changes, everything passes away. Only the totality remains. The world begins and ends without ceasing. At every instant it is at its beginning and at its end . . . In this immense ocean of matter, no single molecule resembles any other, and no single molecule resembles itself for more than a moment: *Rerum novus nascitur ordo* [a new order of things is born]—there's its eternal slogan." Then he sighed and added: "Oh, the vanity of our thoughts! The poverty in glory and in our works! The wretched smallness of our vision! There's nothing substantial except drinking, eating, living, loving, and sleeping. . . . Mademoiselle de l'Espinasse, where are you?"
>
> "I'm here."
>
> Then his face became flushed. I wanted to feel his pulse, but I didn't know where he had hidden his hand. It looked as though he was going through a convulsion. His mouth was half open, and his breath was forced. He gave a deep sigh, and then a fainter sigh, and then another deeper sigh. He turned his head on his pillow and went to sleep . . . At the end of a few moments, I saw a slight smile cross his lips.[20]

Nevertheless, Diderot's ribald celebration of women as objects of male desire is far from the entire picture, in terms of his advocacy for women's emancipation from their religious, social, and educational oppression. Diderot would become a fierce critic of the Christian sacrament of marriage, including, as in Montesquieu, out of genuine concern for women's educability and perfectibility.[21] "I have seen honest women shudder with horror at the approach of their husband", he would write:

I have seen them plunge into a bath, never believing themselves sufficiently cleansed from the filth of their [marital] duty . . . Many women will die without having felt the extremes of *volupté* . . . The highest happiness flees them even in the arms of the man they adore; whereas we [men] can find it lying next to a compliant woman whom we do not even like.[22]

Diderot's 1772 text *On Women* (*Sur la femme*) rails against disadvantages facing women:

more constrained and more neglected in their education, abandoned to the same capricious fate, with a soul that is more mobile, more delicate organs, none of that firmness, natural or acquired, which prepares us for life, reduced to silence in their adulthood.[23]

Yet the *philosophe*'s most extraordinary testament concerning sexuality, women, and marriage is undoubtedly his *Supplement to Bougainville's Voyage (Supplément au voyage de Bougainville, ou dialogue entre A et B sur l'inconvénient d'attacher des idées morales à certaines actions physiques qui n'en comportent pas*). Like *D'Alembert's Dream*, Diderot kept this *Supplement* from publication in his own lifetime.[24] As the penultimate enlightenment text we will look at here, it also brings together nearly every element we have in the previous chapters been reclaiming in the enlightenment: a self-othering that sees European customs through Tahitian eyes, biting anti-theological satire, and anti-colonialist rage.

The origins of the text lie in the 1766–1769 expedition by French explorer Louis-Antoine de Bougainville to the islands of Tahiti. In 1771, Bougainville published his *A Voyage around the World* (*Voyage autour du monde*). According to Tahitian customs, newcomers were greeted by:

people stripped to the waist in the presence of gods and high chiefs, and a high-ranking stranger was often greeted by a young girl swathed in layers of bark cloth who slowly turned around, unwinding the bark cloth from her body until she stood naked.[25]

For the French sailors, who had been aboard ship for six months, such a welcome seemed to portend a terrestrial paradise, or announce that they had arrived at a "New Kythara" peopled by goddesses. Bougainville confesses that it was nearly impossible to maintain his men's discipline—or his own.

With the appearance of Bougainville's chronicle, a literary journal asked Diderot to write a review, waving this red flag before the incorrigible *philosophe*. Diderot responded by writing a fictional philosophical "supplement" to Bougainville's voyage. This *Supplement* features two nameless Europeans, "A" and "B". They set about co-reading and debating what is advertised as an unpublished "supplement" written by Bougainville himself about his Tahitian voyage, too scandalous to go before the censors and the public.[26]

The full subtitle of Diderot's characteristically ludic and elusive text is significant: *Supplement to Bougainville's Voyage, or, a Dialogue Between A and B on the Inconvenience of Attaching Moral Ideas to Certain Physical Action which Do Not Attach/Belong to Them*. Given Bougainville's original, we can know that the "actions" in questions are those attending sexuality. But beyond this, a deeper question looms in Diderot's subtitle. Are societies' moral opinions wholly artificial, with different societies merely "attaching" their arbitrary prejudices onto actions which do not carry them? Or should not morality—and sexual morality, particularly—have its basis in nature, whatever that might mean?

The diegetic "Supplement" which A and B read, with us, opens with the speech of a Tahitian elder (187–192) on Bougainville's and his men's departure. Alongside Diderot's interpolations into *History of the Two Indies* (chapter 5), this speech is amongst the strongest anti-colonialist statements of the eighteenth century. Here again, the critical evaluation of the Europeans' actions has been put by Diderot into the mouth of a non-European Other. "And you, leader of these brigands who obey you, take your vessel swiftly from our shores", the Tahitian Elder begins:

> We are innocent and happy, and you can only spoil our happiness. We follow the pure instinct of nature, and you have tried to efface her imprint from our hearts. Here all things are for all, and you have preached to us I know not what distinctions between mine and thine (187).

From this pointed evocation of Diderot's old friend Jean-Jacques Rousseau's *Discourse on the Origins of Inequality*—a text which had famously argued for the "noble savage"[27]—we pass immediately to the absurdity of the French having arrived on Tahiti and planted their flag to claim it as their own. By what right have these visitors dared to proclaim "this land belongs to the people of France"?, the Elder thunders. How would the French feel if, as in a mirror, the Tahitians arrived on European shores and, planting a piece of cloth in the soil, declared that "these lands belonged to the people of Tahiti?" (188)

The French are neither Gods nor Demons, the Elder reasons, and there is an Aristotelian echo here (188). Elementary moral reciprocity (cf. chapter 3), and those laws of hospitality Diderot was to propound in *History of the Two Indies* (chapter 5), ought to govern concourse between peoples. "You are not slaves; you would suffer death rather than be enslaved, yet you want to make slaves of us!", the Elder protests. "Do you believe, then, that the Tahitian does not know how to die in defence of his liberty?" (188)

French and Tahitian, in the Elder's view, share one human nature: "We respected our own image in you" (188). It is the European who falsely asserts fundamental difference, in a way that flatters his vanity: "This Tahitian, whom you want to treat as a chattel, as a dumb animal; this Tahitian is your brother. You are both children of Nature—what right do you have over him that he does not have over you?" (188)

There are telling biblical, Edenic resonances in the Elder's discourse, setting up the *Supplement*'s ongoing anti-theological plays. "You killed the Tahitian who ran to greet you, crying 'Taio-friend!' ", the Old Man addresses Bougainville,

> because he was tempted by the glitter of your little *serpent's eggs* [jewels]. He gave you his *fruit*; he offered you his wife and daughter; he gave you his hut to live in—and you killed him for taking a handful of those little glass beads without asking your permission (191).

When the Old Man finishes his exordium, urging the Europeans never to return, Diderot affords him an almost Mosaic *gravitas*, able to command the natural elements themselves:

> He finished speaking, and in an instant the throng of natives disappeared. A vast silence reigned over the whole extent of the island, and nothing was to be heard but the dry whistling of the wind and the dull pounding of the waves along the whole length of the coast. It was as though the winds and waters had heard the old man's voice and obeyed him (192).

The most famous of the *Supplement*'s scenes follows soon after. Bougainville's chaplain is recounting the hospitality offered him by Orou, a Tahitian who has learnt the Europeans' tongue:

> When he was about to go to bed, Orou, who had stepped outside with his family, reappeared and presented to him his wife and three girls—all naked as Eve [*sic*]—and said to him: "You are young and healthy and you have just had a good supper. He who sleeps alone, sleeps badly; at night a man needs a woman at his side. Here is my wife and here are my daughters. Choose whichever one pleases you most, but if you would like to do me a favour, you will give your preference to my youngest girl, who has not yet had any children" (194).

Diderot is surely having fun at this moment. But there is a serious point beneath the play. The shocked chaplain immediately protests that "his religion, his holy orders, his moral standards and his sense of decency all prevented him from accepting Orou's invitation" (194). Orou, bemused, then wants to know what this "religion" is, since it forbids you to partake of an innocent pleasure to which Nature, the sovereign mistress of us all, invites everybody. It seems to prevent you from bringing one of your fellow creatures into the world, from doing a favour asked of you by a father, a mother, and their children, from repaying the kindness of a host, and from enriching a nation by giving it an additional citizen (195).

As for the chaplain's morals, as Orou sees things, "your chief duty is to be a man and to show gratitude" to a gracious host. Orou underlines that this is the Tahitian custom. He is wholly within his rights as a father to offer his wife and daughters to his guest. If the chaplain is too tired, that is one thing. If he is worried about his health, that is another. As things stand, he has offended both Orou and the women. Orou thus closes with a further appeal to his guest "to do a good deed and have the pleasure of honouring one of my daughters in the sight of her sisters and friends? Come, be generous" (195).

What on earth is going on here? On one hand, Diderot is placing before his readers, stark naked, the extent of differences between a European and a non-European culture—even (and above all) concerning sexuality, this oldest and most universal of human pastimes. As the text unfolds, and Orou and the chaplain discuss further, we learn that Tahitian sexual customs are opposed to those of Christian Paris in almost every conceivable way. Above all, there is the Tahitian lack of anything like a sense of "sinfulness" about sexuality, its pleasures, and its components of play and display. Nubile young women uncover their breasts and take pride in arousing the young men (190, 204–05, 220–21). As for marriage, unlike in Europe at this time, it is wholly voluntary for both parties, and revocable by either. (It need only last one month, to avoid confusions surrounding paternity [206].) In cases of "divorce", if that is the word, half of the children go with either spouse, becoming a dowry to new marriages (202). In cases where a young woman can attract no partner, her father may without censure sleep with her, and more rarely, a mother may sleep with her son to give him, and the people, children. For the Tahitians consider having children in any circumstances as the greatest gift of nature and joy in life (202).

On the other hand, by arraying before his readers' eyes these cultural differences, Diderot wants to provoke our philosophical reflection. The *Supplement* is once more asking enlightened readers to step outside of their taken-for-granted assumptions for long enough to ask which society's sexual customs might be more "natural", and how we might decide this question. "Is our moral code a better or a worse one than your own?", Orou asks:

This is an easy question to answer. Does the country you were born in have more people than it can support? If it does, then your morals are neither better nor worse than ours. Or can it feed more people than it now has? Then our morals are better than yours (195).

In fact, we see, Tahitian sexual mores are about more than the innocent enjoyment of sexual pleasure, as a boon of nature, and, for Diderot, an affront to Christian prudery. There is also a "biopolitics" of reproduction at issue. Orou comments to the chaplain that "you would find it hard to believe how much our morals have been improved on these points by the fact that we have come to identify in our minds the idea of public and private wealth with the idea of increasing the population" (210). It is this goal which in fact underlies their practice of hosts' offering their daughters to visitors which had so affronted the chaplain:

> When you came, we let you do what you liked with our women and girls. You were astonished and your gratitude made us laugh. You thanked us, even though we were levying the heaviest of all taxes on you and your companions . . . [w]hen you go away, you will leave with us a brood of children (211).

As for how European sexual mores appear in the eyes of the Tahitians, in the classic enlightenment mirror the *Supplement* sets up, the Elder's opening speech already points the way towards what Orou's discourse will confirm. The Christian sense of sexuality is for *them* an unhappy fall:

> The notion of crime and the fear of disease have come among us only with your coming. Now our enjoyments, formerly so sweet, are attended with guilt and terror. That man in black, who stands near to you and listens to me, has spoken to our young men, and I know not what he has said to our young girls, but our youths are hesitant and our girls blush (190).

"I should be sorry to give offense by anything I might say, but if you don't mind, I'll tell you what I think", Orou announces at one point to the chaplain (198). What follows is a strident critique of Christian norms of love, sex, and marriage. For Orou, such customs are unnatural. As such, they are "admirably calculated to increase the number of crimes". He explains:

> When people take it upon themselves to rearrange all ideas of justice and propriety to suit their own whims, to apply or remove the names of things in a completely arbitrary manner, to associate the ideas of good and evil with certain actions or to dissociate them for no reason save caprice, then of course people will blame each other, accuse each other, suspect each other, tyrannize, become jealous and envious, deceive and wound one another, conceal, dissimulate, and spy on one another, catch each other out, quarrel and tell lies. Girls will deceive their parents, husbands their wives and wives their husbands. Unmarried girls— yes, I am sure of it—unmarried girls will suffocate their babies; suspicious

fathers will neglect or show contempt for their own rightful children; mothers will abandon their infants and leave them to the mercy of fate (201).

The chaplain admits that all these sad things happen in Christian Europe. Orou by contrast will have to have the very meaning of the words "fornication", "incest", and "adultery" explained to him, since they are unknown in Tahiti (208). European marriage customs are contrary to nature, secondly, in their demand for permanency and monogamy, when:

> in truth is there anything so senseless as a precept that forbids us to heed the changing impulses that are inherent in our being, or commands that require a degree of constancy which is not possible, that violate the liberty of both male and female by chaining them perpetually to one another? (198–99)

Thirdly, they are unnatural, since they assign ownership of women to men, assuming "that a thinking being, one that has feelings and a sense of freedom, can be the property of another being like himself", a clearly repulsive proposition (198).

Orou's discourse hence resembles nothing so much as what many of Diderot's readers would have recognised as a "natural law" position, ironically close to that of the Catholic Church, which Diderot is here attacking. "Would you like to know what is good and what is bad in all times and places?", Orou asks again:

> Pay close attention to the nature of things and actions, to your relations with your fellow creatures, or the effect of your behaviour on your own well-being and on the general welfare. You are mad if you believe that there is anything in the universe, high or low, that can add or subtract from the laws of nature. Her eternal will is that good shall be chosen rather than evil, and the general welfare rather than the individual's well-being. You may decree the opposite, but you will not be obeyed (200).

As things stand, Orou diagnoses European humanity as prey to a kind of internal "civil war", between the laws of their natures, and the artificial laws imposed by civil and religious authorities (198–99; 218–19). "One day you would be told, on behalf of one of your three masters: 'Kill', and in all good conscience you would be obliged to kill. Another day they might say: 'Steal', and you would be bound to steal. Or: 'Do not eat of this fruit' [*sic*], and you would not dare to eat of it" (199). But laws which deny human nature cannot be followed, however heroically figures like the chaplain may try to do their duty:

These things are so because they must be so, and your society, whose well-ordered ways your chief boasts to you about, can't be anything but a swarm of hypocrites who secretly trample the laws under foot, or a multitude of wretched beings who serve as instruments for inflicting willing torture upon themselves, or imbeciles in whom prejudice has utterly silenced the voice of nature, or ill-fashioned creatures in whom nature cannot claim her rights (202).

To repeat: We once again find ourselves with Diderot's *Supplement* in the presence of a strident critique of European customs, placed by a leading *philosophe* in the mouths of non-European Others: hardly the stuff of unregenerate Eurocentrism. The question of whether Diderot himself wholly "sides" with Orou and the Tahitians against Christian mores and modern European civilization in this text is far more difficult to ascertain.[28] The final discussion between A and B after Orou's discourse breaks off,[29] with B closing with the "assurance" that nowhere on Earth are there people happier than the Tahitians. Nevertheless, Diderot's A is more equivocal, without in any way approaching the kind of stadial Eurocentric narratives we have seen critics of "the enlightenment" charge against all of its proponents. "I have often thought that for every individual the sum total good and bad was different", A reflects:

but that for a species of animals there was a definite aggregate of happiness and unhappiness that was not subject to change. So perhaps, for all our striving, we do ourselves as much harm as good. Perhaps we have only tormented ourselves in order to make both sides of the equation a little larger [by developing more technologically advanced societies] without disturbing in the least the eternally necessary balance between its two sides (226).

One thing which is clear from the *Supplement* is that Diderot accepts Orou's criticisms of the Christian denaturing of sexuality and marriage, including the double standard imposed by men on women. Why is this "act so solemn in its purpose, an act to which nature invites us by so powerful a summons—how did it come about that this act . . . has become the chief source of our depravity and bad conduct?", he has A ask (222). B's answer, which cites Orou's authority and is not challenged by Diderot, recalls Montesquieu's Anais's position in *Persian Letters* (chapter 2). Present European customs reflect the "tyranny" of men, who have converted marriage into an institution for the ownership of women. They benefit political and religious authorities which inculcate artificial ideas of virtue and vice in ordinary people, which they will each by nature nevertheless transgress innumerable times in their lives (223).

WOLLSTONECRAFT, DE GOUGES, AND THE ADVENT OF ENLIGHTENMENT FEMINISM

With Denis Diderot's *Supplement to Bougainville's Voyage*, we stand at the threshold of the development of enlightenment-era feminism. That step will rightfully be taken by two famed women, one English and one French, in the years of the French Revolution. With it, the kinds of critical self-othering which we have seen defines key enlightenment texts from Montesquieu forwards—learning to see oneself in the Other, and from their perspectives—gives place to the direct voicing of the Other's perspectives. In this way, the argumentative arc of this little book also reaches its rightful culmination by considering the vindications of the rights of women we find in Olympe de Gouges and Mary Wollstonecraft.

Olympe de Gouges' *Declaration of the Rights of Woman and the Female Citizen* was issued in early 1791, following the non-take-up of the Women's Petition to the National Assembly by the new revolutionary government.[30] "This revolution will only take effect when all women become fully aware of their deplorable condition, and of the rights they have lost in society", de Gouges contended. The famous opening of the *Declaration* apostrophises the privileged sex: "Man, are you capable of being fair? A woman is asking: at least you will allow her that right. Tell me: what gave you the sovereign right to oppress my sex?"[31]

The ensuing articles of the *Declaration* self-consciously echo and subvert those of the *Declaration of Man and Citizen*, changing the nouns from the exclusive "men" of the latter to the conjunction "men and women". "Woman is born free and remains equal to man in rights. Social distinctions may only be based on common utility", Article 1 contends. "The only limit to the exercise of the natural rights of woman is the perpetual tyranny that man opposes to it", Article 4 charges. In the language of the enlighteners, de Gouges enjoins that "these limits must be reformed by the laws of nature and reason". Women should be granted equal right to public offices:

> All citizens including women are equally admissible to all public dignities, offices and employments, according to their capacity, and with no other distinction than that of their virtues and talents (Article 6).

Article 17, addressing marriage and divorce, like Diderot's *Supplement*, calls for the end of the double standard. Within marriage as outside it, women and men should be equal in the eyes of the law. Either party, as free beings, should be able to end the union. Upon divorce, property should be split evenly between them, if not their progeny, as amongst the Tahitians (see ch. 6). The woman's property should no longer be alienable "without reason", just as the women cannot seize the men's. In case there were any doubt, de Gouges' "Postscript" situates the document squarely in the lineage of the enlightenment, whose cultural and philosophical challenges to the prejudices enshrined by Church and Monarchy had made it possible. "Woman, wake up", de Gouges enjoins her sisters, "the tocsin of reason is resounding throughout the universe: acknowledge your rights".

It is, however, with an Englishwoman, perhaps appropriately when we recall chapter 3, that we must look to find the most philosophically developed vindication of the rights of women which de Gouges had claimed for Frenchwomen in 1791. As Voltaire had looked to the English at the start of the enlightenment, Mary Wollstonecraft looked to the predominant roles we saw women playing in enlightenment Paris as exemplary in *A Vindication of the Rights of Woman*. "In France there is understandably a more general diffusion of knowledge than in any other part of the European world, and I attribute it, in part[ial] measure, to the social intercourse that has long subsisted between the sexes", she writes.[32]

And what then are the philosophical bases of Wollstonecraft's claims on behalf of women? Like the enlightenment monogenists concerning race, like Montesquieu as early as 1721 in *Persian Letters*, she claims that women share a common nature with men, and equal capabilities for reason and virtue. The first chapter of *A Vindication of the Rights of Woman* hence argues that since natural rights are given by God—a key claim of the revolutionary declarations in America and France in the preceding years—it follows that for one segment of society to deny them to another segment is a sin.[33] So, why do men and women seem at present to be so unequal in capacities, and why, indeed, do many women behave so frivolously, like "spaniels" or "toys", in comparison to their men? Drawing on a Lockean idea with which we are well familiar, and which is already present in the *philosophe* Claude-Adrien Helvétius concerning the sexes, *A Vindication of the Rights of Woman* claims that the intellectual inequalities between the sexes were largely due to inequalities of education and opportunity.[34] They hail from the way women are presently nurtured, not from an essential nature, innate preponderance of emotion over intellect, or the like.

As things stand, women are treated by men as potential sexual playthings before marriage, and as decorative ornaments, obedient servants, and child-bearing and -rearing machines thereafter. Their minds are not cultivated, their opportunities are limited. So they can hardly be blamed for being "blown about by every momentary gust of feeling" and subject to "romantic, wavering feeling".[35] "Taught from their infancy that beauty is woman's sceptre, the mind shapes itself to the body, and, roaming around its gilt cage, only seeks to adorn its prison".[36] All of the feminine faults of that time—the affectation of weakness and timidity, which feeds and pleases the male's assumption of superiority, the addiction to cards, gossip, astrology, sentimentality, and literary trash, since women have little access to better entertainments, the absorption in dress and self-admiration, since appearances are so highly valued as means for female advancement—none of these bespeak anything essential, unchangeable, or incontestable, as far as Wollstonecraft is concerned:

> Nature, music, poetry, and gallantry all tend to make women the creatures of sensation . . . and this overstretched sensibility naturally relaxes the other powers of the mind and prevents intellect from attaining that sovereignty which it ought to attain; . . . for the exercise of the understanding, as life advances, is the only method pointed out by Nature to calm the passions.[37]

It is the same argument that Jean-Jacques Rousseau and others had made concerning the "slavish natures" of historically enslaved peoples. They despair of attaining freedom, and become accustomed to their chains and modes of conduct which appease their masters, who then point to these behaviours to justify the subjection.[38] Wollstonecraft attacks the authors of "conduct-books" like James Fordyce and John Gregory, as well as educational philosophers such as Jean-Jacques Rousseau, who argue that a woman does not need a rational education, comparable to that of men.[39] By contrast, along with other female reformers such as the historian Catharine Macaulay and Hester Chapone,[40] Wollstonecraft argues that women were indeed capable of rational thought and deserved to be educated. Men remain stronger physically than women: "Let it not be concluded that I wish to invert the order of things; I have already granted, that, from the constitution of their bodies, men seem to be designed by Providence to attain a greater degree of virtue".[41] Nevertheless, there are the same virtues for men and women:

> I speak collectively of the whole sex; but I see not the shadow of a reason to conclude that their virtues should differ in respect to their nature. In fact, how can they, if virtue has only one eternal standard? I must therefore, if I reason consequentially, as strenuously maintain that they have the same simple direction, as that there is a God.[42]

Wollstonecraft hence advocates that both sexes should be given equal chances to develop mind and body. Boys and girls should be educated together, with the same curriculum and, where possible, the same or equivalent sports. Every woman should be made sufficiently strong in body and competent in mind to earn her own living if necessary. The goal of this education should be moral, intellectual, and spiritual independence. "The most perfect education", she writes, is "an exercise of the understanding as is best calculated to strengthen the body and form the heart. Or, in other words, to enable the individual to attach such habits of virtue as will render it independent".[43]

Wollstonecraft, with this said, does not ask or wish for women to renounce their maternal roles, or their roles as wives. However, she does argue that husbands would benefit from having real equals as their life partners. Wives should be the rational "companions" of their husbands, and even pursue at least some professional careers, should they so choose, at that time a radical proposal. Then she adds, extraordinarily, that "they might, also, study politics . . . Business of various kinds, they might likewise pursue".[44] Indeed, in her earlier *A Vindication of the Rights of Men, in a Letter to the Right Honourable Edmund Burke; Occasioned by His Reflections on the Revolution in France* (1790), Wollstonecraft had already argued that "women ought to have representatives [in Parliament], instead of being governed without having any direct share allowed them in the deliberations of government".[45] The extraordinary radicality of these egalitarian proposals is clear, when we recall that in fact in Europe, women's suffrage (for women over thirty) and the right to stand as MPs would await 1918 in Wollstonecraft's homeland, the green Isle of England. Far from working against marital happiness, and the longevity of Christian marriages, these measures would stop so many men getting bored and seeking out mistresses or the company of other men. Maternal training in nursing, in particular, might make families smaller and stronger.[46] Wollstonecraft's ideal is the educated mother in equal union with an educated male, which we can see is modelled in her own enlightened marriage to William Godwin.[47]

What then of women's sexuality, which we have seen had also become an explicit concern in enlightenment literature? Wollstonecraft, no less than Diderot, advocates for a woman's right to feel, and to confess, physical satisfaction in coitus. She warns both sexes that "love considered as an animal appetite cannot long feed itself without expiring". In that sense, "it is the most evanescent of all passions."[48] Some twentieth-century critics have accordingly seen Wollstonecraft as hostile to female desire, or even charged her with wanting to make women like men.[49] Hers is most certainly what we call an egalitarian—not a difference—feminism, since for Wollstonecraft, in her times, it was precisely the differences in how men and women were understood and treated which she felt needed to be changed. Wollstonecraft hence, for instance, sees no natural or reasonable ground as to why women should be so severely punished throughout their lives for even a single departure from chastity, whilst "men preserve their respectability during the indulgence of vice".[50] Equal in the eyes of God as in their capacities for virtue, there can be no reason to sustain such differences beyond the wish of one sex to maintain prerogatives over the other, based on nothing more substantial than physical strength and unquestioned tradition.

SELF-OTHERING, FROM IMAGINARY TO REAL

With the work of Mary Wollstonecraft, then, we have come full circle in this little book. Montesquieu had called for a radical reconsideration of the theologico-sexual situation in Europe, recognising women's equal capacities for virtue and intelligence (chapter 2). De Gouges and Wollstonecraft answer to this call. The imagined others of Zulema and Anais in *Persian Letters* have become real women, emboldened after two generations of enlightenment social, ethical, and epistemic critique to speak in their own voices and vindicate their own rights. Voltaire had been exiled to England and aspired to transform French culture by holding out countermodels of religious toleration, and new, experimental, and fallibilistic modes of inquiry (chapter 3). With Wollstonecraft, once more, we have an Englishwoman looking across the Channel the other way, to the enlightenment culture of France, as her inspiration to call for equal educational, legal, and even economic and political rights to men. All this, a century before any European nation or satellite would so much as give women the vote. Diderot had appealed to the practices of the Tahitians to challenge European assumptions about the reasonableness of their sexual and marital customs, and plead for the independence of women (as we saw above). De Gouges and Wollstonecraft plead in their own voices, and de Gouges addresses a declaration to the French National Assembly.

The History of the Two Indies, finally (chapter 5), had reached its most radical pitch in Diderot's call for a "Black Spartacus" to rise up and overthrow the colonial oppressors. On 21 August 1791, the slaves of "Saint-Domingue" (Haiti) rebelled against their colonial masters, forcing the French government to grant freedom to people of colour in the colonies in March 1792. In February 1794, their hand being forced by British and Spanish invasions of the island and the need for Haitians' support, the French National Convention abolished slavery in all French colonies:

> Representatives of the French people, until now our decrees of liberty have been selfish, and only for ourselves. But today we proclaim it to the universe, and generations to come will glory in this decree; we are proclaiming universal liberty . . . We are working for future generations; let us launch liberty into the colonies.[51]

Four further years of struggle against the British and Spanish ensued, in which the French became increasingly reliant on independent Haitian forces led by the brilliant, self-educated, freed slave, Toussaint Louverture. Toussaint would assume leadership of the island in 1798, and issue its own independent constitution in 1801. This "Black Spartacus", we are told, kept a quarto edition of Raynal and Diderot's *Histoire philosophique des Deux*

Indes on his study table (chapter 5). Yet, as Sudhir Hazareesingh comments, by independently effecting the Haitian revolution, Louverture "not only reappropriated the *Histoire philosophique*, but brought the text to life in a glorious display of erudition, swagger and wit".[52] Enlightenment ideas, always aimed at changing the world, had passed from the pens of the *philosophes* into the actions of the Others their writings had evoked, and become revolutionary in ways which continue to reverberate today.

NOTES

1. The historical information in the following paragraphs is drawn from Durant and Durant, *The Age of Voltaire*, 286–302.
2. Blackstone, at Mary Wollstonecraft—Equal Rights for Women | Libertarianism. org.
3. Of course, the great majority of the peasants of either sex could not read. In the villages and towns, those who had learned to read seldom read anything other than what concerned their daily work. Whilst the catechism was widely known, only in the cities was knowledge of literature, science, or history typically more widespread. In many rural communities, the municipal authorities could barely write.
4. Curran, *Diderot and the Art of Thinking Freely*, 42–46.
5. Durant and Durant, *The Age of Voltaire*, 298.
6. Durant and Durant, 286–91.
7. At Durant and Durant, *The Age of Voltaire*, 291.
8. Denis Diderot, *The Nun*, trans. Dennis Tancock (London: Penguin, 1972).
9. Philipp Blom, *A Wicked Company: The Forgotten Radicalism of the European Enlightenment* (New York: Basic Books, 2010), 187–88.
10. Durant and Durant, *The Age of Voltaire*, 302.
11. Durant and Durant, "The Salons", in *The Age of Voltaire*, 298–302; Dena Goodman, "Enlightenment Salons: The Convergence of Female and Philosophic Ambitions", *Eighteenth-Century Studies* 22, no. 3, *Special Issue: The French Revolution in Culture* (Spring 1989): 329–50; Annetta Black, "The Lady Salonières of the Enlightenment", The Lady Salonnières of the Enlightenment | ODD SALON.
12. Diderot to Grimm, at Blom, *A Wicked Company*, 227.
13. Durant and Durant, *The Age of Voltaire*, 299–300.
14. She also co-authored an extensive critical commentary on the book of Genesis with Voltaire. See Karen Detlefsen, Émilie du Châtelet (Stanford Encyclopedia of Philosophy) (2014).
15. Blom, *A Wicked Company*, 184–98.
16. Jean-Baptiste de Boyer Marquis d'Argens, *Thérèse the Philosopher*, in *Thérèse the Philosopher and The Story of Mrs. Bois-Laurier*, trans. Charles Carrington (Locus Elm Press, 2014: Kindle Edition). See Blom, *A Wicked Company*, 189–90.
17. Blom, *A Wicked Company*.

18. See Jennifer Riskin, *Science in the Age of Sensibility: The Sentimental Empiricists of the French Enlightenment* (Chicago: University of Chicago Press, 2002); Robertson, esp. *The Enlightenment,* 32–37 with 260–350. See also Sylvana Tomaselli, "Reason", in *The Blackwell Companion to the Enlightenment,* ed. John W. Yolton (Oxford, UK: Blackwell, 1991), 446: "It would be mistaken to think of reason as the rallying cry of Enlightenment thinkers except in so far as it was opposed to faith, and the Age of Reason opposed to the Age of Superstition. If one's gaze shifts away from the battles with l'*Infâme*, then the 'Age of Sentiments', 'Sentimentality', 'Feelings', 'Passions', 'Pleasure', 'Love' or 'Imagination' are apter titles for the movement of ideas in the eighteenth century".

19. Blom, *A Wicked Company,* 185–90.

20. Denis Diderot, *D'Alembert's Dream,* in *Rameau's Nephew and D'Alembert's Dream,* trans. Leonard Tanock (London: Penguin, 1966), 174–75.

21. Blom, *A Wicked Company,* 227–28.

22. Diderot, at Blom, *A Wicked Company,* 227.

23. Diderot, at Blom, *A Wicked Company,* 227.

24. Denis Diderot, *Supplement to Bougainville's Voyage,* in *Rameau's Nephew and Other Works,* trans. Jacques Barzan and Ralph H. Brown (Indianapolis/Cambridge: Hackett Publishing co., 1956), 179–228. In this section, all bracketed page numbers refer to this text and edition.

25. Bougainville, cited in Marion Diamond, "The New Cythara and the Transit of Venus". See Anne Salmond, Aphrodite's Island: The European Discovery of Tahiti (London: Viking, 2016).

26. So, yes, Diderot's *Supplement* features two people reading Bougainville's (non-existent) "supplement" in the text: a characteristic hall of mirrors which Diderot and Voltaire and other enlighteners liked to set up to, in one register as a way to avoid censors assigning controversial opinions to them.

27. Jean-Jacques Rousseau, *Discourse on the Origins of Inequality* (London: Britannica, 1952).

28. See, for examples, D. Garraway, "Parodic Mimicry and Utopia in Diderot's Supplement", in *Postcolonial Enlightenment,* eds. D. Carey et al. (Oxford, UK: Oxford University Press, 2009), 220–31; Sunil Agnani, "*Doux Commerce, Douce Colonisation:* Diderot and the Two Indies of the French Enlightenment", *The Anthropology of the Enlightenment,* ed. by Larry Wolff and Marco Cipoloni (Stanford: Stanford University Press, 2007), 65–84; Sharon A. Stanley, "Unraveling Natural Utopia: Diderot's Supplement to the Voyage of Bougainville", *Political Theory* 37, no. 2 (2009): 266–89.

29. Compare the resounding denunciation of the "barbarism" of asking men (priests) and women (nuns) to become chaste, at 213.

30. Olympe de Gouges, The Declaration of the Rights of Woman (September 1791) · LIBERTY, EQUALITY, FRATERNITY: EXPLORING THE FRENCH REVOUTION (chnm.org).

31. This preface is included here: The Rights of Women by Olympe de Gouges (csulb.edu).

32. Mary Wollstonecraft, "To M. Talleyrand-Perigord, Late Bishop of Audin", in *A Vindication of the Rights of Woman*, Digital Edition 1.0 (Kaysville, UT: Gibbs Smith, 2019), 10. The French, Wollstonecraft claims, also "admit more of mind into their notions of beauty" than her own compatriots. As such, they "give the preference to women of thirty. . . . They allow women to be in their most perfect state when vivacity gives place to reason, and to that majestic seriousness of character which marks maturity".

33. Wollstonecraft, "The Rights and Involved Duties of Mankind Considered", in *Vindication*, 20–28.

34. Wollstonecraft, *Vindication*, esp. 31–44. See Wootton, "Helvétius: From Radical Enlightenment to Revolution"; Ballinger, "The Idea of Social Progress through Education in the French Enlightenment Period".

35. Wollstonecraft, *Vindication*, 91.
36. Wollstonecraft, *Vindication*, 56.
37. Wollstonecraft, *Vindication*, 76.
38. See Jean-Jacques Rousseau, *Social Contract* (London: Britannica, 1952), I, 5.
39. Wollstonecraft, *Vindication*, 51–52, 53–54, 61
40. See Karen Green, "The Rights of Women and the Equal Rights of Men", *Political Theory*, 49, no. 3 (2021): 403–30.
41. Wollstonecraft, *Vindication*, 37.
42. Wollstonecraft, *Vindication*, 37.
43. Wollstonecraft, *Vindication*, 31.
44. Wollstonecraft, *Vindication*, 175.
45. Wollstonecraft, at Will and Ariel Durant, *The Age of Napoleon* (New York: Simon & Schuster, 1975), 365.
46. Wollstonecraft, *Vindication*, 164, 168.
47. Wollstonecraft, *Vindication*, 31, 82, 177, 196.
48. Wollstonecraft, *Vindication*, 38.
49. See Harriet Devine Jump, *Mary Wollstonecraft and the critics, 1788–2001* (London: Routledge, 2003).
50. Wollstonecraft, *Vindication*, 157.
51. Laurent Dubois; John D. Garrigus, *Slave Revolution in the Caribbean, 1789–1804 A Brief History with Documents* (Bedford/St. Martins, 2006), document 26.
52. Sudhir Hazareesingh, *Black Spartacus: The Epic Life of Toussaint Louverture* (New York: Farrar, Straus and Giroux, 2020), 11.

Conclusion
What Was the Enlightenment?

"A day will come when the libels published against the most illustrious people of this century will be raised up from out of the dust by the wicked from the same spirit that dictated them", Denis Diderot wrote in 1782. Here as elsewhere, the great *philosophe* has proven far-sighted. For, if even a sizable part of the evidences we've documented in this book are probative, then thinkers who hail from the political Left find themselves in an especially uncanny position. By the Left, to be clear, I mean anyone who believes in the abiding truth and worth of post-enlightenment ideals of the equal dignity of all human beings, in all peoples' shared capacities for rationality and the virtues, and (as such) in the continuing need to struggle to make the ideals of liberty, equality, and fraternity more meaningful for more people.

This book has set out to show that many of the representations of the enlightenment hailing from different sources over the last generations have been decisively inaccurate: concerning Montesquieu, Voltaire, Diderot, and concerning many other enlightenment philosophers and naturalists. Although not technically "libelous", per Diderot's impassioned rhetoric, these representations are deeply mistaken about, and often seem to be simply unaware of, Voltaire's and the *Encyclopedists'* intellectual and political campaigns for toleration; Montesquieu's, Voltaire's, Jaucourt's, and others' arguments decrying the inhumanity of slavery; or indeed Raynal's, Diderot's, and others' inflammatory denunciations of European colonialism—as well as the direct lineage between the enlighteners' key ideas and the first European feminists led by Mary Wollstonecraft, as well as the revolutionary actions of Toussaint Louverture in Haiti.

Thinkers on the illiberal Right continue to revile the enlightenment campaigns for cultural pluralism, religious toleration, and expanded education, and the *lumières'* critical blows struck against unquestioned prejudice, superstition, and parochial assumptions about "our" superiority. The "thought leaders" of the Alt- and New Right today carry forward, and reheat, criticisms of science, rationality, liberalism, and campaigns for sexual and racial equality looking back to criticisms of the enlightenment from conservative and reactionary thinkers like Edmund Burke, Joseph de Maistre, Donoso Cortes, and Friedrich Nietzsche.

There is nothing surprising in this. What is so worrying is the popular traction that these ideas have been gaining in the new millennium, and what this rising popularity portends for the remainder of the twenty-first century. To trade the historical limitations and the growing problems that face societies, like the United States and Australia, still formally committed to constitutional governance protecting the equal rights of all citizens, for the open embrace of reactionary strong men justifying political illiberty, economic inequality, and ethnonationalist particularisms seems a profoundly dark prospect which will make our present problems and limitations pale in comparison.

Thinkers on the New Left, on the other hand, carry forward the enlightenment-era values of pluralism, toleration, and a concern for the equal dignity of individuals, groups, genders, and peoples. However, they do so whilst targeting the enlightenment as not the first, incomplete moment in European ideas in which these values were advocated by some—indeed, only a small few—thinkers, despite great adversity, but as ironically cut from the same cloth with the forces of reaction against which Montesquieu and the other *lumières* struggled. There is something historically surprising in this, it being a cultural outcome which few people could have predicted as recently as 1960, implicating an understanding of the cultural politics of the enlightenment which its own protagonists, both *philosophes* and their enemies, could hardly have understood.

But this is the present situation. The illiberal Right understands the enlightenment's values but reviles them. The New Left arguably adapts (some of) these same values, whilst (we have tried to show) widely misunderstanding the enlightenment. Many New Leftists share with their Rightist foes an antagonistic attitude towards the intellectual period in Europe in which anti-slavery, anti-colonialism, anti-racism, and feminism all emerged for the first time. Folk on the Right will hence denounce this book for being too "woke" (even though it is enlightening, not "awakening", that we are arguing for!). Many on the New Left may denounce it, since it critically challenges historical assumptions which are very deep-set in the hegemonic forms of "theory" in the academy of the past decades, but too often have remained unexamined. On both counts, the author has to plead "guilty", whilst contesting the terms of the charges.

It would be absurd to claim that the enlightenment represents the unsurpassable high-water mark of European thought, or of the ongoing struggles against economic, socio-political, and other forms of inequity and inhumanity.

Such an idea would have been ludicrous to the *philosophes* themselves. They were all too aware of the inertial forces of Throne, Altar, and prejudice they were pitted against. We have not argued for this idea here. What *The Other Enlightenment* has contended is that the critical self-othering which we see so artfully staged and modulated in Montesquieu, Voltaire, and Diderot—that is, seeking out Others' perspectives, including their criticisms of our ways, and thereby expanding our perspectives to challenge and balance our prejudices—represents a vital school for the cultivation of the kinds of "enlarged thought" needed if even imperfectly pluralistic societies are to remain viable. We must balance the "principle of diversity", which comes from examining the different ways, values, and excellences of other cultures, with "the principle of unity", which comes from seeing the Others' commonalities with us (ch. 2). We must grasp that both we and they, far from being wholly different, share a common condition and forms of fallibility, not trading for a chauvinistic exaltation of our unexamined excellences a symmetrical idolization of anything which is not "us".[1]

There was nothing predetermined about the rise—and there is surely nothing guaranteed about the continuance—of the forms of liberal or pluralistic societies which have arisen in the wake of the enlightenment in many countries. Such societies are, after all, a comparative historical anomaly in the West as elsewhere. Full franchises (including women) were only widely achieved in Europe after 1918, and in a nation like Australia, the indigenous population was only given the vote following a referendum in the 1960s (see ch.6). From the Right, these forms of modern government have always faced theological and reactionary enemies opposed to the "ideas of 1789" pre-shaped by the *philosophes* in France: those demanding, contested, and potentially conflictual bedfellows of "liberty, equality, fraternity". Viewed from the Left, their histories have almost everywhere been tarnished by the dark realities of deep-set racism, the ongoing reproduction of economic and political inequalities beneath ideological appeals to formal liberty and equality, the too-often brutal mistreatment and destruction of indigenous peoples and their cultures, and the continuance of forms of direct political—and indirect economic—imperialism, which the *philosophes* decried, not simply in the absolute monarchies of France and Spain, but the liberal, parliamentary monarchy of Great Britain.

The complacent idea that our regimes are simply the best, right now, or the "end of history", is one which we can well imagine Voltaire or Diderot would revile as a secularization of Christian notions of divine election, as well as a hybristic recipe for the disasters that after 2008 seem to be duly besetting us. *Tout n'est pas bien*, reading Voltaire reminds us; and today, Candide could still make a tour of the globe which would largely pass from one scene of expropriation and violence to the next, with scarcely any oases. Thirty years of the freeing of markets and opening national boundaries to the flows of money have not, as was promised, promoted greater toleration, "post-ideological" harmony, and "trickled down" material prosperity for all. Instead, economic inequality in nations like the United States is approaching levels comparable to that of pre-revolutionary France, in which Diderot wrote. Yet mainstream politics devolves into a sequence of mediatic spectacles and ever-more-decisive culture wars.

Then, in the last decade, we've seen the rise of forms of ethnonationalist authoritarianism which take aim at everything which this book has argued that the enlightenment stood for. We mean, to repeat, a self-reflective, self-limiting culture of scientific inquiry and dialogue, based upon fostering peoples' capabilities for learning to see themselves through the eyes of Others, awake to the propensities we all have to favor flattering, partial and tribal prejudices over what may be true in any larger, independent sense. What the new authoritarianism instead proposes are newly defiant assertions of such prejudices, repackaged via the conduits of charismatic "strong men" as a new authenticity, based in the promises to make our societies "great again" by whitewashing the complexities of history, censoring the culture and dialogue which makes independent inquiry possible, scapegoating minorities, suppressing dissent, fostering an anti-scientific conspiracy culture, and leaving the fundamental socio-economic settings which have led to the present levels of social division almost entirely intact.

This book is hence not only a study in the history of ideas. Interested in the past for the sake of the present and the future, it has tried to freshly reexamine key texts from a neglected, misrepresented, yet vital period in European ideas, in which many of the ideas the postmodernist Left has inherited were first trialed, and wherein many of the values any post-postmodernist Left will need were first defended with great wit, power, and artistry, as well as at great risk. The enlightenment, as a period of the history of ideas, was highly specific. Our issues and challenges today are not the same as those which faced Montesquieu, Voltaire, and Diderot. Likewise, we cannot "return to" Diderot's materialism, Locke's empiricism, or Voltaire's Deism, or many of the other doctrines that different enlightenment *philosophes* set upon, in response to the social issues and scientific developments of their times. It is enlightenment as an ethics of thinking and of inquiry, one which is modelled by the *philosophes*, as against "the enlightenment", that can potentially still inform and inspire us, and which we have maintained has been passed over in polemical criticisms of this period.

Enlightenment as a way of thinking, inquiring, or philosophizing (again, not a doctrine or dogmatism), as we have seen it developed by Montesquieu, Voltaire, and Diderot, is more than a learning "to think for oneself", challenging inherited prejudices, as Kant's "What is Enlightenment?" echoes Diderot (ch. 4). Everyman and -woman tends to consider herself as a model of such intellectual independence—even those who become dupes to conspiracy theories, or forms of religious fundamentalism, who see themselves as bravely challenging "the establishment". Thinking back to Kant's description of the requirements of "common understanding" in *Critique of Judgment*, there is also the need to check one's all-too-human propensities to "relate everything to oneself" and shape one's opinions concerning what is "true" according to what one "likes", wishes, or fears.[2] Mere consistency, Kant's third requirement of common understanding, also cannot guarantee an enlightened cast of mind. For whilst consistency is an intellectual virtue, as Diderot or Voltaire remind us, even fanatics reason coherently on the basis of their foundational delusions. As Karl Popper rejoins much later, the problem with dogmatists is indeed that they tend to find confirmations everywhere for their orienting ideas, so that nothing which contradicts them can be allowed.

This is the importance of Kant's second requirement of common understanding for any enlightenment worthy of the name, as well as for the French enlightenment's key thinkers, as this book has presented them. To break out from the "subjective personal conditions of judgment" towards an "enlarged" perspective, Kant saw—and the French enlighteners practiced—we must practice "shifting [our] ground to the standpoint of others".[3] Montesquieu's, Voltaire's, and Diderot's sense of the importance of this requirement explains why Persians, Quakers, Chinese, foreign philosophers, space travellers, naïves, and the blind have such large walk-on roles in their texts. Catholic Europeans would not critically understand themselves, Montesquieu, Voltaire, and Diderot supposed, until their follies, prejudices, unexamined beliefs, institutions, and failings were revealed to them through the eyes of others, even when those eyes were those of blind sages: "Look at me, Holmes, I have no eyes".[4] One could learn by introducing such others, and out of these others' mouths, that what "we" take as necessary, inevitable, or unquestionably rational contains a good deal of contingency, custom, choice, and, often enough, irrationality. One could also prompt readers to turn their tested ability to see the motes in others' eyes around: as a way to realize that they also have planks in their own eyes, preventing them from seeing clearly.

Finally, we have claimed that enlightenment involved seeing and owning the connection between the ability to "enlarge" one's mind to take in the view of others, and the ability to recognize the limits of our own understandings. If the monad of complacent self-certainty is never broken, light from elsewhere cannot get in. This is the philosophical reason why this book placed such emphasis on Francis Bacon, John Locke, and Pierre Bayle in chapter 1. Recognizing that we do not and cannot know everything, and that we tend to cut corners when examining the world in ways which flatter our present opinions, recommends the need to proceed as if "blind-folded", in Diderot's words in *Thoughts on the Interpretation of Nature* (ch. 4).[5] We can form our opinions about the world well only by proceeding from experience to experience, like the blind man with his cane; withholding assent and avoiding generalizing except with epistemic caution, awake to the ways we have been wrong in the past, and alert to the probability that we will be wrong soon enough in future. One can easily understand how this fallibilist position relates to an opening to the viewpoints of others. We can do with all the help we can get in accumulating diverse experiences, checking them against each other, and staying honest with ourselves. The distance of this program from the hybristic teaching that "knowledge is power" and the project to mindlessly dominate nature and other human beings, which have often been alleged against "the enlightenment" in the last half-century, cannot be overstressed. As Voltaire wrote:

> What is tolerance? It is the appurtenance of humanity. We are all full of weakness and errors; let us mutually pardon each other our follies—it is the first law of nature.[6]

The task of this book has been to try to show, through detailed textual analyses, how central this conception of enlightenment as an ethics of inquiry was, within the work of arguably the three pre-eminent French *philosophes* of the eighteenth century. It is perhaps not meaningful to raise the question of whether a "new enlightenment" is possible today, given the changed socio-political conditions and challenges we face. It is unclear what such a proposal would concretely mean. As political communities become more divided, and as the threats posed by climate change, economic instability, steepling inequalities, heightening alienation, ascending demagoguery, and superpower conflict become more immediate, the tone of public debate is widely becoming more strident and categorical, not more nuanced and tolerant. The enlightenment thinkers' calls to fallibilism, and commitments to experimental modes of inquiry and to seeing one's perspective through the eyes of others—even one's political opponents—can seem like a still small voice, if not an idealistic pipe dream, amidst the loud clamour of partisan argumentation today.

Yet, and precisely because of these cultural shifts, these enlightenment calls—those of the *philosophes* as we have excavated them here, not their legion of polemical critics—in another sense sound out as loudly as ever as I write this in early 2022. If now is not the time for critical voices to advocate for a post-Voltairean culture in which strident self-assertion would be tempered by dialogic doubt; factional dogmata would be tested against ongoing attempts to fallibilistically verify what is true (versus what we might wish or dread); a just attention to particular differences would be balanced by a recovered sense of what unites different groups (and a shared humanity facing increasingly global threats); and a rightful criticism of the deep historical barbarities of Western hybris would be acknowledged, all the while recognizing the vast ethical and political differences which nevertheless separate what Cornell Wests calls the "monstrous tribalism" of today's reactionary ethnonationalisms[7] from forms of constitutional governance enshrining in principle (though rarely enough in fact); the protections of citizens from the arbitrary exercise of power and their rights to publicly protest its excesses—then it is difficult to imagine when such a time could come.

NOTES

1. Cf. Ira Wade, *Intellectual Origins*, 391.
2. Cf. Montesquieu, *Persian Letters*, L59, 76; 3.3 above.
3. Kant, *Critique of Judgment*, §40.
4. Diderot, "Letter on the Blind", 112; cf. 4.4 above.
5. Diderot, *Thoughts on the Interpretation of Nature*, §23; cf. 4.5.
6. PD, "Toleration".
7. In Judith Butler, Cornel West, Glenn Greenwald, "Transcript from the 2021 Holberg Debate: "Identity Politics and Culture Wars", online at https://holbergprisen.no/en/2021-holberg-debate-identity-politics-and-culture-wars.

Bibliography

Agnani, Sunil. "*Doux Commerce, Douce Colonisation:* Diderot and the Two Indies of the French Enlightenment". *The Anthropology of the Enlightenment*, ed. Larry Wolff and Marco Cipoloni, 65–84. Stanford: Stanford University Press, 2007.
Allen, Amy. *The End of Progress: Decolonising the Normative Foundations of Critical Theory.* New York: Columbia University Press, 2017.
Andereggen, Amon. "The Image of the African in the French Collective Psyche". *Peuples Noirs, Peuples Africains* no. 59–62 (1988): 129–40.
Anstey, Peter R. "Locke, Bacon and Natural History". *Early Science and Medicine* 7, no. 1 (2002): 65–92.
Atkinson, Geoffrey. *The Extraordinary Voyage in French Literature from 1680 to 1700.* New York: Columbia University Press, 1920.
———. *The Extraordinary Voyage in French Literature from 1700–1720.* Paris: Champion, 1922.
Bacon, Francis. *Novum Organum*, in *The Works of Francis Bacon . . . : Translations of the Philosophical Works, Volume VIII*, ed. James Spedding et al. New York: Hurd and Houghton, 1869.
———. "Preparative towards a Natural and Experimental History [*Parasceve*]", in *The Works of Francis Bacon, Volume VIII, Translations of the Philosophical Works*, trans. James Spedding et al., 351–72. Boston: Houghton Mifflin, c. 1900.
———. *Advancement of Learning.* London: J. M. Dent & Sons, 1973.
Ball, James. *Post-Truth: How Bullshit Conquered the World.* London: Biteback Publishing, 2018.
Ballinger, Stanley E. "The Idea of Social Progress through Education in the French Enlightenment Period: Helvétius and Condorcet". *History of Education Journal* 10, no. 1/4, Tenth Anniversary Issue (1959): 88–99.
Ballstadt, Kurt. *Diderot: Natural Philosopher.* Oxford, UK: Voltaire Foundation, 2003.
Barber, Kenneth E. "Johann Blumenbach and the Classification of Human Races", *Encyclopedia.com.* https://www.encyclopedia.com/science/encyclopedias-almanacs-transcripts-and-maps/johann-blumenbach-and-classification-human-races.

Bayle, Pierre. *The Historical and Critical Dictionary: Selections*, trans., with an introduction and notes by Richard H. Popkin. Indianapolis/Cambridge: Hackett Publishing Co., 1965.
———. *Various Thoughts on the Occasion of a Comet*. Albany: State University of New York Press, 2000.
———. *Philosophical Commentary on the Words of the Gospel*, ed. with an introduction by John Kilcullen and Chandran Kukathas. Indianapolis, IN: Liberty Fund, 2005.
Beiner, Ronald. *Nietzsche, Heidegger, and the Far Right*. Philadelphia: University of Pennsylvania Press, 2018.
Benot, Y. *Diderot: De l'athéisme à l'anticolonialisme*. Paris: François Maspero, 1970.
Bernasconi, Robert, and S. Cook, eds. *Race and Racism in Continental Philosophy*. Bloomington: Indiana University Press, 2003.
Bernasconi, Robert, and T. Lott, eds. *The Idea of Race*. Indianapolis, IN: Hackett, 2000.
Black, Annetta. "The Lady Salonières of the Enlightenment", https://www.oddsalon.com/the-lady-salonnieres-of-the-enlightenment.
Black, Jeremy. *A Brief History of Slavery*. New York: Little, Brown Book Group, 2011.
Blom, Philipp. *A Wicked Company: The Forgotten Radicalism of the European Enlightenment*. New York: Basic Books, 2010.
Blumenberg, Hans. *The Legitimacy of the Modern Age*, trans. Robert M. Wallace. Cambridge: Massachusetts Institute of Technology Press, 1983.
Boucher, Geoffrey, and Henry Martyn Lloyd. *Rethinking the Enlightenment*. Lanham, MD: Lexington Books, 2017.
Brewer, Daniel. *The Discourse of Enlightenment in Eighteenth-Century France: Diderot and the Art of Philosophising*. Cambridge, UK: Cambridge University Press, 2006.
———. *The Enlightenment Past: Reconstructing Eighteenth-Century French Thought*. Cambridge, UK: Cambridge University Press, 2008.
Brittain, Christopher. "Washing His Hands of the Enlightenment: A Critique of John Milbank", *Theology and the Crisis of Engagement Essays on the Relationship of Theology and the Social Sciences*, ed. Jeff Nowers, 58–76. Nestor Medina. Eugene, OR: Pickwick Press, Wipf and Stock, 2014.
Bruno, Michael, and Eric Mandelbaum. "Locke's Answer to Molyneux's Thought Experiment", *History of Philosophy Quarterly* 27, no. 2 (2010): 165–80.
Buck-Morss, Susan. *Hegel, Haiti, and Universal History*. Pittsburgh: University of Pittsburgh Press, 2009.
Bury, J. B. *The Idea of Progress*. Gutenberg E-books, 2010. https://www.gutenberg.org/files/4557/4557-h/4557-h.htm.
Cassam, Quassim. *Vices of the Mind: From the Intellectual to the Political*. Oxford, UK: Oxford University Press, 2019.
Cassirer, Ernst. *The Philosophy of the Enlightenment*. Boston, MA: Beacon Press, 1955.
Chakrabarty, Dipesh. *Provincialising Europe: Postcolonial Thought and Historical Difference*. Princeton, NJ: Princeton University Press, 2007.

Chisick, Harvey. "Looking for Enlightenment", *History of European Ideas* 34, no. 4 (2008): 570–82.
Cicero, Marcus Tullius. *Tusculan Disputations*. Loeb Classical Library 141, trans. J. E. King. Cambridge, MA: Harvard, 1927.
Cohen, H. Floris. *How Modern Science Came Into the World: Four Civilizations, One 17th-Century Breakthrough*. Amsterdam: Amsterdam University Press, 2012.
Corneanu, Soranu. *Regimens of the Mind*. Chicago: University of Chicago Press, 2011.
Cors, Alan Charles. *Voltaire and the Triumph of the Enlightenment*. Available at https://www.thegreatcourses.com/courses/voltaire-and-the-triumph-of-the-enlightenment.html.
Crocker, Lester G. *Nature and Culture: Ethical Thought in the French Enlightenment*. Baltimore, MD: John Hopkins University Press, 1963.
Cronk, Nicholas. "The Voltairean Genre of the *Conte Philosophique*: Does It Exist?". *Enlightenment and Narrative: Essays in Honour of Richard A. Francis by Colleagues and Friends*, ed. P. Robinson, Nottingham French Studies, 48, no. 3 (2009): 61, 80, 81.
Cronk, Nicholas, and J. L. Shank. "Introduction". In N. Cronk and J. L. Shank, eds. *Micromégas and Other Texts (1738–1742), Les oeuvres complèts de Voltaire, 20c*. Voltaire Foundation. Oxford, UK: Oxford University Press, 2017.
Curran, Anthony S. *Diderot and the Art of Thinking Freely*. New York: Other Press, 2019.
d'Alembert, Jean-Baptiste le Rond, and Denis Diderot. "Preliminary Discourse". In *The Encyclopedia of Diderot and d'Alembert Collaborative Translation Project*, trans. Richard N. Schwab and Walter E. Rex. Ann Arbor: Michigan Publishing, University of Michigan Library, 2009. http://hdl.handle.net/2027/spo.did2222.0001.083.
d'Argens, Jean-Baptiste de Boyer Marquis. *Thérèse the Philosopher*, in *Thérèse the Philosopher and the Story of Mrs. Bois-Laurier*, trans. Charles Carrington. Locus Elm Press, 2014: Kindle Edition.
de Gouges, Olympe, "The Declaration of the Rights of Woman". https://revolution.chnm.org/d/293/.
Descartes, René. *Discourse on Method*, trans. E. Haldane, 41–68. In *Descartes, Spinoza*. Chicago: Britannica Great Books, 1952, vol. 31.
Detlefsen, Karen. "Émilie du Châtelet". *Stanford Encyclopedia of Philosophy*. 2014. https://plato.stanford.edu/entries/emilie-du-chatelet/.
Diamond, Marion. "The New Cythera and the Transit of Venus". Blog. *Historians Are Past Caring*, 2012. https://learnearnandreturn.wordpress.com/2012/06/05/the-new-cythera-and-the-transit-of-venus/.
Diderot, Denis. *Indiscreet Jewels*. Project Gutenberg e-book. https://www.gutenberg.org/files/54672/54672-h/54672-h.htm.
———. *Essai sur les règnes de Claude et de Néron et sur la vie et les écrits de Sénèque pour servir d'introduction à la lecture de ce philosophe*. Paris: L'Imprimerie de J. J. Smith et al., 1792 [orig. 1782].

———. "Letter on the Blind for the Use of Those Who See". In Margaret Jourdain, ed. and trans., *Diderot, the Early Philosophical Works*. Chicago and London: Open Court Publishing, 1916.

———. *Supplement to Bougainville's Voyage*, in *Rameau's Nephew and Other Works*, trans. Jacques Barzan and Ralph H. Brown, 179–228. Indianapolis/Cambridge: Hackett Publishing, 1956.

———. *D'Alembert's Dream*, in *Rameau's Nephew and D'Alembert's Dream*, trans. Leonard Tanock. London: Penguin, 1966.

———. "Eclecticism". In Denis Diderot, *The Encyclopedia*, ed. and trans., Stephen J. Gendzier. New York: Harper, 1967.

———. *The Nun*, trans. Dennis Tancock. London: Penguin, 1972.

———. "System", in Stephen J. Gendzier, trans., *The Encyclopedia of Diderot and d'Alembert Collaborative Translation Project*. Ann Arbor: Michigan Publishing, University of Michigan Library, 2009. http://hdl.handle.net/2027/spo.did2222.0001.321.

———. "Philosophy". In *The Encyclopedia of Diderot and d'Alembert Collaborative Translation Project*, trans. Julia Wallhager. Ann Arbor: Michigan Publishing, University of Michigan Library, 2015. http://hdl.handle.net/2027/spo.did2222.0003.145.

Dombowsky, Don. *Nietzsche and the German Autumn*, 2020. https://www.researchgate.net/publication/347839446_Friedrich_Nietzsche_and_The_German_Autumn_Don_Dombowsky_C2020.

Doron. Claude-Olivier. "Race and Genealogy: Buffon and the Formation of the Concept of 'Race' ", *Humana Mente: Journal of Philosophical Studies* 22 (2012): 75–109.

Dubois, Laurent, and John D. Garrigus. *Slave Revolution in the Caribbean, 1789–1804: A Brief History with Documents*. Bedford/St. Martins, Document 26, 2006.

Duflo, Calas. *Diderot, Philosophe*. Paris: Honoré Champion, 2003.

Du Marsais, César Chesneau. "Philosopher", in Dena Goodman, trans., *The Encyclopedia of Diderot and d'Alembert Collaborative Translation Project*. Ann Arbor: Michigan Publishing, University of Michigan Library, 2002. Online at http://hdl.handle.net/2027/spo.did2222.0000.001.

Durant, Will. *The Story of Philosophy*. New York: Simon & Schuster, 1926.

Durant, Will, and Ariel Durant. *The Story of Civilization, Volume VIII: The Age of Louis XIV*. New York: Simon & Schuster, 1963.

———. *The Story of Civilization, Volume IX: The Age of Voltaire*. New York: Simon & Schuster, 1965.

Eagleton, Terry. *The Illusions of Postmodernism*. Cambridge, UK: Blackwell Publishers, 1996.

Edelstein, Dan. *The Enlightenment: A Genealogy*. Chicago: University of Chicago Press, 2010.

Ehrenreich, Barbara, and John Ehrenreich. "The Professional-Managerial Class". *Radical America* (March–April 1977).

———. "The New Left: A Case Study in Professional-Managerial Class Radicalism", *Radical America* (May–June 1977).

Eze, Emmanuel. "Hume, Race, and Human Nature", *Journal of the History of Ideas*, vol. 61, no. 4 (2000): 691–98.
Faye, Emmanuel. *Martin Heidegger: The Introduction of Nazism into Philosophy*, trans. Michael B. Smith. New Haven and London: Yale University Press, 2009.
Ferrone, Vincenzo. *The Enlightenment: History of an Idea*, trans. Elisabetta Tarantino. Princeton, NJ: Princeton University Press, 2015.
Forst, Rainer. "Pierre Bayle's Reflexive Theory of Toleration", *Nomos* 48 (2008): 78–113.
———. *Toleration in Conflict: Past and Present.* Cambridge, UK: Cambridge University Press, 2013.
Foucault, Michel. *The Birth of the Clinic*, trans. M. Sheridan Smith. London: Tavistock, 1973.
———. *Discipline and Punish*, trans. Alan Sheridan. New York: Vintage, 1979.
———. "What is Enlightenment?", trans. Catherine Porter. In *Ethics: Subjectivity and Truth, Volume 1 of The Essential Works of Foucault, 1954–1984*, ed. Paul Rabinow. New York: New Press, 1997.
Frank, Manfred. *What Is Neostructuralism?*, trans. Sabine Wilke and Richard Gray. Minneapolis: University of Minnesota Press, 1989.
Garraway, D. "Parodic Mimicry and Utopia in Diderot's Supplement". In D. Carey et al., eds. *Postcolonial Enlightenment*, 220–31. Oxford, UK: Oxford University Press, 2019.
Gaukroger, Stephen. *The Collapse of Mechanism and the Rise of Sensibility: Science and the Shaping of Modernity, 1680–1760.* Oxford, UK: Oxford University Press, 2011.
———. *The Natural and the Human.* Oxford, UK: Oxford University Press, 2016.
Gay, Peter. *The Enlightenment: An Interpretation, Volume I: The Rise of Modern Paganism.* New York: W. W. Norton & Co., 1995.
———. *The Enlightenment: An Interpretation, Volume II: The Science of Freedom.* New York: W. W. Norton & Co., 1995.
Goldberg, David Theo. *Racist Culture: Philosophy and the Politics of Meaning.* London: Wiley-Blackwell, 1993.
Goodman, Dena. "Enlightenment Salons: The Convergence of Female and Philosophic Ambitions", *Eighteenth-Century Studies* 22, no. 3, *Special Issue: The French Revolution in Culture* (Spring 1989): 329–50.
Gordon, Daniel. "On the Supposed Obsolescence of the French Enlightenment". In Daniel Gordon, ed., *Postmodernism and the Enlightenment*, 201–21. London: Routledge, 2001.
Goulbourne, Russell. "Diderot and the Ancients". In *New Essays on Diderot*, ed. James Fowler, 13–30. Cambridge, UK: Cambridge University Press, 2014.
Green, Karen. "The Rights of Women and the Equal Rights of Men". *Political Theory* 49, no. 3 (2021): 403–30.
Gutting, Gary. *Thinking the Impossible: French Philosophy since the 1960s.* Oxford, UK: Oxford University Press, 2013.
Habermas, Jurgen. *Philosophical Discourse of Modernity*, trans. Frederick G. Lawrence. Cambridge: Massachusetts Institute of Technology Press, 1987.

Hadot, Pierre. *Philosophy as a Way of Life*, trans. M. Chase. London: Wiley-Blackwell, 1995.
Harrison, Peter. *The Fall of Man and the Foundation of Modern Science*. Oxford, UK: Oxford University Press, 2009.
Hasan, Rumy. *Modern Europe and the Enlightenment*. Sussex, UK: Sussex University Press, 2021.
Hazareesingh, Sudhir. *Black Spartacus: The Epic Life of Toussaint Louverture*. New York: Farrar, Straus and Giroux, 2020.
Heidegger, Martin. *On Hegel's Philosophy of Right*, trans. Andrew J. Mitchell. London: Bloomsbury, 2014.
Himmelfarb, Gertrude. *The Roads to Modernity: The British, French and American Enlightenments*. London: Vintage, 2008.
Holub, Robert. *Crossing Borders: Reception Theory, Poststructuralism, Deconstruction*. Madison: University of Wisconsin Press, 1992.
Israel, Jonathan. *Radical Enlightenment*. Oxford, UK: Oxford University Press, 2001.
———. *Enlightenment Contested*. Oxford, UK: Oxford University Press, 2006.
———. *A Revolution of the Mind: Radical Enlightenment and the Intellectual Origins of Modern Democracy*. Princeton, NJ: Princeton University Press, 2010.
———. *Democratic Enlightenment: Philosophy, Revolution and Human Rights, 1750–1790*. Oxford, UK: Oxford University Press, 2013.
———. "Enlightenment, The". *The Encyclopedia of Political Thought*. Wiley Online Library, 2014. https://onlinelibrary.wiley.com/doi/10.1002/9781118474396.wbept0317.
Jacob, Margaret C. *The Radical Enlightenment: Pantheists, Freemasons and Republicans*. London: George Allen and Unwin, 1981.
James, C. L. R. *The Black Jacobins: Toussaint L'Ouverture and the San Domingo Revolution*, 2nd ed., rev. New York: Vintage, 1963.
Jaucourt, Louis, chevalier de. "Slave Trade". In *The Encyclopedia of Diderot and d'Alembert Collaborative Translation Project*. Ann Arbor: Michigan Publishing, University of Michigan Library, 2007. <http://hdl.handle.net/2027/spo.did2222.0000.114>. Trans. of "Traite des nègres", *Encyclopédie ou Dictionnaire raisonné des sciences, des arts et des métiers*, vol. 16. Paris, 1765.
Jimack, P. "Introduction" to *A History of the Two Indies: A Translated Selection of Writings from Raynal*, edited and selected by P. Jimack. London: Routledge, 2006.
Judy, Ronald. "Kant and the Negro". *Surfaces* 1 (1991). https://doi.org/10.7202/1065256a.
Jump, Harriet Devine. *Mary Wollstonecraft and the Critics, 1788–2001*. London: Routledge, 2003.
Junker, Thomas. "Blumenbach's Theory of Human Races and the Natural Unity of Humankind". In *Johann Blumenbach*. London: Routledge, 2018.
Kant, Immanuel. *Critique of Judgment*, trans. with introduction and notes by J. H. Bernard (2nd ed., rev.). London: Macmillan, 1914.
———. "An Answer to the Question: What is Enlightenment?". In *Political Writings*, ed. H. S. Reid. Cambridge, UK: Cambridge University Press, 1991.
Keegan, Susanne. *History of Slavery*. UK: Grange Books, 1997.

Keohane, Nannerl O. *Philosophy and the State in France: The Renaissance to the Enlightenment.* Princeton, NJ: Princeton University Press, 1980.
Kessler, Sanford. "Religion and Liberalism in Montesquieu's Persian Letters", *Polity* 15, no. 3 (Spring 1983): 380–96.
Kimball, Roger. "Introduction: The Dictatorship of Relativism". *The New Criterion*, January 2009. https://newcriterion.com/issues/2009/1/introduction-the-dictatorship-of-relativism.
Laidlaw, G. Norman. "Diderot's Teratology", *Diderot Studies* 4 (1963).
La Vopa, Anthony J. "A New Intellectual History? Jonathan Israel's Enlightenment". *Historical Journal* 52, no. 3 (2009): 717–38.
Leibniz, Gottlieb W. *Theodicy: Essays on the Goodness of God, the Freedom of Man and the Origin of Evil*, trans. E. G. Hubbard. London: Routledge & Kegan Paul, 1951.
Litti, Antoine. "Comment écrit-on l'histoire intellectuelle des Lumières? Spinozisme, radicalisme et philosophie", *Annales HSS* 1 (janvier–février 2009): 171–206.
Lloyd, Genevieve. *Enlightenment Shadows.* Oxford, UK: Oxford University Press, 2013.
Locke, John. *Essay on the Human Understanding*, with an introduction by Mark G. Spencer. London: Wordsworth Classics of World Literature, 2014.
———. *On the Conduct of the Human Understanding.* https://www.earlymoderntexts.com/assets/pdfs/locke1706.pdf.
———. "Fundamental Constitution of Carolina". https://www.ncpedia.org/fundamental-constitutions.
Losurdo, Domenico. *Friedrich Nietzsche: Aristocratic Rebel.* Leiden: Brill, 2020.
Lukacs, Gyorgy. *Destruction of Reason*, trans. Peter Palmer. India: Askar Books, 2017.
Malik, Kenneth. "On the Enlightenment's 'Race Problem' ". *Pandaemonium.* https://kenanmalik.com/2013/02/13/on-the-enlightenments-race-problem.
Mannies, Whitney. "Denis Diderot and the Politics of Materialist Skepticism". In *Skepticism and Political Thought in the Seventeenth and Eighteenth Centuries*, ed. John C. Laursen and Gianni Paganini. Toronto: University of Toronto Press, 2015.
Manuel, Frank E. *The Eighteenth Century Confronts the Gods.* Cambridge MA: Harvard University Press, 1959.
Mason, Haydn. "Crime and Punishment: Voltaire (1694–1778), Commentaire sur le livre des délits et des peines (1766)". In *French Writers and their Society, 1715–1800.* London: Palgrave Macmillan, 1982.
Mason, John Hope. *Irresistible Diderot.* London and New York: Quartet, 1992.
McCarthy, Thomas. "The Critique of Impure Reason: Foucault and the Frankfurt School", *Political Theory* 18, no. 3 (1990): 437–69.
Milbank, John. *Theology and Social Theory.* London: Wiley-Blackwell, 1990.
Montaigne, Michel de. "The Apology of Raymond Sebond". In *The Complete Essays of Michel de Montaigne*, trans. Donald R. Frame. Stanford, CA: Stanford University Press, 1965.
Montesquieu, Charles-Louis de Secondat, Baron de La Brède. *Persian Letters*, introduction by Andrew Kahn, trans. Margaret Mauldon. Oxford, UK: Oxford University Press, 2008.

———. *The Spirit of Laws*, trans. Thomas Nugent. Chicago: Britannica Great Books 38, 1952.
Mosher, Michael. "Reviewed Work(s): Radical Enlightenment: Philosophy and the Making of Modernity, 1650–1750, by Jonathan I. Israel", *Political Theory* 32, no. 3 (June 2004): 427–31.
Moyn, Samuel. "Mind the Enlightenment", *The Nation*, May 12, 2010.
———. "A Response to Jonathan Israel", *History News Network*, HNN Special: Debating the Enlightenment. https://historynewsnetwork.org/article/128433.
Muenck, Thomas. "The Enlightenment as Modernity: Jonathan Israel's Interpretation Across Two Decades," *Reviews in History*, 15 (2016). https://reviews.history.ac.uk/review/2039.
Muthu, Sankar. *Enlightenment against Empire*. Princeton, NJ: Princeton University Press, 2003.
Nablow, Ralph Arthur. "Was Voltaire Influenced by Lucian in 'Micromégas' ", *Romance Notes* 22, no. 2 (1981): 186–91.
Neumann, Franz. *Behemoth: The Theory and Practice of National Socialism, 1933–1944*. Chicago: Ivan R. Dee, 2009.
———. *Democratic and Authoritarian State*. New York: Free Press, 1957.
Newman, Brooke N. *Dark Inheritance: Blood, Race, and Sex in Colonial Jamaica*. New Haven and London: Yale University Press, 2018.
Nietzsche, Friedrich. *Beyond Good and Evil*, trans. R. J. Hollingdale. London: Penguin, 2003.
O'Neill, Aaron. "Slaves Brought from Africa to the Americas", *Statista*, at https://www.statista.com/statistics/1143207/slaves-brought-from-africa-to-americas-1501-1866/.
———. "Number of Slaves Taken from Africa by Region, Country", *Statista*, at https://www.statista.com/statistics/1150475/number-slaves-taken-from-africa-by-region-century/.
Pagden, Anthony. *The Enlightenment and Why It Still Matters*. Oxford, UK: Oxford University Press, 2013.
Papazoglou, Alexis. "The Post-Truth Era of Trump Is Just What Nietzsche Predicted". *The Conversation*, December 14, 2016. https://theconversation.com/the-post-truth-era-of-trump-is-just-what-nietzsche-predicted-69093.
Pearson, Roger. *The Fables of Reason: A Study of Voltaire's "Contes Philosophiques"*. Oxford, UK: Oxford University Press, 1993.
Popkin, Jeremy D. *You Are All Free: The Haitian Revolution and the Abolition of Slavery*. Cambridge, UK: Cambridge University Press, 2010.
Powell, Jim. "Mary Wollstonecraft—Equal Rights for Women". Blog. *Libertarianism.org*, https://www.libertarianism.org/publications/essays/mary-wollstonecraft-equal-rights-women.
Rasmussen, Dennis. *The Pragmatic Enlightenment: Recovering the Liberalism of Hume, Smith, Montesquieu, and Voltaire*. Cambridge, UK: Cambridge University Press, 2013.

———. "Contemporary Political Theory as an Anti-Enlightenment Project". In Geoff Boucher and Henry Martyn Lloyd, eds. *Rethinking the Enlightenment: Between History, Philosophy, and Politics*. Lanham, MD: Lexington Books, 2017.
Richards, Xander. "Was David Hume Racist? Here's the Scottish Philosopher's Racist Comment in Full", *The National*, 14 September 2020.
Riskin, Jennifer. *Science in the Age of Sensibility: The Sentimental Empiricists of the French Enlightenment*. Chicago: University of Chicago Press, 2002.
Robertson, Ritchie. *The Enlightenment: The Pursuit of Happiness, 1680–1790*. New York: HarperCollins, 2021.
Rousseau, Jean-Jacques. *Discourse on the Origins of Inequality*. London: Britannica, 1952.
———. *Social Contract*. London: Britannica, 1952.
Salmond, Anne. *Aphrodite's Island: The European Discovery of Tahiti*. London: Viking, 2016.
Schleisser, Eric. "Jonathan Israel, Democratic Enlightenment: Philosophy, Revolution, and Human Rights, 1750–1790," *Oeconomica: History, Methodology, Philosophy* 4, no. 4 (2014): 651–57.
Schmidt, James, ed. *What Is Enlightenment? Eighteenth-Century Answers and Twentieth-Century Questions*. Berkeley: University of California Press, 1996.
Schorsch, Jonathan. *Jews and Blacks in the Early Modern World*. Cambridge, UK: Cambridge University Press, 2004.
Sharpe, Matthew. "What of All the Others?" In Geoffrey Boucher and Henry Martyn Lloyd, eds., Boucher, *Rethinking the Enlightenment*, 61–87. Lanham, MD: Lexington Books, 2017.
———. "The State as the Being of the Volk: State, Führer and the Political in Heidegger's Seminars during the Kairos". In Thanos Zartaloudis, ed., *Law and Philosophical Theory: Critical Intersections*. London: Rowman & Littlefield, 2018.
———. "The Topics Transformed: Reframing the Baconian Prerogative Instances", *Journal of the History of Philosophy* 56, no. 3 (2018): 429–54.
———. "Rhetorical Action in the *Rektoratsrede*: Calling Heidegger's Gefolgschaft", *Philosophy & Rhetoric* 51, no. 2 (2018):176–201.
———. "From Amy Allen to Abbé Raynal: Critical Theory, the Enlightenment and Colonialism", *Critical Horizons* 20, no. 2 (2019): 178–99.
———. "Camus and Diderot: Modern Rebellion, Before the Terror". In Matthew Sharpe, Peter Francev et al. eds., *Camus among the Philosophers*, 91–112. Leiden, Netherlands: Brill, 2019.
———. "Critique, Metacritique, and Making the (World of) Difference: Losurdo on the Paradoxes of Nietzsche Reception", *Historical Materialism* (2022, in press).
Sharpe, Matthew, and Michael Ure. *Philosophy as a Way of Life: History, Dimensions, Directions*. London: Bloomsbury, 2021.
Shea, Louisa. *The Cynic Enlightenment: Diogenes in the Salon*. Baltimore, MD: John Hopkins University Press, 2010.
Shklar, Judith. *Montesquieu*. Oxford, UK: Oxford University Press, 1987.
Smith, Justin E. H. "The Enlightenment's 'Race' Problem, and Ours", *New York Times*, February 13, 2013.

Spivak, Gayatri. *Critique of Postcolonial Reason: Towards a History of the Vanishing Present*. Cambridge, MA: Harvard University Press, 1999.
Stanley, Sharon A. "Unraveling Natural Utopia: Diderot's Supplement to the Voyage of Bougainville", *Political Theory* 37, no. 2 (2009): 266–89.
Strauss, Leo. *Persecution and the Art of Writing*. Chicago: University of Chicago Press, 1948.
———. "Preface", *Spinoza's Critique of Religion*. Chicago: University of Chicago Press, 1965.
Taine, Hippolyte A. *The Origins of Contemporary France, Volume 1: The Ancient Regime*, trans. John Durand. Project Gutenberg, 2008 [1880]. https://www.gutenberg.org/files/2577/2577-h/2577-h.htm.
Talbot, A. "The Influence of Travel Literature on the Work of John Locke", in *"The Great Ocean of Knowledge"*, 143–59. Leiden, Netherlands: Brill, 2010.
Taylor, Charles. *A Secular Age*. Cambridge, MA: Harvard University Press, 2018.
Todorov, Tzvetan. *In Defence of the Enlightenment*, trans. Gila Walker. London: Atlantic Books, 2010.
Tomaselli, Sylvana. "Reason", in *The Blackwell Companion to the Enlightenment*, ed. John W. Yolton, 446. Oxford, UK: Blackwell, 1991.
Tunstall, Katherine. *Blindness and Enlightenment: An Essay: With a new translation of Diderot's "Letter on the Blind" and La Mothe Le Vayer's "Of a Man Born Blind"*. London: Continuum, 2011.
Van Damme, Stéphane. "The philosophe/philosopher", in Daniel Brewer, ed., *The Cambridge Companion to the French Enlightenment*, 153–66. Cambridge, UK: Cambridge University Press, 2014.
Vartija, Devon. "Revisiting Enlightenment Racial Classification: Time and the Question of Human Diversity", *Intellectual History Review* (2020). DOI 10.1080/17496977.2020.1794161. https://www.tandfonline.com/doi/pdf/10.1080/17496977.2020.1794161.
Voltaire. "Law [Natural]". In *The Works of Voltaire, Volume VI (Philosophical Dictionary Part 4)*. Online Library of Liberty. https://oll.libertyfund.org/title/fleming-the-works-of-voltaire-vol-vi-philosophical-dictionary-part-4.
———. "Virtue: Section I", *The Project Gutenberg eBook of Voltaire's Philosophical Dictionary*. https://www.gutenberg.org/files/18569/18569-h/18569-h.htm.
———. "Poem on the Lisbon Disaster", trans. Joseph McCabe, in *Toleration and Other Essays / Poem on the Lisbon Disaster*. Wikisource. https://en.wikisource.org/wiki/Toleration_and_other_essays/Poem_on_the_Lisbon_Disaster.
———. *The Ignorant Philosopher*, in *The Complete Romances of Voltaire*. New York: Walter J. Black, 1927.
———. "General Reflection on Man". In *Philosophical Dictionary*. Selected and trans. H. I. Woolf. New York: Dover, 1928.
———. "We Must Take Sides", in *Selected Works of Voltaire*, trans. J. McCabe. London: C. A. Watts & Co., 1948.
———. *Micromégas*. In I. Wade, ed., *Voltaire's Micromégas: A Study in the Fusion of Science, Myth, and Art*, 119 ff. Princeton, NJ: Princeton University Press, 1950.

———. "Zadig". In *Viking Portable Voltaire*, ed. Ben Ray Redman, 329 ff. London: Viking Penguin, 1977.
———. *Traité de métaphysique*, ed. W. H. Barber, in *The Complete Works of Voltaire, Volume 14*. Oxford, UK: Voltaire Foundation, 1989 [1736].
———. *Philosophical Dictionary*, trans. Thomas Besterman. London: Penguin, 2004.
———. *Philosophical Letters, or Letters Regarding the English Nation*, ed. and with an introduction by John Leigh, trans. Prudence L. Steiner. Indianapolis/Cambridge: Hackett Publishing Company, 2007.
———. *Candide*, trans. Robert M. Adems, ed. Nicholas Cronk. New York, London: W. W. Norton, 2016.
———. *Treatise on Toleration*, trans. Desmond M. Clarke. London: Penguin, 2017.
Vyverberg, Henry. *Historical Pessimism in the French Enlightenment*. Cambridge, MA: Harvard University Press, 1958.
———. *Human Nature, Cultural Diversity, and the French Enlightenment*. Oxford, UK: Oxford University Press, 1989.
Wade, Ira. *Voltaire's Candide: A Study in the Fusion of History, Art, and Philosophy*. Princeton, NJ: Princeton University Press, 1959.
———. *Intellectual Development of Voltaire*. Princeton, NJ: Princeton University Press, 1969.
———. *Intellectual Origins of the French Enlightenment*. Princeton, NJ: Princeton University Press, 1971.
———. *The Structure and Form of the French Enlightenment, Volume 1: Esprit Philosophique*. Princeton, NJ: Princeton University Press, 1977.
———. *The Structure and Form of the French Enlightenment, Volume 2. Esprit Revolutionnaire*. Princeton, NJ: Princeton University Press, 1977.
West, David. *Continental Philosophy: An Introduction*. London: Wiley-Blackwell, 2010.
Wheeler, Joseph M. "Tributes to Voltaire", in *The Sincere Huron, Pupil of Nature*. Musaicum Books, 2017.
Wigelsworth, Jeffrey W. *Deism in Enlightenment England*. Manchester, UK: Manchester University Press, 2009.
Williams, Henry Smith. *History of Science, Volumes II–IV*. New York, London: Harper & Brothers, 1904.
Wilson, Catherine. "The Enlightenment Philosopher as Social Critic", *Intellectual History Review* 18, no. 3 (2008): 413–25.
Witteveen, Joeri. "Linnaeus, the Essentialism Story, and the Question of Types", *TAXON* 69, no. 6 (2020).
Wolfe, Charles T. "Epigenesis and/as Spinozism in Diderot's Biological Project". *The Life Sciences in Early Modern Philosophy*, ed. Ohad Nachtomy and Justin E. H. Smith. Oxford, UK: Oxford University Press, 2014.
Wolker, Robert. "Projecting the Enlightenment." In *After MacIntyre: Critical Perspectives on the Work of Alasdair MacIntyre*, ed. John Horton and Susan Mendus, 108–26. Notre Dame, IN: University of Notre Dame Press, 1994.
Wollstonecraft, Mary. *A Vindication of the Rights of Woman: With Strictures on Political . . . , Volume 1*. London: J. Johnstone, 1796.

———. "To M. Talleyrand-Perigord, Late Bishop of Audin". In *A Vindication of the Rights of Woman*, Digital Edition 1.0. Kaysville, UT: Gibbs Smith, 2019.

Wootton, David. "Helvétius: From Radical Enlightenment to Revolution", *Political Theory*, vol. 28, no. 3 (2000): 307–33.

Index

African peoples, slavery, slaves: attitudes towards, conceptions of, 14, 45, 76, 109, 111–13, 116, 117, 118, 119–20, 122, 123
D'Alembert, Jean le Rond, 27, 79, 89, 101, 115, 122, 137, 138
Allen, Amy, 124, 126
Americans, indigenous, first nations peoples, x, 45, 46, 48, 53, 60, 76, 111, 112, 118, 119, 120, 122, 127, 149
Anais (in PL), 57–60
anti-colonialism, 87, 121–25, 149, 158
Aristotle, Aristotelian, 8, 24, 26, 27, 66, 115, 119, 142
atheism, possibility of virtuous atheists, 11, 35–37, 38, 88, 89, 97, 98, 99, 114,
authoritarianism, authoritarian Right, 160

Bacon, Francis (and idols of the mind), x, 8, 12, 13, 22, 26–31, 34, 35, 36, 38, 50, 52, 67, 69, 70, 73, 74, 82, 91, 92, 93, 101, 102, 103, 161
Baudrilllard, Jean, 2
Bayle, Pierre: *Historical and Critical Dictionary*, 35, 75, 80, 128; *Philosophical Commentary*, 37;

Various Thoughts on the Occasion of a Comet, 13, 34, 35, 97
Biology, 25, 88, 98, 110, 116, 119
Biopolitics, 145
Blind, the; blindness, ix, x, 6, 14, 48, 52, 90–105, 161–62
Blumenbach, Johann Friedrich, 120–21
Buffon, Comte de, 88, 115, 120, 121

Calas, Jean, 79, 82
Censorship, 22, 23, 43, 48, 49, 50, 69, 72, 88, 92, 104, 160
China, Chinese (also attitudes towards), ix, x, 25, 45, 48, 60, 64, 65, 70, 124, 161
Christ, Jesus, 68, 81, 91, 139
Christianity, Christian ideas, Christians, ix, 5, 11, 13, 23, 25, 26, 27 28, 34, 35–37, 43, 46, 49, 51, 56, 57, 58, 67–69, 74, 75, 79, 81, 91, 103, 112, 113, 114, 115, 126, 135, 139, 140, 144–47, 151, 159
Cicero, Marcus Tullius, 8, 28, 64, 66, 88
Clarke, Samuel, 98–99
colonialism, imperialism, 4, 9, 14, 45, 78, 110–11, 115, 116, 125, 157
Confucius, 64, 66
culture wars, 3, 4, 6, 15, 110, 160
Cunegonde (in *Candide*), 76, 77

177

Cynicism, Cynics (philosophy, philosophers), 95

De Gouges, Olympe, 14, 148–49, 151
Deism, 11, 14, 67, 78, 79–80, 82, 88, 103, 160
Democracy, 1, 6, 88, 89, 137
Derrida, Jacques, 2, 6
Descartes, René, 7, 21, 26, 31, 70–71, 89, 91, 93, 102
despotism (absolute one man rule), 15, 51, 52, 53–57, 59–60, 124
Diderot, Denis: *D'Alembert's Dream*, 115, 137, 140, 141; "Eclecticism," in *Encyclopedia*, 87–88; *History of Two Indies* (interpolations), 14, 121–25; *Indiscreet Jewels*, 100–101, 139; *Letter on the Blind*, x, 2, 14, 87, 88–105, 115, 137, 162; *Supplement on Bougainville's Voyage*, 14, 140–47; *Thoughts on the Interpretation of Nature*, 101, 104, 162
diversity, principle of (diversifying principle), 47, 65, 116, 117, 121, 159

Education, 87
Elder (Tahitian, Mosaic speech thereof), 142–43
Encyclopedia (*Encyclopédie, ou Dictionnaire raisonné des sciences, des arts, et des métiers*), 7, 8, 13, 27, 63, 79, 87, 88, 89, 101, 118–19, 122, 127, 157
"enlightenment, the" (artificially unified polemical idea of), 10–12, 115, 162
Epictetus (Stoic), 64
Epicureanism, 8, 27, 46, 64, 79, 98, 100
Epigenism, 98, 100, 115
epistemic virtues, critique[s] of epistemic egoism, x, 28, 29–30, 35, 37, 38, 50, 52, 70, 71, 73, 74, 81, 82, 92, 98, 99, 152, 162
epistemology, including as culture of the mind, 29, 33, 99, 103, 115

evil, problem of, 15, 37, 57, 64–65, 75, 77, 78, 81, 99, 122, 123, 145, 146
experiment, experimental philosophy, experimentation, 2, 8, 9, 10, 13, 28, 29, 32, 38, 70, 74, 77, 89, 91, 100–102, 105, 111, 116, 127, 152, 160, 162

fanaticism, 37, 79–82, 161
feminism, 5, 9, 14, 139, 148, 151, 157, 158
Forst, Rainer, 36
Foucault, Michel, ix, 2, 4, 6, 11, 23

God, Christian and Deist views of, pagan gods, 14, 24, 25–28, 31, 33–37, 38, 46, 50, 57–59, 64, 68, 69, 70, 71, 74, 75, 78, 79, 80, 81, 88, 91, 92, 94, 96, 98–99, 113, 119, 139, 141, 142, 149, 150, 151

health, sanitation, 2, 22, 45, 136, 143, 144
Heidegger, Martin, 3, 4, 110, 127
Helvétius, Claude-Adrien, 89, 138, 149
D'Holbach, Baron, 4, 88, 89, 114, 122, 137
Hume, David, 66, 109, 113, 115, 116

identitarianisms (New Left and Right), 3, 4, 6, 163
inequality, 66, 108, 113, 115, 116
Israel, Jonathan (distinction of moderate and radical enlightenments), 10, 11, 62, 65, 78, 88–89, 116, 117, 121, 122, 124

Jacob, Margaret, 21
Jaucourt, Louis de, 118–19, 127, 157

limits of understanding, self-limiting forms of inquiry (also need for), x, 8, 10, 11, 12, 13, 28, 30–32, 33, 37, 38, 64–65, 70, 71, 74, 75, 90, 91, 95, 103, 111, 119–20, 127, 160, 161

Linnaeus, Carl, 115, 119–20, 121
literature, literary dimensions of enlightenment texts, ix, x, 4, 7, 8, 9–10, 23, 26, 32, 34, 43, 45, 46, 48, 60, 63, 65, 67, 77, 82, 88, 97, 136, 138, 139, 149, 150, 151
Lloyd, Genevieve, xi, 50
Locke, John: *Essay on Human Understanding*, 29, 30–33; *On the Conduct of the Understanding*, 30–31
Louis XIV (King), 23, 24, 49, 50, 56, 69, 113
Louis XV, 2, 23, 92
Lucretius, Titus, 98

Macintyre, Alisdair, 10
Manicheanism (& Martin the Manichean), 75, 78
marriage (critique, comparative), 9, 44, 55, 57, 135–36, 139, 140, 141, 144, 145, 147, 148, 149, 151
metaphysics, 7, 8, 13, 31, 43, 64, 65, 75, 76, 77, 80, 82, 88, 89, 94–97, 100, 102, 103, 104, 114, 115, 116
mirror, mirroring (exercise), 28, 46, 47–51, 53, 60, 82, 93, 142, 145
monogenism, 114, 116–117, 120, 121, 125, 149
monsters, 14, 25, 35, 92, 99, 101
Montesquieu, Charles-Louis de Secondat, Baron de La Brède: *Persian Letters*, 13, 21, 24, 38, 43–53, 57–60; *Spirit of the Laws*, 53–57
Morality, x, 11, 13, 25, 26, 35–36, 38, 44, 46–47, 64, 65–66, 77, 79, 80, 81, 88, 89, 94, 95, 96, 97, 103, 109, 114, 117–19, 122–23, 124–26, 138, 139, 142–43, 144–45, 150
moral sentiments, 66, 88, 95
Mussolini, Benito, 3

natural law, 66, 118, 146
New Left, 3, 6, 109, 158

Newton, Sir Isaac, 13, 24, 25, 62, 63, 64, 67, 69, 70, 73, 88, 98, 99, 115, 138
Nietzsche, Friedrich, 4, 7, 110, 158

Orou, 143–46
Other, seeing oneself through, x, 3, 14, 42, 47, 48, 50, 60, 99, 123, 124, 148, 151, 153, 159
L'Oueverture, Toussaint, 152, 157

Pagden, Anthony, 122, 124
Pangloss (in *Candide*), 76, 77, 78
Pascal, Blaise, 25, 72
philosophe versus other philosophers, 8, 80, 117, 123, 157
physics, 25, 31, 63, 64, 74, 88, 96, 115, 116
Plato, Platonism, 27, 64, 96, 97, 100, 110, 140
Polygenism, 114, 116, 117
postmodernism, post-structuralism, xi, 1, 2–4, 32, 37, 38, 109–110, 116, 160
post-truth (concept, condition), 1, 2, 3, 4
prejudice, prejudices (unexamined beliefs), 3, 9, 12, 14, 28, 30, 34, 52, 60, 76, 77, 80, 82, 87, 91, 105, 109, 110, 113, 114, 121, 123, 142, 147, 149, 157, 159, 160–62
Pufendort, Samuel von, 118

Quakers, ix, x, 13, 60, 68–69, 93, 161

race, racial theory, racial theories, 3, 4, 6, 14, 89, 94, 109, 110, 112, 113, 114, 115 117, 118, 118–21, 123, 125, 126, 149, 158
Rasmussen, Dennis, 4
Raynal, Abbé de, 14, 87, 116, 121–22
rationalism, and critique of, 6, 10, 63, 71, 76, 89, 91, 93
reformation, the, 11, 12, 23, 24, 26, 47, 59, 63
relativism, 3, 16

renaissance, the, 11, 12, 23, 24, 26, 47, 59, 63, 137
revocation of Edict of Nantes, 24, 49, 113,
revolution[s], French, American, Haitian, 10, 21, 53, 148, 151, 157
Rica (in *PL*), 43, 44, 48, 49–50, 57, 60, 67, 68

Saunderson, Nicholas, 96–100, 103, 105
Scepticism, 31, 32, 36, 60, 63, 64, 89, 90, 114
sciences, the (including life sciences), 8, 11, 24–25, 27, 38, 70, 88, 96, 98, 101, 103, 115, 119–21
seraglio, 44, 51–53, 55, 56, 57–60, 70, 139
Self-othering, ix, xi, 14, 38, 43, 60, 67, 72, 82, 93, 111, 123, 141, 148, 152, 159
sex, sexuality, sexual difference, homosexuality, eroticism, 3, 4, 6, 14, 22, 44, 45, 51, 55, 56, 57, 58, 59, 60, 89, 135, 137, 139, 140, 141–47, 148, 149, 150, 151, 152, 158
slavery, slave trade, transatlantic, 4, 9, 11, 14, 15, 45, 55, 59, 76, 78, 109–13, 115, 117–19, 122, 123, 125, 142, 150, 157, 158
Socrates, 10, 13, 64, 71, 97, 110
Spinoza, Baruch, 7, 22, 64, 65, 79, 89
Stoicism, 8, 27, 50, 51, 89, 128
system, spirit of (critique of), 4, 7, 10, 18, 24, 27, 47, 70, 73, 74, 77, 78, 88, 89, 96, 101–102

Tahiti, Tahitians, x, 140–47
Theology, 68, 103
tolerance, toleration, x, 2, 3, 4, 9, 11, 12, 13, 19, 23, 34, 36–37, 38, 44, 50, 51, 63, 68, 69, 75, 78, 79, 81–82, 89, 152, 157, 158, 160, 162
torture, 22, 24, 79, 89, 117, 147
travel tales, 45–47

universality of morality, truth-claims, 4, 12, 47, 65, 66, 115–16
universities, university teaching[s], 8, 9, 22, 26, 27, 137

virtue, the virtues, x, 11, 12, 29, 47, 51, 53, 54, 57, 58, 59, 64, 66, 68, 95, 117, 126, 136, 147, 148, 149, 150, 151, 152, 157, 161
Voltaire: *Candide*, 5–6, 13, 22, 75–78, 79, 82, 99, 112, 117, 159; *Ecrasez l'infâme*, 13, 79–80; *English Letters, Letters on the English*, 13, 60, 67–72, 73, 74, 93, 101, 138; *Micromégas*, 64, 65, 67; *Philosophical Dictionary*, 6, 6, 63, 79, 81, 118, 127; "Poem on the Lisbon Disaster," 75–76; *Treatise on Metaphysics*, 64, 65, 67, 116; *Treatise on Toleration*, 79; *Zadig*, 64, 67

Wade, Ira, 45, 46, 47, 64, 116
Wollstonecraft, Mary: *Vindication of the Rights of Men*, 151; *A Vindication of the Rights of Women*, 14, 148, 149–51, 152, 157
Women, femininity conditions of, views on, 9, 11, 13, 14, 22, 28, 40, 43, 48, 51, 55–56, 57–60, 64, 67, 79, 112, 120, 125, 135–39, 140–141, 144–47, 148–51, 152, 159

Zulema (in *PL*), 57–59

About the Author

Matthew Sharpe teaches philosophy and psychoanalytic studies at Deakin University. He is the author of *Camus, Philosophe: To Return to Our Beginnings* (Brill, 2014/15), coauthor of *Philosophy as a Way of Life: History, Dimensions, Directions* (Bloomsbury, 2021), *The Times Will Suit Them: Postmodern Conservatism in Australia* (Allen & Unwin, 2008), and *Understanding Psychoanalysis* (Acumen, 2008; Routledge, 2017), and co-translator of Pierre Hadot, *Selected Writings: Philosophy as Practice* (Bloomsbury, 2020). He has published professional chapters and articles on a variety of subjects spanning political theory, critical theory, psychoanalytic theory, and the history of philosophy, as well as articles on subjects of public concern for *The Conversation, ABC Online, Modern Stoicism*, and other venues. He has a lasting interest in the history of the idea of philosophy as a practice which effects changes in people and the world, rather than being only a retired or scholarly endeavor, which is reflected in his ongoing teaching on psychoanalysis, and also his work on Stoicism today. He also works increasingly on the ideas and growing scope of the anti-liberal Far Right, about which he is deeply concerned. He is a husband and father of two children, living in Melbourne, Australia.

www.ingramcontent.com/pod-product-compliance
Lightning Source LLC
Chambersburg PA
CBHW021829300426
44114CB00009BA/383